THE
COMPLETE
IDIOT'S
GUIDE® TO

C#
Programming

by David Conger

ALPHA

A Pearson Education Company

In memory of my father, who left us a legacy that will endure forever.

Copyright © 2002 by David Conger

For marketing and publicity, please call: 317-581-3722

The publisher offers discounts on this book when ordered in quantity for bulk purchases and special sales.

For sales within the United States, please contact: Corporate and Government Sales, 1-800-382-3419 or corpsales@pearsontechgroup.com

Outside the United States, please contact: International Sales, 317-581-3793 or international@pearsontechgroup.com

Publisher: *Marie Butler-Knight*
Product Manager: *Phil Kitchel*
Managing Editor: *Jennifer Chisholm*
Acquisitions Editor: *Eric Heagy*
Development Editor: *Clint McCarty*
Production Editor: *Billy Fields*
Copy Editor: *Molly Schaller*
Illustrator: *Chris Eliopoulos*
Book/Cover Designer: *Trina Wurst*
Indexer: *Angie Bess*
Layout/Proofreading: *Svetlana Dominguez, Becky Harmon*

Contents at a Glance

Contents

Introduction

This is not a traditional book introduction. The introductions to most computer books spend a great deal of time telling you why you should buy this book. I'm not going to give you the hard sell. You want to learn how to program computers; that's the reason you pulled this book off the shelf.

Learning to program computers has traditionally not been easy. But it's easier now than it has ever been. The C# programming language and the .NET Frameworks, both developed by Microsoft Corporation, make the task of writing programs simpler to master than ever before.

As a writer, my job is to get you up and running in C# as rapidly as possible. I've been a software developer for 20 years now. Over those 20 years, I've written a lot of software in many different languages, taught college classes in programming, and written some programming books. With this book, I take you along the pathway to programming success. You'll avoid many of the pitfalls novice programmers often make. You'll learn the essentials of programming in C# without a lot of fuss. You'll get results *fast*.

Software and Hardware Requirements

To program in C#, you need the following:

- ◆ Visual Studio.NET
- ◆ A computer that runs Windows 2000

If you're wondering whether you can write C# programs on Windows 95 or Windows 98, the answer is (sadly) no. Visual Studio.NET does not run on any version of Windows prior to Windows 2000.

Relax and Have Some Fun

My advice is to have some fun and enjoy the experience of learning C#. I think you'll be pleased and surprised at how soon you'll be producing programs that look professional.

So, enough talk. Let's get going.

Advice Along the Way

Techno Talk

This type of box defines words and phrases that all programmers need to know.

Programming Pitfalls

These boxes warn you of potential hazards that you might encounter while programming in C#.

Data Bit

These boxes contain notes and tips that provide you with useful programming information.

From the Knowledge Bank

These boxes contain useful insider information nuggets that teach you something new.

Special Thanks to the Technical Reviewer

The Complete Idiot's Guide to C# Programming was reviewed by an expert who double-checked the accuracy of what you'll learn here, to help us ensure that this book gives you everything you need to know about C#. Special thanks are extended to Christopher McGee.

Trademarks

All terms mentioned in this book that are known to be or are suspected of being trademarks or service marks have been appropriately capitalized. Alpha Books and Pearson Education, Inc., cannot attest to the accuracy of this information. Use of a term in this book should not be regarded as affecting the validity of any trademark or service mark.

Part 1

Getting Started

Your Aunt Millie has been telling you for years that someone as bright as you should be in computers. "It's a good living," she always says.

So you've decided to take her advice and you want to learn to write programs. In the early days of computing, you generally had to have a Ph.D. in math or engineering to program computers. These days, life is much better. With some basic knowledge of the most important components of computers and how they work, you can literally be writing useful programs in just weeks.

This part provides you with an overview of how computers work. It also describes the basics of writing a C# program.

Chapter 1

Jumping Feet First

In This Chapter

◆ How computers "think" and "talk"
◆ The contents of computer programs
◆ Using text editors and program editors
◆ Writing source code
◆ Translating source code to binary
◆ Finding and fixing program errors

Although many science fiction movies and TV shows feature computers that think, talk, and program themselves, today's computers are not nearly that advanced. Anyone who writes computer programs must understand some basic facts about how computers process information.

The first thing to know about computers is that, unlike you, they can't think. They have no judgment. Computers do exactly what we tell them to do. This is frustrating if what we *tell* them to do is not quite what we *want* them to do. Unfortunately, there is no button on any computer labeled, "Do what I mean, not what I say." So it's up to you and me, as programmers, to communicate with computers in a way they'll understand.

The Language of Computers

All computers store programs and information as binary numbers. Binary numbers are numbers in base 2. In binary, there are only two digits to count with, 0 and 1. Humans generally count with base 10, so we're used to counting with 10 numbers; 0, 1, 2, 3, 4, 5, 6, 7, 8, and 9. In the computer industry, the binary digits 0 and 1 are referred to as *bits*.

Techno Talk

A **bit** is a binary digit. It can be either a 0 or a 1.

Data Bit

The prefix kilo- on the word kilobyte usually refers to 1,000 of something. For example, a kilometer is 1,000 meters, and a kilogram is 1,000 grams. However, in computers, a kilobyte is 1,024 bytes, not 1,000. The number 1,024 is a power of two. A group of bytes that is a power of two in size is easier for the computer to work with. So, since the early days of computing, the convention has been to have 1,024 bytes in a kilobyte.

If you aren't familiar with base 2 (most people aren't), you might want to take a look at Appendix B, which explains the binary and hexadecimal numbering systems. Fortunately, though, you and I don't have to use binary to write most computer programs.

The bits in a computer are organized into *bytes*. A byte is eight bits. A group of 1,024 bits is one *kilobyte*. 1,000 kilobytes is one *megabyte*. 1,000 megabytes is one *gigabyte*.

Although this a seems like a mouthful of geek speak (it is), we need to know what bits and bytes are to get a clear picture of what's going on in a computer.

Memory

When they are running, computers store their instructions (programs) and data in memory. To understand C# and program in it well, we must have a solid understanding of what memory is and how it works.

A computer's memory is a collection of microchips that can hold binary numbers. The binary numbers can be either program instructions or data. The microprocessor in a computer retrieves each instruction in a program one by one. It then performs the task specified in the instruction.

Although it's a bit of a childish example, you can think of a computer's microprocessor as a little gnome or elf inside your computer. The gnome follows the instructions you give him, and he works very, very fast. In this example, memory can be thought of as the gnome's scratch pad. He uses it to do his work.

To be manageable, the bits in memory are grouped into bytes. Every byte in memory has an address. The address specifies the byte's location in memory. In this way, memory is similar to a long road with houses along the side. Every house on the road has an address. Each house holds people and their stuff (too much stuff, if their house is anything like mine). If you want to pick up your friend who lives along this road, you drive to her address, knock on her door, and she comes out.

Like this imaginary row of houses, memory is a sequence of locations. Each location has a unique address, and each location can hold something. That something is a binary number. If you want a computer to fetch a binary number from memory, you give the microprocessor an instruction that tells it to go to a particular address in memory and read the number that's there.

The memory that a microprocessor uses is called *random access memory*, or *RAM*. If RAM does not have an electrical current flowing to it, it loses the information it is storing. Essentially, it "forgets" everything it knows every time the power goes out.

Computers have other devices, such as disks, that serve a similar function as memory. Unlike memory, disks "remember" their contents when you turn off your computer. But disks are too slow to keep up with microprocessors. So computers store programs and data on disks. When you run a program or load a data file, the computer loads it into memory.

> **From the Knowledge Bank**
>
> Over the last 20 years that I've been in computing, the amount of memory in computers has grown unbelievably. I can remember when it was normal for personal computers to have 8 kilobytes (often abbreviated as 8K). These days, it is not uncommon to have 128 to 256 megabytes of memory in our computers.

Techno Talk

Random access memory (**RAM**) is where a microprocessor stores its programs and data. Every time you turn off your computer, RAM "forgets" everything it contains.

What Is a Computer Program?

Microprocessors execute binary instructions stored in memory to accomplish tasks. A collection of instructions is called a *program*. Computer programs are also called *application programs*, *applications*, *software*, and *application software*. These terms all refer to a group of instructions that enable a computer to accomplish a particular task.

Programs enable a computer to become a particular type of tool. For instance, a word processing program enables a computer to be a tool for typing and formatting text. A music program turns a computer into a tool for composing, recording, and playing music. Accounting programs make the computer into an accounting

Techno Talk

A computer's RAM is also called its **primary storage**. Hard and floppy disks are examples of **secondary storage**.

Techno Talk

Computer programs are known by various names. These include **application programs, applications, software,** and **application software.**

tool. The nice thing about computers is that they can be used as many different types of tools. It's just a matter of getting the right software.

Microprocessors execute binary instructions. They process binary data. In the early days of computing, the instructions for a program were input into a computer in binary using toggle switches. The programmer set the switches into the on or off positions to represent 1s or 0s. Next, he pressed a button that told the computer to store the instruction in memory and get ready to receive the next instruction. After a while, even people who really enjoyed flipping switches decided that there had to be a better way.

Programming Languages

To enable people to better communicate instructions to computers, some very smart person figured out that programmers could write instructions that are similar to words in human languages. A computer could then translate these written instructions into binary instructions. We call the translation programs *compilers* or *interpreters* (more on these later).

From the Knowledge Bank

I spent many years programming computers before I realized one basic fact: Computer programmers are people who spend inordinate amounts of time communicating with inanimate objects.

Not everyone can say that about themselves. (Of course, maybe they wouldn't want to.)

The first programming language was called Assembly language, or Assembler. Assembly language used instructions such as MOV and LOAD to tell the microprocessor to move data from one memory location to another and to load data from memory. There was often a one-to-one relationship between a microprocessor's binary instructions and the same instructions written in Assembly language. As a result, Assembly language programs tended to be rather arcane and hard to understand.

To make programming easier, programmers developed clearer, higher-level languages. These languages used instructions that were more like human languages (primarily English) than Assembler. Researchers at companies and universities invented hundreds, if not thousands, of programming languages. Some languages that were popular early on include Basic, Pascal, Fortran, and Cobol.

In the 1970s, a language called C was invented at Bell Labs. It proved to be one of the most popular and flexible languages ever conceived. The C programming language is the direct ancestor of C#. Programming languages such as C and C# are considered higher-level than Assembly language because one instruction C or C# usually translates into many instructions in binary.

Tools of the Trade

Recall that programs are groups of instructions that tell a computer how to accomplish a particular task. We write programs in programming languages like C#. As we write them, we save them as a file on the computer's disk. Programmers call these files *source files*. Each statement in a source file is an instruction to the computer.

Building a computer program is like building, well … a building. It requires tools. And part of building programs is learning what the necessary tools are and how to use them well.

I'm the first to admit that I'm a complete idiot when it comes to carpentry tools. You might feel that way about the tools needed for programming. However, getting started with them is a lot easier than it first appears.

Techno Talk

Source files contain the instructions we write for our programs. The instructions in a source file are called **source code.**

Program Editors

Text editors or program editors are used to create the source files for programs. A *text editor* is a computer program that enables you to type text into a document in a computer's memory. Text editors also let you save the document as a file. *Program editors* are text editors that are specialized for use by programmers.

Most operating systems come with a text editor included. For instance, Windows includes Notepad, and Unix typically ships with vi or emacs. Program editors are easy to get at any software store. Compilers (which are covered in the next section) almost always come with a program editor of some kind.

When it comes to program editors, every programmer has his or her preference. Many just use the one that comes with the compilers they have. However, there are companies that do nothing but write program editors. These companies produce software that is very flexible and very customizable. As you become more familiar with programming, it's a good idea to look around at the program editors on the market. Choosing the one that best fits the way you work can save you a lot of time.

Which editor is the best one? That depends entirely on you. Some program editors enable you to write *macros*. A macro is a group of commands that the software understands. These editors enable you to store your macros in files, and execute the instructions in the macros whenever you want. Macros help you automate repetitive tasks.

However, macros might not be important to you. What is? Is it important that you can work with many files at once? If so, then you need to pick an editor that enables you to do

Techno Talk

A **macro** is a set of commands recognized by a computer program. These commands are stored in a file and can be executed whenever you need them. In this way, a macro is very much like a computer program. The difference is that a macro is executed by a program.

that easily. Do you need to work with extremely large source files? Check to see if there is a size limit to a program editor before you buy it.

Before you buy a program editor, always check to be sure that it works with the other tools you have. Specifically, you want to be able to run your compiler without having to exit your editor. Look in editor's advertisement material (read the box) to see whether you can use it with your compiler. In the vast majority of cases, the answer will be yes. However, it's wise to check before you buy.

Compilers and Linkers

I've mentioned compilers several times now without really saying much about them. Recall that instructions written in C# must be translated into binary so that the microprocessor is able to execute them. Doing that translation is the job of a compiler.

There is also another type of program, called an *interpreter*, that translates programming statements into binary. The difference between a compiler and an interpreter is that a compiler translates the entire program at once. The translated program can then be executed repeatedly without having to be translated again.

Techno Talk

You must have a compiler or interpreter to translate your computer program into binary format (unless you want to program in binary, ugh!). A **compiler** translates all of the statements in your source code and then saves them in a binary form. An **interpreter** translates one instruction from your source code into binary, and then executes the binary code. It then moves on to the next statement in your source code. Compiled programs need to be compiled only once. Interpreted programs must be interpreted each time they're run.

An interpreter, on the other hand, reads one line from the source file, translates it, and executes it. It does this for each line in the source file. Every time you run the program, the interpreter must do the translation again.

As you might expect, compiled programs run faster than interpreted programs. Almost all of the programs you will ever use are compiled.

Until recently, the process of compiling a program followed a standard model. The C# programming language uses a new method of converting source code into executable code. To understand how it works, we first have to know what's been done traditionally.

For most of the history of programming, compilers translated source code into *object code*. Object code is a set of binary instructions. However, object code cannot be executed by the microprocessor. It is an intermediate form. Before object code can be executed, it must be linked. A specialized program, called a *linker* (as you might expect), performs the linking step. The linker outputs the final executable program.

Techno Talk

Linkers are programs that convert the object code created by compilers into executable programs.

So the traditional process of making executable programs is as follows:

1. You use a program editor to write your source code and store it as text in a text file.

2. You use a compiler to compile the source code into object code.

3. You use a linker (discussed next), to convert the object code into an executable program.

The traditional process of creating a computer program is shown in the Figure 1.1.

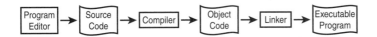

Figure 1.1

The traditional process of writing, compiling, and linking a program.

You might ask, "What does the linker link to?" Every program you write must be linked to some standard libraries of code that come with your compiler. It can also be linked to other libraries that you write, or that you buy.

Libraries? What's this about libraries?

Yes, it's true. You can write libraries of code. These are not programs by themselves. Code libraries contain pieces of program code that you can use over and over again in many different programs. Libraries are distributed as object code, and then others link these libraries to their programs.

Currently, you can buy many different types of libraries. Compilers have some standard libraries that their manufacturers publish with them. For example, later in this book, we'll use Windows Forms (to make it easier to build professional-looking programs. The code for Windows Forms is a library that Microsoft distributes with its compilers. To use Windows Forms, you must link your program to the appropriate library.

Data Bit

You can write libraries of code that you can sell or give to other programmers. This saves them a lot of time when writing their programs.

Figure 1.2 shows the sets for building programs again. However, it also includes the process of linking to libraries.

Figure 1.2

Linking your program to libraries.

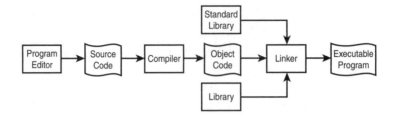

All of this is actually easier than it sounds. Typically, when you run a compiler, it calls the linker for you. As far as you're concerned, the compile and link actions are all done in one step. You might have to specify which libraries to link to. However, modern development tools make this very easy and straightforward.

You might remember that I said that C# does not use the traditional model of compiling and linking. I haven't specified how it operates differently. For now, I'm not going to. The reason is that this view of compiling and linking works perfectly until you're ready to start programming with the .NET Framework and Windows Forms. At that point, I'll go into more detail.

Another reason for not going into details about this process right now is that the process itself is invisible to you. To write your C# programs, you'll use the version of Visual Studio provided with this book. Visual Studio makes the entire process of converting source code to executable code as simple as pressing a function key on your keyboard.

The main reason that I've presented the traditional model of compiling and linking is so that you'll be able to build your programs. You also need to know this so that you'll have enough background to understand the error messages you'll get when you compile and link.

Using this approach makes it easy to get up and running quickly. You're not bogged down with details that you don't need to know right now. However, if you're curious, you can peek ahead at Part 5.

Debuggers

Every program you ever write will contain errors. Depressing, isn't it?

As a result, every programmer must obtain a debugger. These days, most compilers ship with excellent debuggers. A debugger is a program that enables you to execute a program line by line, just as if it were interpreted. With this capability, you can see exactly how your program operates.

Good debugging programs enable you to step over areas of source code that already work. Stepping over code means executing a bunch of instructions without watching it execute each line.

With a debugger, you can watch the values of data in memory. This is important. You must be able to see how your data changes as your program runs. This capability enables you to see when your data gets changed to invalid values. That tells you which program instructions you need to change.

Debuggers also enable you to set *breakpoints.* When you set a breakpoint in your program code, it causes program execution to stop. However, a breakpoint does not end the program. All of the data is still intact in memory. If you tell it to, the debugger can make your program resume execution. You can have your program execute one statement, then stop and wait for your next command. Alternatively, you can just tell the debugger to resume normal execution of the program. You're the boss.

Typically, you'll write, compile, link, and test your program. As you test it, you'll find some problems with it. Do not be upset or frustrated. This is normal. No one ever writes a program perfectly the first time.

When you find that your program contains an error, load it into the debugger. Just take a guess as to where it might be going wrong. Set a breakpoint in the code just before the spot you think is causing the problem. Then execute your program normally.

Techno Talk _____

A **debugging program,** or **debugger,** enables you to inspect your program as it executes. This helps you find errors.

Techno Talk _____

Using a debugger to set a breakpoint causes program execution to stop at the statement you select in the source code. It does not end the program. You can examine the program's data to determine whether there is a problem, and what the problem is. After you're done looking at the code. You can resume program execution.

From the Knowledge Bank

Testing programs is so important that it is a profession in itself; knowing how to program opens up more than one career path to you.

If your program crashes or generates incorrect data before it hits the breakpoint, move your breakpoint closer to the beginning of the program. If the breakpoint occurs first, then execute your program in the debugger one line at a time. Watch your data carefully. Think about each instruction as the computer executes it. Try to foresee any problems that the instruction might cause. If it looks okay, move on to the next instruction.

As you move through your program in this manner, you can watch it make its mistakes. Execute it repeatedly in the debugger until you understand where it's going wrong. Then you'll need to rewrite your source code to fix the problem.

Having It All: Integrated Development Environments

Computing is not a very old profession when compared with jobs such as farming or architecture. The tools used by computer professionals have changed tremendously since I started in the industry 20 years ago. (Twenty years! Where has the time gone?) One of the nicest changes I've seen in the toolsets used by programmers is the advent of integrated development environments, or IDEs.

An IDE combines a compiler, linker, debugger, and possibly other tools, into a single working environment. From your point of view, they look like one program.

Using an IDE also enables you to easily specify all of the source files and libraries that the compiler uses to create your program. Professional programs are typically made up of many source files. They might also include several libraries. A major advantage of an IDE is that, in most cases, you can simply drag and drop source files and libraries into your project. The IDE knows to compile the source files and link to the libraries.

This is a huge advance. You don't have to memorize arcane commands to get your program to compile and link. After you specify which files are in your project, you simply press a button or choose a command from a menu. Poof! You get a compiled program. If you've never suffered through creating make files, and using command-line compilers and linkers, you really don't know how good you have it. And if you don't know what make files are, don't ask. Just be glad for your IDE.

Using an IDE also enables you to debug your application in your program editor. This helps you find and fix program bugs more rapidly.

Typically, your IDE provides you with a menu of tools to which you can add other programs you use for software development. It's a great help to be able to invoke all your tools from the same menu. When programming under graphical user interfaces, it is very common to use a tool that enables you to watch the exchange of information between your program and the operating system. Your IDE often enables you to invoke such tools from a single menu.

In my opinion, the two most important tools for programmers are their editors (or IDEs) and their debuggers. An editor or IDE that you are happy with enables you to quickly write code with a minimum of distractions or frustrations. It enables you to set up your working environment and develop code just the way you want to. And having a debugger with lots of features and an interface that you easily understand saves you many, many hours of work. It also decreases your frustration levels as you labor to find bugs in your source code.

Compilers and linkers are important also. But, in an IDE, they do their work with such little fuss or fanfare that they don't influence your development experience nearly as much as your IDE and debugger.

Techno Talk

The term **graphical user interface** is abbreviated as **GUI**. The abbreviation GUI is pronounced "gooey."

If your computer offers a graphical user interface, you do not have to type commands to the operating system. Instead, the operating system offers graphical elements and symbols that enable you to communicate with it. A graphical user interface displays menus, dialog boxes, onscreen buttons, edit boxes, and drop-down lists. GUIs usually use both keyboards and mice as input devices.

Examples of GUIs include Macintosh Finder, Microsoft Windows, Motif, KDE, and Gnome.

The Least You Need to Know

- The instructions that a microprocessor executes are always binary numbers. Computers store data as binary numbers.

- Microprocessors keep their data and instructions in memory. Memory is also called RAM, and it is measured in bytes, kilobytes, megabytes, and gigabytes.

- Programs contain collections of instruction for the microprocessor to execute.

- A program editor is used to write programs in languages such as C#. Program editors save C# commands in source files.

- Compilers translate source files into object files. Object files are in binary, but they are not executable programs.

- Linkers link object files to libraries. After the program is linked, it can be run.

- Every program you write will contain errors. Debuggers enable you to watch what is going on in your programs. This helps you find and fix program errors.

- Integrated development environments (IDEs) are extremely convenient. They unite your program editor, compiler, linker, and debugger into a single development environment.

The View from 10,000 Feet: Introducing C# and Visual Studio

In This Chapter

- ◆ A brief overview of the C# language
- ◆ The relationship of C# to C, C++, and Java
- ◆ An introduction to Microsoft's Visual Studio .NET

Obviously, you've chosen to learn to program in Visual C#, or you wouldn't be reading this book. You also already know that C# is the hot new programming language from Microsoft.

But, C# is much more than that. With C#, you can learn to quickly develop professional-looking Windows applications with Windows Forms, as demonstrated in Part 5 of this book.

C, C++, and C#

C# is derived from the C and C++ programming languages. Languages derived from C have always been favorites with many programmers. However, C was designed by very bright, programmers who held advanced degrees in subjects that make my head hurt. As a result, C is a very powerful tool, if you know and understand the internal workings of computers in great detail. If you don't (most of us don't), it can be a struggle to learn to use C well.

The C programming language was created at Bell Labs in the 1970s. In the 1980s, Bjarne Stroustrup, also working at Bell Labs, extended C to include object-oriented programming techniques.

Data Bit

The philosophy behind the C programming languages was to create a language that would let you do pretty much what you want to do, even if it is quite odd. In fact, it's often been said that C gives you enough rope to do anything you want, even hang yourself with great speed and efficiency.

What is object-oriented programming? Chapter 12 discusses object-oriented programming in detail. For now, let's just say that object-oriented programming takes computer programming languages to a higher level. It makes programming easier and faster (at least, that's the intent).

The C++ programming language became very popular by adding object-oriented techniques to C. However, that did not necessarily make it a truly object-oriented programming language. Whenever you stated that it was, there was always someone in the crowd ready to argue the point (it's mostly a matter of definitions).

One of the advantages of C is that it has a very compact syntax. Unfortunately, C++ does not share that compactness with C. C++ adds many new keywords and operators. (Keywords and operators are covered in later chapters.) The long and short of it is that C++ is not an easy language to learn to program well with. It can surprise even veteran programmers at times.

However, don't think that I am putting C++ down in any way. It is an excellent language. When it came out, it was a great step forward. However, one has to be realistic and understand that every programming language has its strengths and weaknesses.

C# and Java

In the 1990s, C++ provided the basis for a new step forward in programming languages. The Java language, developed at Sun Microsystems, overcomes many of the shortcomings of C and C++. It is a truly object-oriented programming language. It is also extremely *portable*, meaning programs written in Java can run on many different types of computers.

Portability makes Java an excellent programming language for the World Wide Web. Java programs can be attached to Web pages and executed on the user's computer when it loads the page. In general, it does not matter what type of computer or Web browser is running the Java program. It should run just fine under any browser. That is the theory, anyway; it doesn't *always* happen in practice.

Techno Talk

A **portable** program is one that can be easily moved to a different type of computer or a different operating system.

Data Bit

Programs are ported in different ways. Here are some examples:

- If a program you write on a Macintosh runs on a PC as well, it is portable at the binary level. You need to use special techniques to make programs portable at the binary level.

- If you write a program on a Windows computer, put the source code on a Linux computer, recompile, and it runs okay, your program is portable at the source code level. It is not portable at the binary level.

So, **binary level portability** means that programs run on different operating systems or different types of computers. **Source level portability** means you have to recompile the program when you port it.

In addition, it is very common to have to make some modifications to the source code when you port a program. The more changes you need to make, the less portable your program is.

Portability is a kind of "holy grail" for programmers. Everyone seeks it, but true portability is difficult to find.

Sun Microsystems controls the standard for the Java language. C# is Microsoft's answer to Java. C# and Java share many features. They are both object oriented; they both have a cleaner syntax than C++; and they are both designed to be much more portable that C or C++.

Java, being a few years old, has a huge following in the software industry. At the time of this writing, it is not clear whether C# will displace Java as the language of the Web. However, it *is* clear that C# is rapidly becoming a popular language and a powerful force in the computer industry.

C#, like Java, can be easily extended for developing World Wide Web applications. Everything you learn in this book is applicable to writing programs for the Web. You can extend the techniques presented in this book by using the .NET (pronounced "dot net")

Framework. With the .NET Framework, writing Web programs using Web Forms is extremely similar to writing Windows Forms programs. When you've finished reading this book, it's a good idea to look into Web Forms programming.

Microsoft Visual Studio

Currently, Microsoft Visual Studio .NET (Visual Studio version 7) is the only compiler for C#. Microsoft is taking steps to submit the C# language specification to a standards organization to make it possible for anyone to create a C# compiler.

A Ton of Tools

After installing Visual Studio .NET and setting your profile information, you see the opening screen shown in Figure 2.1. This opening screen enables you to start a new project or open an existing one. The next section explains projects in detail.

Figure 2.1

From the Visual Studio .NET opening screen, you can create or open projects.

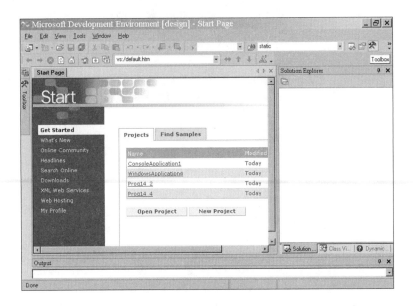

After you create or open a project, Visual Studio displays its IDE window. Visual Studio divides its IDE window, shown in Figure 2.2, into multiple panes. Each pane contains one or more tabbed panels. The panels enable you to interact with source files or IDE tools. As you can see from the number of windows and panels, there are a lot of tools available. It's okay if you don't understand what each tool is at this point. But it's important to be able to find each tool when you need it.

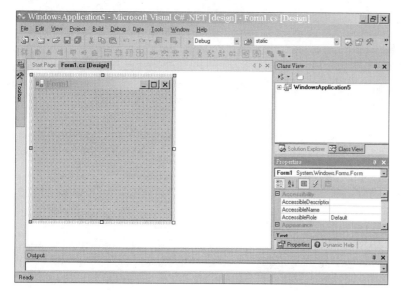

Figure 2.2

The Visual Studio .NET IDE window. This is how Visual Studio looks when you're creating the user interface for a Windows program.

The left pane of the Visual Studio window shows a work area that's called the design palette, or the designer. The design palette enables you to build Windows applications by dragging and dropping components onto the palette surface. The components come with Visual Studio in its Windows Forms library. You learn how to use them in Part 5 of this book.

Notice that the left pane is a tabbed window. See the tabs on top of the left pane? The one with the bold text in its title is tab for the design palette. Visual Studio often displays several tab in this window. The other tabs generally display your source files. They are editor windows. Each source file you load into an editor window has its own tabbed panel. You view a file by clicking on its tab.

Visual Studio's upper right pane displays the current solution and project. Microsoft calls this pane the Solution Explorer. Like the left pane, the right pane is a tabbed window. Clicking the tabs along the bottom of the pane displays the Class View. This shows you all of the classes in your program. Classes are presented in Chapter 12.

In the lower right pane, you'll find the Dynamic Help and the Properties window. Make friends with the Dynamic Help window. It is a great tool. While you're developing your program, Dynamic Help displays a list of help topics. The list changes, depending on what you're doing. If you need help, look in the Dynamic Help list first.

At the top of the Dynamic Help window are three small icons. One looks like a book. When you click it, Visual Studio displays the table of contents for its online help. The second icon at the top of the Dynamic Help window looks like a piece of paper with a question mark on it. When you click that icon, Visual Studio opens up its Index window. You can use the index to search for information on a topic by keyword. The third icon at the top of the Dynamic Help window brings up Visual Studio's Search window. It enables you to search through the entire collection of online documentation.

The Properties window isn't important until Part 5. Then, you use it often.

Having It Your Way

One of the nice things about Visual Studio's user interface is that you can easily configure it. The simplest way to do that is to drag the tabs of various panels to different panes.

For example, I like to combine the contents of the two panes on the right. To do so, I point my mouse cursor at the tab of a panel in the lower right pane, hold my mouse button down, and drag it to the tabs in the upper right pane. If you drag the tab of the Dynamic Help to the tabs in the upper right pane, the Dynamic Help panel moves to that pane. I repeat this process for any of the panels that might appear in the lower right-hand pane. For the last panel in the lower pane, you have to drag its title bar rather than its tab. Figure 2.3 shows how Visual Studio looks when you configure its interface in this way.

Figure 2.3

This is how I like Visual Studio to look. I encourage you to configure its appearance to suit your tastes.

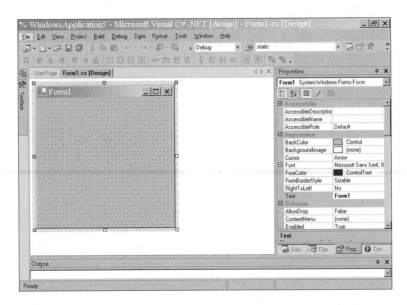

Doing this gives more space to the individual panes. I generally find the default configuration too cramped. When I use it, I'm constantly having to resize the right-hand panes.

When you compile and link programs, Visual Studio prints messages in the Output window. By default, it displays the Output window across the bottom of its main program window.

I find this configuration very inconvenient. It's difficult to have enough room for everything. I drag the Output window into the same pane as the Solution Explorer. I also put the window for error messages there.

By combining the windows in this way, I'm able to work with the designer and the editor on the left. Everything else goes on the right. I click the tabs on the right to show the window I need to work with at the moment. I find this very handy. The drawback of this configuration is that I have to click the tabs a lot. However, I don't find this inconvenient.

Take time to arrange Visual Studio's interface in a way that suits you. It makes your development experience more pleasant. In addition, you tend to work more efficiently when things are the way you like them.

Data Bit

Giving more space to the individual panes really improves their readability. If I want, I can set Windows to use a larger font to display the text in Visual Studio's various panes. This might not be important to those of you who are under 30. However, as you get into your late 30s and early 40s, you'll really appreciate this capability in software. I know I do.

Solutions and Projects

In addition to creating executable programs, Visual Studio .NET enables you to create components. Components are reusable pieces of code stored in libraries. The libraries that contain C# components are called *assemblies*.

So what's that got to do with making C# programs? The short answer is that it affects the terminology used in Visual Studio. In Visual Studio lingo, you must create a solution and a project to build a program.

Say what?

Programmers build professional C# programs from many source files. They also combine their source files with components from assemblies. To combine all of the source files and assemblies into one program, you create a *project*.

Projects can be either programs or components. You can create more than one project in a *solution*. In professionally written software, it's not unusual to have several projects in one solution. Typically, some of them are components. At least one of them is a program.

Techno Talk

Libraries that contain C# components are called **assemblies**.

You combine one or more source files to make a Visual Studio **project**.

A **solution** is a collection of one or more projects.

It's confusing at first, I know. But you aren't creating components in this book, so you're able to create a project and a solution in one step. That makes life much simpler.

The Solution Explorer shows a list of all of the projects, source files, and assemblies in the current solution. If you accidentally close a design or edit window in which you want to work, the Solution Explorer provides a quick way to open it back up. Just double-click the file's name in the Solution Explorer's list. Visual Studio pops it up in an edit or design pane on the left.

The Least You Need to Know

- C# was derived from C and C++.
- C# shares many similarities with Java.
- Like C++ and Java, C# extends the basic syntax C into object-oriented programming.
- Microsoft Visual Studio enables you to compile and link C# programs at the press of a button.
- In addition to a compiler and linker, Visual Studio provides an editor, integrated debugger, the Solution Explorer (for managing projects), and an extensive online help system.

Chapter 3

Writing Programs in C#

In This Chapter

- ◆ How to write a C# program
- ◆ Namespaces
- ◆ Application classes
- ◆ The `Main()` function
- ◆ The `ReadLine()`, `Write()`, and `WriteLine()` functions

After just a couple of short chapters, you've learned enough to start programming. All of that stuff about bits and bytes—the most boring part of learning to write software—is all behind you. From now on, things get more interesting because you're writing programs and seeing the results of your efforts.

Creating Visual C# Programs

Visual Studio can create several different types of programs. In Parts 1 through 4 of this book, you make console programs. In Part 5, you build Windows Forms programs.

Console programs do not use a graphical user interface. They input and output text. Windows Forms programs use a GUI.

To create a console application, follow these steps:

1. From Visual Studio's main menu, select **Project.**

2. In the **New Project** dialog box, click **Visual C# Projects** in the **Project Types** list.

3. Select **Consol Application** in the **Templates** list, then click **OK.**

To create a Windows Forms application, follow these steps:

1. From Visual Studio's main menu, select **Project.**

2. In the **New Project** dialog box, click on **Visual C# Projects** in the **Project Types** list.

3. Select **Windows Application** in the **Templates** list, then click **OK.**

When you create a project using these steps, Visual Studio creates a solution for you.

Hello, C#—a First Program

Your first C# program is a consol application. Traditionally, everyone's first program in a new programming language is called "Hello, World." This program is very similar; it's called, "Hello, C#."

Writing "Hello, C#"

When you create your console application, Visual Studio generates a file for you called Class1.cs. To change the name of this file, place your mouse cursor over the file name in the Solution Explorer. Recall that Visual Studio displays the Solution Explorer in a panel on the upper right of your work area.

With the mouse cursor pointing at the filename, click your mouse's secondary button. Visual Studio displays a context-sensitive menu that contains a list of all actions you can perform on whatever you selected. This menu is called the context menu.

Data Bit

For right-handed people, the left button is the mouse's primary button. Its right button is the secondary button. If you use a left-handed mouse, the primary button is the right button. The left button is the secondary button.

Pointing the mouse cursor at something and clicking the primary button is often called "left-clicking" it. Pointing at something and clicking the secondary button is typically referred to as "right-clicking" it.

Rather unfair to left-handed people, in my opinion. But that's the way it is.

Select **Rename** in the context menu. When you do, Visual Studio displays a box that enables you to edit the file name. Type

```
HelloCSharp.cs
```

and then press **Enter.** The name of the file is now HelloCSharp.cs.

You're now ready to start editing the program itself. Visual Studio displays the contents of the source file in an edit window. The contents of the panel look like Listing 3.1.

Listing 3.1　The Source Code That Visual Studio Generates for You

```
using System;

namespace ConsoleApplication1
{
    /// <summary>
    /// Summary description for Class1.
    /// </summary>
    class Class1
    {
        /// <summary>
        /// The main entry point for the application.
        /// </summary>
         [STAThread]
        static void Main(string[] args)
        {
            //
            // TODO: Add code to start application here
            //
        }
    }
}
```

Edit the contents of the file to match Listing 3.2 (the changes are shown here in bold).

Listing 3.2　The "Hello, C#" Program

```
using System;

namespace ConsoleApplication1
{
    /// <summary>
    /// Summary description for HelloCSharp class.
    /// </summary>
    class HelloCSharp
```

continues

Listing 3.2   The "Hello, C#" Program   (continued)

```
{
    /// <summary>
    /// The main entry point for the application.
    /// </summary>
    [STAThread]
    static void Main(string[] args)
    {
        // Say hello, C#.
        System.Console.WriteLine("Hello, C#.");
        // All done.
    }
}
}
```

Now select **Build** from the main menu. In the **Build** menu, choose **Build Solution.** If you've typed the changes exactly as is shown here, Visual Studio shows the output in Figure 3.1.

Figure 3.1

Visual Studio's output when you compile the "Hello, C#" program.

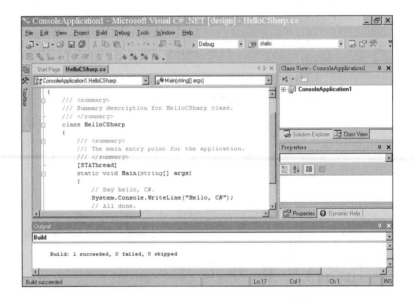

As you can see, the Visual Studio opens a new pane containing a summary of the results of compiling and linking the program. If you've made any mistakes, they're listed here. Otherwise, it tells you that the build succeeded.

If you made any typing errors, go back and fix them now. Then rebuild the program. Repeat the process until the build succeeds.

If you run the program from inside Visual Studio or by double-clicking its filename, you might not see the output. That's because Windows closes the output window as soon as it's finished. To see the output of the program, open a command window, switch to the directory containing the program, and run it from the command line.

Running "Hello, C#" in the Debugger

Another way to see the output of this program is to run it under the debugger. Begin by scrolling the file HelloCSharp.cs until you can see line 17. The editing area is usually white. To the left of the editing area is a thin margin. Click your mouse's main button in the margin to the left of line 17. Red highlighting appears on line 17, and a red dot is displayed in the left margin, as shown in Figure 3.2. Congratulations! You've just set a breakpoint.

Techno Talk

Errors that the compiler finds during the build process are called **syntax errors**. Those aren't the only kind of errors that can occur in a program. There's still the possibility of **logical errors**, which occur when we put incorrect instructions in our programs.

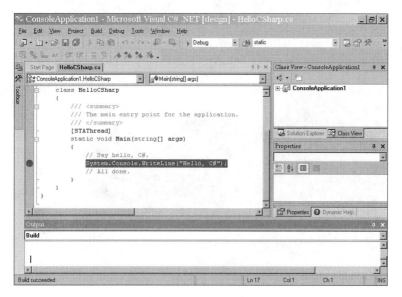

Figure 3.2

A breakpoint in the debugger.

With the breakpoint in place, you're ready to run the program. Press the **F5** key on your keyboard. Visual Studio runs your program until it reaches line 17. At that point, the Visual Studio's debugger halts execution. You should see a yellow arrow in the left margin on line 17. Also, line 17 should be highlighted in yellow, as shown in Figure 3.3.

Figure 3.3

Execution is stopped on line 17 of "Hello, C#".

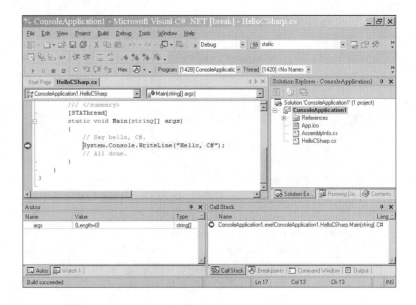

In your Windows Taskbar (usually across the bottom of your screen) is an icon for your Hello, C# program. Click that icon, and a window filled with black appears.

Switch back to Visual Studio, and press **F10**. This advances the program one line. Now switch to the output window again. As shown in Figure 3.4, the words "Hello, C#" are printed to the console window.

Figure 3.4

Hello, C#.

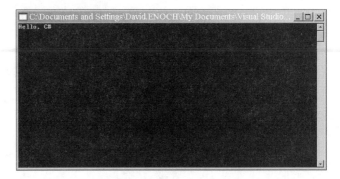

Switch back to Visual Studio and press **F5** again. This tells the debugger to continue running the program. It finishes execution and closes its console window.

Parts of a Visual C# Program

Although the "Hello, C#" program doesn't really do anything important, it demonstrates all of the essential parts of a C# program. Let's look at these in detail.

Listing 3.3 shows the source code for the
"Hello, C#" program again. This time, I've
numbered the lines. Line numbers make it
easier for me to indicate which part of the
source code we're discussing. From now on,
I'll show all of the source code in this book
with line numbers. You can't put line numbers
in your source files when you write C# programs.
The compiler will generate an error if you do.

Programming Pitfalls

CAUTION

Do not put line numbers
in your source code. The only
reason I use line numbers in this
book is to make it easier to present the material.

Listing 3.3   The Source Code for the "Hello, C#" Program

```
1     using System;
2
3     namespace ConsoleApplication1
4     {
5         /// <summary>
6         /// Summary description for HelloCSharp class.
7         /// </summary>
8         class HelloCSharp
9         {
10            /// <summary>
11            /// The main entry point for the application.
12            /// </summary>
13            [STAThread]
14            static void Main(string[] args)
15            {
16                // Say hello, C#.
17                System.Console.WriteLine("Hello, C#.");
18                // All done.
19            }
20        }
21    }
```

Using Comments

Any line in a C# source file that begins with the characters // is a comment. The compiler
completely ignores it. Comments are there just for you and I. They make our programs
more readable to others (and ourselves).

Visual Studio can use the comments that begin with three slashes (like this ///) to generate
XML program documentation files. XML, and generating XML documentation files, is
beyond the scope of this book.

C# also supports comments that span more than one line. These are delimited with the /* and */ symbols.

```
/* Here is a C# comment
that spans more than one
line of code. The C# compiler
completely ignores all of this
text. */
```

Stating the Namespace

The first C# statement to look at in the "Hello, C#" program is on line 3. It creates a namespace for the console application. In the C# world, a namespace serves a function that is similar to telephone country codes in the real world.

Suppose I live in a country called Elberta. Suppose also that in Elberta, our country code is 989. I can call anyone in Elberta without having to dial 989 before the phone number. However, if I want to call someone who lives in North Listonia (also an imaginary country), I have to dial the country code for North Listonia before the rest of the phone number.

C# namespaces work similarly. A namespace defines what is "local" and what is "long distance" to the current place in the program.

Using namespaces helps programmers avoid name conflicts. Recall from Chapter 2, "The View from 10,000 Feet: Introducing C# and Visual Studio," that C# programs must be linked to libraries before they can become executable programs. Later chapters talk about creating variables, functions, classes, and other C# language elements. Each of these needs a unique name. It is possible that the name you create for one of them might be the same as a name in a library to which your program links. Two different things with the same name can cause problems.

Data Bit

Adding namespaces to C# programs helps avoid name conflicts. Creating a namespace for your program tells the C# compiler what is "local" and what is "long distance."

Let's say I'm writing a program that contains a class called Snert. At this point, it doesn't matter what a class is, or what it does, or why I would name it Snert (an odd name, indeed). The important point is I've created something in my program that has the name Snert. Now imagine that I link my program to a library that also contains a class called Snert. When I use the name Snert in my program, to which Snert am I referring, the one I made or the one in the library?

Namespaces help clear up the confusion. If I create a class called Snert in the namespace ConsoleApplication, all references to Snert are to the local one. If I want to access the one outside the immediate namespace, I must specify it explicitly, like this:

```
MyLibrary.Snert
```

Putting the name MyLibrary before the name Snert tells the compiler that I am not using the local Snert; rather, I'm "dialing long distance," so to speak. I am referring to the Snert in the namespace MyLibrary, not the one in ConsoleApplication.

Every C# program you write should have its own namespace. Create a namespace by using the namespace keyword, followed by the namespace's name. The opening and closing braces (the symbols { and }) contain the contents of the namespace. The opening brace for the ConsoleApplication namespace is on line 4 of the "Hello, C#" program. The closing brace is on line 21.

The using Directive

Line 1 of the "Hello, C#" program contains the statement

```
using System;
```

Every C# program should contain this directive. The using directive tells the C# compiler which namespaces your program uses. In this case, it states that the "Hello, C#" program uses the System namespace. If you use a namespace that is not defined in the current file, you must put the using directive in your program.

The only namespace defined in the "Hello, C#" program is ConsoleApplication. However, the program also uses the System namespace. Therefore, it requires the directive

```
using System;
```

at the beginning of the file.

Programming Pitfalls

Do not forget to put the using directive at the beginning of your program for each namespace that the program uses.

The Application Class

Every C# program must have an application class. The application class must contain a Main() function. What is a class? What is a function?

Data Bit

Classes are presented in Chapter 12. There is a simple definition of functions later in this chapter. Functions are described in detail in Chapter 4.

Hang onto those questions for later. At this point, it doesn't matter what classes and functions are. I know that might not be a very satisfying answer, but it was my experience as a college professor that trying to tackle every detail at once only confuses learners. I've had better luck by occasionally waving my hands at some details and saying, "Just put it in there for now. I'll explain it later." I usually also told them, "I thank you in advance for your patience."

You create an application class with the `class` keyword, followed by the name of the application class. Like namespaces, the contents of the class occur between opening and closing braces. For the `HelloCSharp` application class, you'll find the opening brace on line 9, and the closing brace on line 20.

Main(), the Beginning and Ending of Everything

Every application class must have a `Main()` function. The `Main()` function is called the program entry point. This is where the program begins execution. If there is no `Main()` in the application class, the compiler generates errors. Putting more than one `Main()` into a program also causes errors.

Data Bit

The beginning of `Main()` is the starting point for every C# program. The program executes the statements in `Main()` one after the other. When `Main()` is done, the program ends.

The declaration of `Main()` must follow the form shown on line 14 of "Hello, C#." Following the same pattern as namespaces and classes (and many other things in C#), the contents of `Main()` are contained in opening and closing braces. You can find them on lines 15 and 19, respectively.

Everything that happens in a C# program begins with `Main()`. In this case, the program just prints the words, "Hello, C#" to the screen.

Printing Text to the Screen

The "Hello, C#" program used the statement …

```
System.Console.WriteLine()
```

… on line 17.

`WriteLine()` is actually a function. Simply put, functions are chunks of program code with names. Every function contains C# statements. `Main()` is a function, and so is `WriteLine()`. The only real difference between them is that you write `Main()`, and `WriteLine()` is written for you. It's found in a library containing the System namespace. Functions are presented in detail in Chapter 4.

Techno Talk

A string of literal text is a text string that is typed directly into your program code. **Literal text** is not a program instruction; it is data (information) contained in your program's source code.

The `WriteLine()` function prints text on the screen. The text must be contained in the `WriteLine()` function's parentheses. The "Hello, C#" program prints a string of *literal text*. You must enclose all literal text in quote marks.

After WriteLine() prints the text you give it, it performs a *line feed* by moving the cursor to the beginning of the next line on the screen.

The WriteLine() function can print other things besides literal strings. You learn what those are in Chapter 4.

Techno Talk

When a C# statement performs a **line feed,** it moves the cursor to the beginning of the next line.

Getting Input from the Keyboard

Getting text from the keyboard is about as straightforward as writing it to the screen. Listing 3.4 shows a variation on the Hello, C# program to demonstrate.

This version of the program asks the user's name, and then says hello. As before, I've put the lines with changes into a boldface type.

Listing 3.4

```
1    using System;
2
3
4    namespace ConsoleApplication1
5    {
6        /// <summary>
7        /// Summary description for HelloCSharp class.
8        /// </summary>
9        class HelloCSharp
10        {
11            /// <summary>
12            /// The main entry point for the application.
13            /// </summary>
14            [STAThread]
15            static void Main(string[] args)
16            {
17                string inputString;
18
19                // Get the user's name.
20                System.Console.WriteLine("Please tell me your name.");
21                inputString = System.Console.ReadLine();
22
23                // Say hello.
24                System.Console.Write("Hello, ");
25                System.Console.WriteLine(inputString);
26                // All done.
```

continues

Listing 3.4   (continued)

```
27              }
28          }
29      }
```

This version of the program provides an overview of variables, which are discussed in detail in Chapter 4. A variable is name for a location in memory. Your program defines the name and the type of data that can be stored there. This program stores a string of characters in memory. To do so, it uses the String type.

Line 17 declares a string variable to hold text. The name of the variable is inputString. On line 20, the program prints a prompt for the user. Line 21 uses the ReadLine() function to get the user's response.

ReadLine() retrieves a line of text from the keyboard. It stops program execution until the user types in a string. When the user presses the Enter key, it continues. When it does, it returns the text it retrieved to the program. The program uses the C# assignment operator to store it in the variable. The assignment operator is the equal sign.

> **Data Bit**
>
> The WriteLine() and Write() functions do basically the same thing. Their only real difference is that WriteLine() performs a line feed. Write() does not.

The result of line 21 is that the program gets one line of text from the user and saves it in inputString.

The program prints "Hello, " on line 24. Notice that it uses the Write() function instead of the WriteLine() function. The difference between these two functions is that WriteLine() performs a line feed, and Write() does not. As a result, the output printed by the statement on line 25 is on the same line on the screen as the word "Hello."

Line 25 uses WriteLine() to print the string in inputString. Here's a sample run of the program. The characters that I typed in at the prompt are shown in bold.

```
Please tell me your name.
David
Hello, David
```

The Least You Need to Know

♦ You create two types of programs in this book: console applications and Windows Forms applications.

♦ Namespaces define what is "local" and what is "long distance" in a program. Every C# program must define a namespace.

♦ In a C# program, the using keyword specifies which namespaces the program uses.

◆ Every C# program must define an application class.

◆ The entry point for a C# program is the Main() function. Every C# program must have exactly one (no more, no less) Main() function in its application class.

◆ The WriteLine() function prints a line of text on the screen, followed by a line feed.

◆ The Write() function prints a line of text on the screen, but does not perform a line feed.

◆ The ReadLine() function gets a line of text from the keyboard.

Part 2

Programming from the Ground Up

You're ready to start writing programs! Your Aunt Millie would be proud.

In this part, you'll learn about the nuts and bolts of C# programs. By the time you finish the next few chapters, your programs will be performing calculations and communicating with users. You'll learn to build your programs from blocks of code that you can use over and over. And you'll even take a look at a rather fanciful way to get to the Moon.

Chapter 4

Basic Building Blocks: Variables and Functions

In This Chapter

- ◆ What variables are and how to create them
- ◆ How to name and use variables
- ◆ The C# simple data types
- ◆ What functions are and how to create them
- ◆ How to name and use functions

Variables in C#

Every program processes data of some kind. Recall from Chapter 1 that as computers run, they keep their programs and data in memory. You may remember that a computer's memory is a long sequence of locations that can store binary information. Every memory location has a unique address. Fortunately, C# does not make us juggle all of those address numbers in our programs. It enables us to create names for memory locations. Named memory locations are *variables*.

At most of the places I have worked, the company provided mailboxes for its employees. Usually, these mailboxes consist of a series of numbered slots on a wall. When you join the company, they often put your name on the mailbox. It stays there until you leave the company (hopefully, for a better-paying job).

Variables in memory work very much like these mailboxes. You can put a name on a numbered memory location. The name is understandable to humans, and stays there until the variable goes away or the program ends. The program can identify the variable by its unique name. It uses the named location to store information.

Every variable must have a name. The names should be descriptive. You must use the following rules when creating variables:

♦ Variable names must start with a letter.

♦ Variable names can contain letters, numbers, and the underscore character (_).

♦ Variable names are case sensitive; the names MyVariable and myVariable refer to two different variables.

♦ The C# keywords cannot be used as variable names. (We'll talk more about keywords later.)

♦ Every variable must have a specified data type.

Techno Talk _____

The **data type** of a variable specifies what kind of data the variable holds. Character variables hold characters, numeric variables hold numbers, and so on.

Techno Talk _____

Simple data types are data types that are built into the C# programming language.

What Is a Data Type?

The C# language enables us to write programs that process data, such as numbers, characters, and strings. Each of these is a different type of data. When you create variables in your programs, the C# language requires that you state what type of data the variables hold. Every variable must have a *data type*.

Many data types are available for use in your programs. Some of these are built into the C# language. They are called the *simple data types*. The .NET Framework provides more.

Table 4.1 provides a list of all the simple data types in C#.

Table 4.1   C# Simple Data Types

Type	Description
sbyte	8-bit signed integer
byte	8-bit unsigned integer

Type	Description
short	16-bit signed integer
int	32-bit signed integer
long	64-bit signed integer
ushort	16-bit unsigned integer
uint	32-bit unsigned integer
ulong	64-bit unsigned integer
float	Single-precision floating point number
double	Double-precision floating point number
bool	Boolean value (true or false)
char	Unicode character
decimal	Precise decimal value

The simple data types are divided into the categories of integers, real numbers, characters, and logical values.

Integers

Integers are numbers that do not contain a decimal point. Table 4.2 shows numbers that are integers and numbers that are not.

Table 4.2   Integers and Nonintegers

Integers	Not Integers
125	125.521
10000	0.00001
–515151	–51.5151
0	1.01
8	8.0

In Table 4.2, the numbers that are not integers all contain decimal points. If it contains a decimal point, it is not an integer. This is true even if the number after the decimal point is 0. So, as the table shows, 8 is an integer, but 8.0 is not.

The integer group of data types includes sbyte, byte, short, int, long, ushort, uint, and ulong. Some of these types are signed and others are unsigned.

Signed numbers can be positive or negative. The types sbyte, short, int, and long are all signed integers.

Unsigned numbers can only hold values that are greater than or equal to 0. No negative values are allowed. The unsigned integer types are `byte`, `ushort`, `uint`, and `ulong`.

From the Knowledge Bank

A given integer type can only hold so many different numbers. For example, an `int` is a 32-bit signed number. That means an `int` can hold 4,294,967,296 (2^{32}) values. About half of those numbers are dedicated to the negative values, and the rest are for positive values. So this integer's data range is from −2,147,483,648 to 2,147,483,647 (including 0).

Unsigned integer types dedicate their entire data storage to numbers that are 0 or greater. So, for instance, a `uint` is a 32-bit unsigned integer. Because it's 32 bits, it can also hold 4,294,967,296 (2^{32}) values. Its data range is from 0 to 4,294,967,295.

If your program does not use negative numbers, it's helpful to use unsigned integers. They provide a greater range of positive numbers.

Real Numbers

In math, real numbers are numbers that contain fractional parts. In C#, this means numbers with decimal points, as shown in Table 4.3. They include the `float`, `double`, and `decimal` data types.

Table 4.3   Numbers with Fractional Parts

125.521
0.00001
−51.5151
1.01
8.0
0.0

CAUTION

Programming Pitfalls

Round-off errors occur when you try to put too many digits into a floating point number.

The C# documentation calls the `float` and `double` data types *floating point types*. It calls the decimal a *precise type*. When using the `float` and `double` data types, it is possible to get *round-off errors*. A round-off error occurs because the number in a data type cannot be exactly represented. For example, the `float` data type has 32 bits to contain information. That gives it only seven digits of significance. The number 123456789.123456789 requires more than 32 bits to store, so it's rounded off. The `double` type has 64 bits, giving 15 significant digits.

If you want to avoid round-off errors, use the `decimal` type. It contains 128 bits. That gives it 28 significant digits. That should be accurate enough for most uses of your computer.

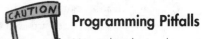

Programming Pitfalls

Using the decimal type can eliminate round-off errors. However, because the size of the variable is larger, it slows the program down a bit. You have to decide which is more important, accuracy or speed. You can't have both.

Characters

In addition to numbers, your program can store characters in variables. Characters are letters, such as A or B. Because all data in a computer must be stored as numbers, the characters in character variables are numbers as well. Programs tell the C# compiler to treat the values in character variables as characters rather than numbers by declaring the variables as type `char`.

All the characters in `char` variables come from the Unicode character set. The Unicode character set is a large group of characters that contains most of the characters people need. It includes characters from many languages. The English alphabet is in it, so are all the letters in the French, Spanish, and German alphabets. It also includes characters from Hebrew, Chinese, Japanese, and many more languages.

Because the Unicode set is so large, I won't type them all for you here. Instead, I'll refer you to Appendix C which contains a chart of the *ASCII* character set.

When computers were first invented, they only used characters for English. The character set used by almost all computers was the ASCII character set. In the ASCII character set, there are 127 characters. The Unicode character set contains the ASCII character set as its first 127 characters. This makes Unicode software backward-compatible with ASCII-based software.

Techno Talk

ASCII stands for American Standard Code for Information Interchange.

As you can see from Appendix C, the ASCII character set contains upper- and lowercase characters. It also has numbers, punctuation marks, and other useful symbols.

Logical Values

Chapter 8 shows how computers can make limited decisions. When they do, they usually use variables of type `bool`. The word `bool` is short for Boolean.

Boolean variables can hold either true or false. Because they are the basis of computer logic, Boolean variables are also called logical variables.

Using Variables

Listing 4.1 contains a program that declares an integer variable.

Listing 4.1   Declaring an Integer Variable

```
1    using System;
2
3    namespace Prog4_1
4    {
5        /// <summary>
6        /// Summary description for Class1.
7        /// </summary>
8        class ApplicationClass
9        {
10           /// <summary>
11           /// The main entry point for the application.
12           /// </summary>
13           [STAThread]
14           static void Main(string[] args)
15           {
16               int totalWood = 42;
17
18               System.Console.Write("How much wood would a ");
19               System.Console.Write("woodchuck chuck, if a ");
20               System.Console.Write("woodchuck\ncould chuck ");
21               System.Console.Write("wood?");
22               System.Console.WriteLine("\nThe answer is {0}",
23                                         totalWood);
24           }
25        }
26    }
```

This is the output of the program:

```
How much wood would a woodchuck chuck, if a woodchuck
could chuck wood?
The answer is 42
```

Line 16 declares an integer variable. Using the equal sign, it sets the variable to an initial value of 42. In C#, the equal sign is called the *assignment operator*. It always assigns the value on the right to the variable on the left.

The program prints a question for the user on lines 18–21. It prints the answer on lines 22 and 23. Notice that it uses both the Write() and WriteLine() functions.

The string that Write() prints on line 20 looks a bit odd the first time you see it. It contains the characters '\n' between the words "wood-chuck" and "could." Although it looks like two characters, the C# compiler sees it as one. It is called the *newline character*. It forces a *line feed* after Write() prints the word "woodchuck."

Data Bit _____

Reminder: The Write() function prints a string to the screen. The WriteLine() function prints the string, followed by a line feed.

From the Knowledge Bank

The terms *newline* and *line feed* are often used interchangeably in C# programming. Most programmers who come from a C or C++ background prefer the term "newline." In C and C++ programming, the term "line feed" means that the cursor moves to the next line, but not necessarily to the beginning of the line. C and C++ programmers use the term "carriage return" to indicate when the cursor moves to the beginning of a line. Technically, a newline indicates that both a line feed and a carriage return are performed.

The WriteLine() statement spans lines 22 and 23. The C# compiler does not care about that at all. It completely ignores the indentation and newlines in source code. They are only there to make the code readable to us. The only time a newline or extra space makes a difference is when it is between quote marks.

Techno Talk _____

Programmers refer to indentation, spaces, and newlines in source code as **white-space**. The C# compiler ignores whitespace.

If I were to change lines 22 and 23 of the program to the following …

```
22          System.Console.WriteLine("\nThe answer
23                              is {0}",totalWood);
```

… the C# compiler would complain with several error messages. It wants the starting and ending quote marks of a string on the same line of code.

Looking closely at the WriteLine() statement on lines 22 and 23 shows how C# programs print variables. When a program prints variables to the screen, it must give a *format string* for Write() or WriteLine(). The format string occurs first in the parentheses.

In this example program, the format string is "\nThe answer is {0}". It tells WriteLine() to print a newline, followed by the characters "The answer is ". It then contains a *format specifier*, which is {0}. Format specifiers tell `Write()` and `WriteLine()` what variables to print. They also indicate how the output should look. The format specifier {0} tells `Write()` and `WriteLine()` to print the first variable after the format string. So on lines 22 and 23, `WriteLine()` prints the characters in the format string, followed by the value in `totalWood`.

If there is more than one item in a function's parentheses, the items must be separated by commas. Because the compiler doesn't care about whitespace, it doesn't matter if there is a newline after a comma. The C# compiler sees lines 22 and 23 as one statement.

Functions in C#

Professional programs are long. Often, they contain hundreds of thousands of lines of source code. It usually takes a team of people (or several teams) to write them.

Given the length of most programs, it doesn't make sense to try to fit all of that source code into `Main()`. Instead, programmers divide programs into *functions*.

A function is a block of C# source code to which you assign a name. You write the function once, and then repeatedly use the source code it contains throughout your program. When a program executes a function's code, we say that it calls or invokes the function.

Data Bit

In the context of classes, which are presented in Chapter 12, C# functions are usually called *methods*.

We write functions to perform a task or a small group of tasks. Every function should be written so that programmers who use the function do not need to know anything about its internal workings. This simplifies the use of functions. There are many things in our lives that work this way.

Like a Microwave Oven

Consider a microwave oven. What does a microwave oven do?

Well, it heats things. That's its purpose, or function.

Every microwave oven has a door on the front. That's how we get cold food into the oven. Microwave ovens have a control pad or knob on them. You use the control pad or knob to tell the oven how long and at what temperature to cook your food. The oven also has a cord that plugs into the wall socket. That's how you get electricity into it.

A microwave oven has three definite input values: cold food, information, and electricity. It has at least one output value: hot food. There are specific ways in which to enter the input values. Cold food goes in the door. Information goes in the keypad or knob.

Electricity goes in the power cord. There is a specific way to get the output value out: You open the door and pull out the food. Be careful—it's hot.

C# functions work in a similar manner. A function accomplishes a definite purpose, just like a microwave oven. Most of us don't have a clue as to what goes on in a microwave oven's internal workings. It doesn't matter. We can use it without that information. You should write all your functions so that they are just the same. If you understand what to put into a function, how to put it in, and what comes out, you should be able to use the function in your programs.

Here's a pop quiz. What functions have you already seen in the example programs?

Time's up. The functions you've already seen in the same programs are `Read()`, `Write()`, `WriteLine()`, and `Main()`. Do you know how `WriteLine()` gets characters to the screen? It doesn't matter. As long as it does its job, you and I don't care how it works.

The reason I'm stressing this point is that the main purpose of breaking programs into functions is to create manageable and reusable chunks of program code. It's only when we write functions in a way that hides their internal workings that those functions are manageable and reusable.

If I write functions that you need and you have to know their internal workings to use them, you won't be very happy with me. Imagine if microwave ovens worked that way, as well as phones, cars, and so on. I don't know much about cars, and I'm happy to keep it that way. If I had to know everything about their internal workings to make them go, I wouldn't get out much. I'm too busy to learn that stuff.

Techno Talk

A function that hides its internal workings is called a **black box function**. The technique of hiding the internal workings of a function is called **implementation hiding**.

How Do I Make a C# Function?

To create a function, first give it a name. Every function in a namespace must have a unique name. C# functions also require parameter lists and return types.

Data Bit

Namespaces were first introduced in Chapter 3. They partition the program into sections. This tells the compiler which names are "local" and which are "long distance."

Function Names

The names for functions follow the same rules as the names for variables. However, they use a different style.

By C# convention, variable names begin with a lowercase letter; any other words in the variable name begin with an uppercase letter. The convention for functions is to capitalize all words in their names. Function names should also be descriptive. Table 4.4 lists some good function names and some that are not so good.

Table 4.4   Good and Bad Function Names

Good Names	Bad Names
CalculateInterest	Print
CalculateArea	Calc Area
ManageWorkFlow	DoBob'sJob
Print_All_Tables	Print$All%Tables

Data Bit

If you don't remember the rules for naming variables, look back at the section called "Variables in C#" earlier in this chapter.

As the table of function names shows, there are many ways to make proper and improper function names. The name CalculateInterest is good because it describes what the function does. It also describes the context in which one would use the function. Calculating interest is something you would expect to do in a financial application.

On the other hand, the name Print is not good because it doesn't really describe what the function does. By looking at it, you can tell it prints something. But what? There's no way of knowing that by looking at the name. You'd have to look at the source code to find out. Any time you have to examine a function's source code to understand what it does, that the function is not a black box. It does not hide its implementation.

Like CalculateInterest, the name CalculateArea describes what the function does. The name Calc Area, shown in the column of bad function names, does the same thing. However, it contains a space. That is not allowed in C# function names.

ManageWorkFlow is descriptive, but DoBob'sJob is not. Someone new to the company who is working on the code might have no idea who Bob is or what he does. Also, what happens when Bob leaves? Will the function be renamed DoMary'sJob? Either way, the C# compiler does not allow function names that contain apostrophes.

The name Print_All_Tables follows a different style than is common in C# by using underscore characters between the words. This is perfectly okay. Although it is not the most common style, as long as you use it for all function names in the program, it's fine.

The name #Print$All%Tables contains the #, $, and % characters. They are not allowed in C# function names.

Getting Data In

Functions have parameter lists enclosed in parentheses. Programs use parameter lists to pass information into functions. Essentially, each parameter is a variable that only the function can see.

The following list contains a group of function names that demonstrates how to create parameter lists.

Table 4.5   Functions with Parameter Lists

CalculateCircleArea(double circleRadius)

ValidateRange(int minValue,int maxValue)

IsYesOrNo(char userInput)

DrawCircle(int centerX,int centerY,float radius)

Wait()

As this group of function names shows, each parameter must have its own type. Parameter lists can contain more than one parameter. They don't have to be the same type. If there is more than one parameter in the list, they must be separated by commas. If parameters are not required for a function, you can leave the parameter list empty.

Getting Data Out

All functions also have a return type. A return type is the type of the data a function sends back to the program that called it. Functions send information back by using the `return` keyword.

The `return` statement causes program execution to jump back to the program that called the function. Therefore, it should occur at the end of the function.

The `FindCircleArea()` function, shown in Listing 4.2, demonstrates how to use the `return` statement in a function.

Data Bit _____

C# keywords have special meaning in the language. They are reserved, so they cannot be used for variable or function names.

Listing 4.2   Returning a Value from a Function

```
1     double FindCircleArea(double radius)
2     {
3         // Area = pi times radius squared.
```

continues

Listing 4.2   Returning a Value from a Function   (continued)

```
4          double area = 3.14159 * radius * radius;
5          return (area);
6     }
```

The FindCircleArea() function returns data of type double. The statement …

```
return (area);
```

… on line 5 sends the value in the variable area back to whatever program calls the FindCircleArea() function.

Time to Tinker: Space Travel Made Easy

When I was a young boy, I read a Dr. Seuss book about a turtle that wanted to see more, so he piled the other turtles in the pond up in a tall stack.

To demonstrate variables and functions in a C# program, I'm going to ask you to suspend your disbelief for a moment. Let's pretend that space travel is possible with the method used by Dr. Seuss's turtles. The program shown in Listing 4.3 calculates how many people it would take to reach the Moon if everyone in the group stood on top of the other.

Listing 4.3   Space Travel, Dr. Seuss Style

```
1     using System;
2
3     namespace Prog4_3
4     {
5         /// <summary>
6         /// Summary description for Class1.
7         /// </summary>
8         class ApplicationClass
9         {
10            /// <summary>
11            /// The main entry point for the application.
12            /// </summary>
13            [STAThread]
14            static void Main(string[] args)
15            {
16                PrintProgramIntro();
17
18                double distanceToMoon;
19                double averageHumanHeight;
20
21                // The Moon is 250,000 miles away.
```

```
22              distanceToMoon = 250000.0;
23
24              // Use 5'6" as the average height of a person.
25              averageHumanHeight = 5.5;
26
27              distanceToMoon = MilesToFeet(distanceToMoon);
28              double totalPeopleRequired =
29                  distanceToMoon/averageHumanHeight;
30              // Print the answer.
31              System.Console.Write("The total number of ");
32              System.Console.WriteLine(
33                  "people required to cover {0} miles is {1}",
34                  FeetToMiles(distanceToMoon),
35                  distanceToMoon);
36          }
37
38          static void PrintProgramIntro()
39          {
40              System.Console.Write("This program calculates ");
41              System.Console.Write("how many people it would ");
42              System.Console.Write("take to reach the Moon\nif ");
43              System.Console.Write("they stood one on top of ");
44              System.Console.WriteLine("the other.");
45          }
46
47          static double MilesToFeet(double numberOfMiles)
48          {
49              return (numberOfMiles * 5280);
50          }
51
52          static double FeetToMiles(double numberOfFeet)
53          {
54              return (numberOfFeet/5280);
55          }
56
57      }
58  }
```

The Main() function in Listing 4.3 begins by calling the function PrintProgramIntro(). When it does, program execution jumps down to line 38. Notice that PrintProgramIntro() does not require any parameters. Therefore, its parameter list is empty.

The PrintProgramIntro() function prints a description of what the program does. When it reaches the closing brace on line 45, the function ends. Program execution jumps back to line 16, and the program continues.

> ### From the Knowledge Bank
>
> Every time a program calls a function, program execution jumps to that function's code. A program can call a function as many times as it needs to. Each time, program execution jumps back to the functions code. This enables you to create more compact programs. Any code that you use more than once should go into a function. Also, any code that you could potentially use in another program should be considered as a candidate for becoming a function.

On lines 18 and 19, the program declares two variables. They are both of type `double`. The program uses the assignment operator on line 22 to assign the value 250000.0 to the variable `distanceToMoon`. On line 25, it assigns 5.5 to the variable `averageHumanHeight`.

The program calls the function `MilesToFeet()` on line 27. It passes the value in the variable `distanceToMoon` through the parameter list. Program execution jumps to line 47. The value in `distanceToMoon` is copied into the parameter `numberOfMiles`. This parameter is local to `MilesToFeet()`. `Main()` cannot access `numberOfMiles`; neither can the function `FeetToMiles()`.

> ### From the Knowledge Bank
>
> To simplify the code, I've made all of the functions in this program `static`. At this point, I'm going to ask for your patience again, wave my hands at this issue, and say, "I'll explain it later. Thank you for your support."

The `MilesToFeet()` function assumes that the value in `numberOfMiles` is a distance in miles. Its purpose is to convert that to the same distance in feet (apologies to those of you who use metric, but I'm too old to start thinking in meters and kilometers). It does this by multiplying the value in `numberOfMiles` by 5280. In C#, the multiplication operator is the asterisk character (*).

The `MilesToFeet()` function does not assign the value it calculates to a variable. Instead, it just returns the result of the calculation. When it does, program execution jumps back to line 27.

Back on line 27, the program assigns the return value of the `MilesToFeet()` function to the variable `distanceToMoon`. It might seem strange to have the same variable on both sides of the assignment operator. However, it doesn't bother the C# compiler a bit. Everything on the right side of the assignment operator is done before anything on the left is looked at. So this statement tells the compiler to pass the value in `distanceToMoon` to the function `MilesToFeet()`. When `MilesToFeet()` returns, the assignment operator assigns the return value back to `distanceToMoon`. As a result, `distanceToMoon` now contains the distance to the Moon in feet rather than miles.

The next step in the program is to calculate how many people it takes to cover the distance between the Earth and Moon. The program does this on lines 28 and 29. The C# compiler is not bothered by the fact that this is spread out over two lines. The extra whitespace doesn't matter.

From the Knowledge Bank

The stuff on the right and left sides of assignment operators has formal names. Everything on the right of the equal sign is an RValue. Everything on the left is called an LValue.

The reason these have formal names is because there are specific rules for what can be an RValue and what can be an LValue.

On lines 31–35, the program prints the result of the calculation. Examine line 31 closely. The call to `WriteLine()` is formatted a bit different from those you saw earlier in this chapter. None of the parameters are on the same line as the function call. Again, the C# compiler is not bothered by this extra whitespace.

The format string on line 33 contains two format specifiers. The specifier `{0}` tells `WriteLine()` to print the string `"people required to cover "`, and then print the value in the first parameter after the format string. That parameter happens to be a function call. Recall that the program converted originally had the distance to the Moon in miles. But it converted that distance to feet. The program needs the distance in miles back again. So it invokes the `FeetToMiles()` function. It passes the value in `distanceToMoon` through the parameter list.

Program execution jumps to line 52. The value in `distanceToMoon` is copied into the parameter `numberOfFeet`. The function expects a distance in feet. It performs a division to calculate that same distance in miles. It then returns the result back to `Main()`.

When `FeetToMiles()` returns, program execution returns to line 34. The return value is passed as a parameter to the `WriteLine()` function. The format specifier `{1}` on line 33 tells `WriteLine()` to print the value in the second parameter after the format string.

From the Knowledge Bank

One of the rules for RValues and LValues states that the return value from a function can never be used as an LValue. However, programs can use it as an RValue.

With that, the `Main()` function ends, and so does the program.

The Least You Need to Know

- ◆ Variables are names for memory locations. C# programs use them to store data in memory without having to refer to the memory location's address number.

- ◆ Every variable must have a type. The type specifies what kind of data can be stored in the variable.

- ◆ Programs use the assignment operator to store values in variables.

- ◆ The C# language provides a variety of simple data types. These are the types that are built into the C# programming language.

- Functions are reusable blocks of source code that have a name.
- If a function is well written, you do not need to know its internal workings. All you need to know is the function's purpose, what information it requires in its parameter list, and what information it returns.
- A parameter list is a list of data items that can be passed into the function.
- A return value is a data item that the function sends back.

Doing Math the Computer's Way

In This Chapter

◆ C# math operators

◆ Rules for using C# math operators

◆ Using C# increment and decrement operators

Nobody likes math. Well … very few people like math. But we all have to deal with it to some extent or another, and so do computers. The difference is that computers are excellent at math.

This is a good thing. It means that we can get computers to do things that most of us don't like to deal with. If we want to do that, we have to understand a bit about how computers do math.

Because computers can't think for themselves, they perform mathematical operations using very strict rules. Even if you don't know it, you understand most of those rules already. Because we're people and not computers, you and I are able to infer rules as we learn. After we figure out the rules for doing things, we don't think about those rules again. We just follow them.

Computers are not that way. To do math (or any other task) they must have a set of rules explicitly spelled out. To get computers to do math properly, you and I have to understand and remember the rules they use.

Numeric Operators

The C# programming language provides the essential operators you might expect. Also, it offers some additional operators that often come in handy.

Addition, Subtraction, Multiplication, and Division

C# has operators for performing the most common math operations: addition, subtraction, multiplication, and division. The symbols that it uses for these operations are shown in Table 5.1.

Table 5.1   The Basic C# Math Operators

Operation	Symbol
Addition	+
Subtraction	-
Multiplication	*
Division	/

These operators generally act in the way you would expect from your experience with using calculators. However, sometimes they give answers that can depend on the type of the data. Suppose, for instance, that you write these lines of code into a program.

```
int thisVariable, thatVariable = 5;
thisVariable = thatVariable/2;
```

What gets stored in `thisVariable`?

Of course, 5 divided by 2 is 2.5. But `thisVariable` is an integer. Integers can't hold numbers with fractional parts. As a result, the program throws away the fractional part and stores 2 in `thisVariable`.

This version of the code gives a different answer.

```
int thatVariable = 5;
double thisVariable;

thisVariable = thatVariable/2;
```

In this case, the variable `thisVariable` is a `double`, one of the floating point data types. It can hold numbers with fractional parts. After these lines of code are executed, `thisVariable` contains the value 2.5.

Modulus

The modulus operator, which is the % sign, gives the remainder of an integer division. Here's the code we saw previously.

```
int thisVariable, thatVariable = 5;
thisVariable = thatVariable/2;
```

Because this is an integer division, the fractional part of the answer gets thrown away. That fractional part is the remainder. The answer to the equation 5 divided by 2 is 2 with a remainder of 1. 2 * 2 is 4, plus the remainder of 1 equals 5.

Using the modulus operator, programs can find remainders, as shown in this example code.

```
int thisVariable, theOtherVariable, thatVariable = 5;

thisVariable = thatVariable/2;
theOtherVariable = thatVariable%2;
```

As before, `thisVariable` contains 2 after a program executes this code. `theOtherVariable` contains the remainder of the division, which is the value 1.

Assignment Operators

You've already seen the assignment operator, which is the equal sign. However, C# also gives us some additional assignment operators. Consider the following code.

```
aVariable = aVariable + 20;
```

This line of code tells the computer to take the value in `aVariable` and add 20 to it. Next, store the result back into `aVariable`. C# gives us a nice shorthand way of doing this, as shown in this next line of sample code.

```
aVariable += 20;
```

This version uses the += operator to do the same thing as the previous line of code. It takes the value in `aVariable`, adds 20 to it, and stores the result back into `aVariable`.

Here's another use of the += operator. Suppose that the value `aVariable` is 10, and the value in `someVariable` is 50. What do you think is stored in `aVariable`?

```
aVariable += someVariable - 20;
```

If the answer you got is 40, you're correct. When using any kind of C# assignment operator, the program does everything on the right of the operator first. So in this example, it first does the subtraction and gets a result of 30. Next, it adds the contents of `aVariable`, which gives 40. Finally, it stores the 40 back into `aVariable`.

The += operator isn't the only assignment operator of this kind that C# offers. Table 5.2 shows some more.

Table 5.2   The C# Assignment Operators

Operator	Description
+=	Add the value on the right to the variable on the left, store the results in the variable on the left.
-=	Subtract the value on the right from the variable on the left, store the results in the variable on the left.
*=	Multiply the value on the right by the variable on the left, store the results in the variable on the left.
/=	Divide the value on the right into the variable on the left, store the results in the variable on the left.
%=	Find the remainder of dividing the value on the right into the variable on the left, store the results in the variable on the left.

Techno Talk

A compound assignment operator is an operator composed of an assignment operator prefixed with another operator.

In C and C++ programming literature, the operators in Table 5.2 are commonly called operator-assign operators, because they are made of an operator and an assignment. The Microsoft C# documentation calls them *compound assignment operators*.

As you can see from Table 5.2, C# offers compound assignment operators that correspond to all of the math operators presented so far. There are others for non-mathematical operations that are presented later.

Precedence

Earlier in this chapter, I mentioned that there are specific rules for performing math operations in C#. Now that you've seen some of the operators, it's time to look at the rules by which they are used.

Suppose your program contains the function DoSomething(), shown in Listing 5.1.

Listing 5.1   Precedence in Math Operations

```
1    void DoSomething(int p1,int p2,int p3)
2    {
3        int v1,v2;
4
```

```
5          v1 = p1 + p2 - p3;
6          v2 = p1 - p2 * p3 + v1;
7    }
```

Line 5 shows an equation with two operators. The question is, which one is done first?

Because people who read English read from left to right, our natural inclination is to process this equation the same way. Most of us would perform the addition first, then the subtraction. C# programs process it in exactly the same way.

C# handles the equation on line 6 a bit differently. According to the rules by which C# programs process math operations, the multiplication is done first. Next, the program performs the subtraction. Finally, it does the addition.

The order of evaluation of math operators is called *precedence*. Every operator in C# has precedence. Operations with higher precedence are performed before operations with lower precedence. For a complete list of all C# operators and their precedence, please see Appendix D.

If you want to, you can change precedence using parentheses. A look in the precedence chart shows that parentheses have very high precedence. The code …

Techno Talk

An operator's **precedence** specifies the order in which it is evaluated in a program.

```
a = b + c * d;
```

… performs the multiplication first, then the addition. To change that, add parentheses, like this:

```
a = (b + c) * d;
```

The parentheses force the addition to be done first, then the multiplication.

Precedence sometimes causes mathematical expressions to be evaluated in ways that we might not expect. To illustrate this idea, here's a pop quiz.

The statement …

```
a *= b + c;
```

… is equivalent to which of the following?

  a) a = (a + b) * c;

  b) a = (a * b) + c;

  c) a = a * (b + c);

  d) a = a * b + c;

To find the answer, let's look at each possible choice in turn. Answer a) is obviously wrong because it switches the positions of the operators. Most of us would choose b) or d). But a look at the precedence chart in Appendix D shows that these statements are the same. The answer is c).

Most of us would think that, because multiplication has higher precedence than addition, answer c) could not be right. However, looking at the precedence chart shows that the *= operator has much lower precedence than the + operator. Therefore, the addition is performed first, then the multiplication and assignment.

My advice is, if you're not sure how an equation will be evaluated, force the precedence with parentheses.

A Little More or Less

It's often the case that our programs need to increase or decrease the contents of a variable by one. Increasing it by one is called *incrementing* it. Decreasing it by one is called *decrementing* it.

C# gives us two operators for incrementing and two for decrementing. The difference between the two sets of operators is in when the increment or decrement is performed. This is illustrated in Listing 5.2.

Listing 5.2   A Postincrement and a Preincrement

```
1     int a, b, c = 5;
2
3     a = c++;
4     b = ++c;
```

Line 1 of Listing 5.2 declares three variables: a, b, and c. It also sets c to 5. Line 3 increments the variable c. In addition, it stores a value in a. This type of increment is called a *postincrement*. It tells the C# compiler to use the value in the variable for other operations on the line first, then perform the increment. The *preincrement* on line 4 tells it to perform the increment first, then use the value in the variable for other operations.

Techno Talk _____

A **postincrement** in a program causes the value in a variable to be used for other operations first, then incremented. A **preincrement** causes the value to be incremented first, then used for other operations.

Because line 3 uses a postincrement on the variable c, the assignment is performed first. Next, the program increments c. After line 3 is executed, the variable a contains 5 and c contains 6.

Line 4 behaves differently. It uses a preincrement. Therefore, it performs the increment first, and then uses the value in c for the assignment. After line 4 is executed, both b and c contain the value 7.

Predecrement and postdecrement follow this same pattern.

Areas and Edge Lengths

It's time for some practice. Create a project in Visual Studio and type the program from Listing 5.3 into it. Compile, link, and run the program.

Listing 5.3   Shape Values Code

```
1    using System;
2
3    namespace prog5_1
4    {
5        /// <summary>
6        /// Summary description for ApplicationClass.
7        /// </summary>
8        class ApplicationClass
9        {
10           /// <summary>
11           /// The main entry point for the application.
12           /// </summary>
13           [STAThread]
14           static void Main(string[] args)
15           {
16               // Prompt the user for a radius.
17               System.Console.Write("Please enter the ");
18               System.Console.Write("integer radius of a ");
19               System.Console.Write("circle in the range of :");
20               System.Console.Write("0-9: ");
21
22               // Read it from the keyboard.
23               char userInput = (char)System.Console.Read();
24
25               // Throw away the newline.
26               System.Console.Read();
27               System.Console.Read();
28
29               // It is a char. Convert it to an int.
30               int radius = CharToInt(userInput);
31
32               // Calculate the area and the circumference.
```

continues

Listing 5.3   Shape Values Code   (continued)

```
33          double area = CircleArea(radius);
34          double edgeLength =
35              CircleCircumference(radius);
36
37          System.Console.Write("\nThe area of a circle ");
38          System.Console.WriteLine(
39              "with a radius of {0} is {1}.",
40              radius,
41              area);
42          System.Console.Write("The circumference of a ");
43          System.Console.WriteLine(
44              "circle with a radius of {0} is {1}.",
45              radius,
46              edgeLength);
47
48          // Prompt the user.
49          System.Console.Write("\nPlease input the length ");
50          System.Console.Write("of a rectangle in the ");
51          System.Console.Write("range of 0-9:");
52
53          // Read it from the keyboard.
54          userInput = (char)System.Console.Read();
55
56          // Throw away the newline.
57          System.Console.Read();
58          System.Console.Read();
59
60          // It is a char. Convert it to an int.
61          int length = CharToInt(userInput);
62
63          // Prompt the user.
64          System.Console.Write("\nPlease input the width ");
65          System.Console.Write("of a rectangle in the ");
66          System.Console.Write("range of 0-9:");
67
68          // Read it from the keyboard.
69          userInput = (char)System.Console.Read();
70
71          // Throw away the newline.
72          System.Console.Read();
73          System.Console.Read();
74
75          // It is a char. Convert it to an int.
76          int width = CharToInt(userInput);
77
```

```
78              // Calculate the area and edge length.
79              area = RectangleArea(length,width);
80              edgeLength = RectangleEdgeLength(length,width);
81
82              System.Console.Write("\nThe area of a rectangle ");
83              System.Console.Write("with a length ");
84              System.Console.WriteLine(
85                  "of {0} and a width of {1} is {2}.",
86                  length,width,area);
87              System.Console.Write("The edge length of a ");
88              System.Console.Write(
89                  "rectangle with a length of {0}",
90                  length);
91              System.Console.WriteLine(
92                  " and a width of {0} is {1}.",
93                  width,edgeLength);
94
95          }
96
97      static int CharToInt(char theChar)
98      {
99          int theAnswer;
100
101          theAnswer = (int)theChar - (int)'0';
102          return (theAnswer);
103      }
104
105     static double CircleArea(int radius)
106     {
107         return (3.14159 * radius * radius);
108     }
109
110     static double CircleCircumference(int radius)
111     {
112         return (2 * 3.14159 * radius);
113     }
114
115      static double RectangleArea(int length,int width)
116      {
117         return (length * width);
118      }
119
120      static double RectangleEdgeLength(
121          int length,
122          int width)
123      {
124         return (2 * length + 2 * width);
```

continues

Listing 5.3 Shape Values Code (continued)

```
125              }
126
127         }
128    }
```

Here's a sample run of the program. My input is shown in bold.

```
Please enter the integer radius of a circle in the range of :0-9: 3

The area of a circle with a radius of 3 is 28.27431.
The circumference of a circle with a radius of 3 is 18.84954.

Please input the length of a rectangle in the range of 0-9:4

Please input the width of a rectangle in the range of 0-9:5

The area of a rectangle with a length of 4 and a width of 5 is 20.
The edge length of a rectangle with a length of 4 and a width of 5 is 18.
```

This program begins by prompting the user for input on lines 17–20. It gets the user's input on line 23. The return type of the Read() function is int. However, what it's getting is characters.

Data Bit

Although it's somewhat confusing, there are very good reasons why the return type of the **Read()** function is **int** rather than **char**. These reasons are presented in Chapter 11; however, the summary of that discussion is that **Read()** must return integers so it can get characters that have a negative value. Specifically, it must be able to return an end-of-file character (EOF). On most computers, EOF has a value of −1.

To convert the integers that Read() returns into characters, the program uses a *type cast*. Type casting is done by putting the type to which you want to convert in parentheses next to the function or variable name. A type cast is good for one statement only. So the (char) in front of System.Console.Read() on line 23 tells the C# compiler to treat the return value of Read() as a character *for that statement only*. As a result, the variable userInput gets the character that the user enters on the keyboard.

Programming Pitfalls

A type cast changes the type of the variable or function for one statement only.

On most systems, after your program calls the Read() function to get a character, it must throw away a carriage return and a line feed. This is caused by buffered input. The details of buffered input are given in Chapter 11. This program throws away the carriage return and the line feed by calling Read() twice more, as shown on lines 26–27.

The program calls a function named CharToInt() on line 30. This function converts a character in the range of '0' through '9' into a number in the range of 0–9. When the program calls this function, the character in userInput is passed into the parameter list and execution jumps to line 97.

The CharToInt() function performs the conversion by subtracting ASCII values. A quick look at the ASCII chart in Appendix C shows that the character '0' has the lowest ASCII value of the characters '0' through '9'. By type casting the parameter theChar and the character '0' into integers, the program can perform math with them. Pretty tricky, don't you think?

Of course, this conversion demonstrates the syntax of the subtraction operator. The use of the - operator is pretty much as most people expect.

Programming Pitfalls

Type casts enable you to change the types of variables and function return values. This can be very good. It can also be very problematic. It is possible to type cast a value to be something that just isn't right. So be sure you know *exactly* what you're doing when you use a type cast.

On line 102 of the program, the function returns the results of its conversion, and program execution jumps back to line 30. The program stores the value returned by the CharToInt() function in the variable radius.

The program calls the CircleArea() function on line 33. It passes the value in radius into the function. Program execution jumps to line 105. The value in the parameter list is copied into the parameter called radius.

The CircleArea() function calculates the area of a circle, and returns it on line 107. Program execution jumps back to line 33, where the program assigns the value from CircleArea() into the variable area.

On lines 34 and 35, the program calls CircleCircumference(). It copies the value in radius into the parameter list, and jumps to line 110. After performing the calculation on line 112, it returns its results and jumps back to lines 34–35. The program assigns the return value from CircleCircumference() into the variable edgeLength. It prints the area and circumference on lines 37–46.

Programming Pitfalls

The name radius in the CircleArea() function refers to the parameter radius, not the variable radius in Main(). Although this can be confusing, it is a common practice for programmers.

Remember that C# uses the * rather than an × for multiplication. Both the `CircleArea()` and `CircleCircumference()` use the multiplication operator.

The rest of the `Main()` function repeats the same pattern for rectangles. It prompts the user for the length and width of a rectangle on lines 49–76. As before, it converts the characters it reads into integer digits (lines 61 and 76). It also throws away the carriage returns and line feeds that it reads (lines 57–58 and 72–73). On line 79, it calls the `RectangleArea()` function to calculate the area of a rectangle with the specified length and width. It calls `RectangleEdgeLength()` to find the total edge length of the rectangle.

> **Data Bit**
>
> The edge length of a rectangle is more correctly called its perimeter. In a professional program, it's generally best to use the most correct terms possible for function names. Therefore, the function `RectangleEdgeLength()` should really be called `RectanglePerimeter()`.

Again, the `RectangleArea()` function demonstrates the multiplication operator. The `RectangleEdgeLength()` shows the use of addition and multiplication in the same equation (line 124). Precedence dictates that the multiplications are performed first, then the addition.

The program finishes by printing the area and edge length of the rectangle on lines 82–93.

The Least You Need to Know

- ◆ C# provides operators for addition, subtraction, multiplication, and division. It also has an operator for finding the remainder of an integer division. This operator is called the modulus operator (%).
- ◆ C# contains several assignment operators. In addition to the basic assignment, it also has compound assignment operators. These perform an operation, and then do the assignment.
- ◆ All C# operators have precedence. Operators with higher precedence are performed first.
- ◆ C# provides two increment and two decrement operators.
- ◆ The preincrement and predecrement operators perform their operations first, and then let the value be used for other operations.
- ◆ The postincrement and postdecrement operators let the value be used for other operations first, then perform the increment or decrement.

Chapter 6

Classy Language

In This Chapter

◆ Software objects

◆ Member Data

◆ Member Functions

◆ Classes

◆ Some objects from the .NET Framework

Although the simple data types presented in Chapter 4 are extremely useful, programmers usually also need access to more complex data types. C# contains several. One example is strings, which is the topic of Chapter 7.

Being the extremely powerful language that it is, C# enables you to create your own data types. In fact, it contains the capability to create a special kind of data type called a *software object*. For this reason, C# is called an object-oriented programming language.

This chapter introduces software objects so that you can begin to use them in your programs. In Chapter 12, you'll learn how to build your own objects.

What Is an Object?

Objects are data types defined by you, the programmer. All objects contain data. The data in an object is called *member data*.

One of the primary purposes of software objects is to hide, or *encapsulate*, the member data. That might sound odd, but it's true. You do not want every statement in a program to have direct access to the data in your object. If they did, any statement could put your data into an invalid state. Invalid data is a very common source of program errors. Encapsulation helps control access to the data. As a result, it's harder for the data to get into an invalid state.

Because an object's data is not directly accessible to the rest of the program, the object must provide *member functions* that give indirect access to the data. The member functions of an object define all of the operations that programs can perform on that data type.

Objects enable programmers to create data types that model or simulate something. It can be something real, or something imaginary.

For instance, if you were writing a program for airplane designers to use, you would probably create a wing object. The wing object would simulate an airplane wing in the program. Using the wing object, your software could predict how a real airplane wing would work. In this way, your software object would model something real.

Now think about bank accounts. There really is no such thing as a bank account. You can't touch a bank account, or paint it purple. It doesn't exist (especially mine). It's a concept or idea. We have nice little bankbooks that describe the state of the account. We have nifty cards that enable us to walk up to machines and do things with bank accounts (take money out). We pretend that bank accounts are real because doing so has advantages for us.

A significant portion of the software written in this world was created to process bank accounts. Many, many programs contain objects that model bank accounts. It's an idea that we find useful, so we model it in software.

An object's member functions have direct access to its data. This enables the functions to change the data, get its current value, and perform validation checks on it. When a program calls a member function to store a value in a member data item, the member function should ensure that the value it received from the program is valid. If not, it should not store the value into the object. This keeps the object in a known and valid state at all times.

Another benefit of member functions is that they hide the implementation of the object. If you write an object, I don't have to know how its member functions are implemented in order to use them. I just have to know what they do, what information they need, and what information they return.

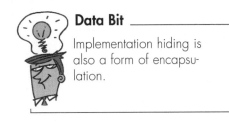

Data Bit _____

Implementation hiding is also a form of encapsulation.

Classes as Objects

C# implements objects with *classes*. Classes have member data and member functions. They provide encapsulation through data and implementation hiding.

The member data in a class can be any valid C# data type. That means that any class can contain member data items that are themselves classes.

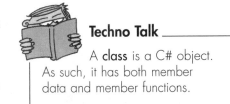

Techno Talk _____

A **class** is a C# object. As such, it has both member data and member functions.

Because all classes are data types, you can use them to declare variables in your programs. You perform operations on them by calling their member functions.

Declaring Class Variables

Programs declare class variables in the same way they declare any other variables. They state the type name and the variable name.

Let's suppose that you are writing a game and you create a class called `dragon`. The `dragon` data type contains member data that describe its size, health level, current emotional state, hunger level, and fire-spitting distance.

To declare a dragon variable in your program, use the same declaration style you used for simple data types. Like this.

```
dragon norbertTheDragon;
```

You can initialize most class variables when you declare them. Some, however, cannot be initialized. It depends on how they're written.

Calling Member Functions

After declaring a class variable in your program, you use it according to the interface of functions that the programmer defined for it. Classes usually support the most common operations. For instance, it would be very reasonable to be able to use the assignment operator with the dragon class.

```
dragon dragonOfTheEasternMountain;
dragonOfTheEasternMountain = norbertTheDragon;
```

Class variables support operations such as assignment because a programmer wrote an assignment operator for that class. The assignment operator is one of the class's member functions.

Member functions can do anything that is sensible for the type. For instance, the dragon class would undoubtedly have the member functions in Table 6.1.

Table 6.1   Member Functions for the dragon Class

Function Name	Description
SpitFire	Causes someone or something in the game to be toasted.
Fly	Makes a dragon fly to a location.
Walk	Makes a dragon walk to a location.
Eat	Better not be around when this function gets called.
Fight	Watch out for this one too.
Flee	Not called very often.

The purpose of calling a member function is to perform operations on object. When your program calls a member function, it must use the object. It states the object name, followed by a period, followed by the function name. Here's an example:

```
norbertTheDragon.Fly(flightPathX,flightPathY);
```

This statement calls the dragon class's Fly() function on the dragon variable norbertTheDragon. This function call only affects the variable norbertTheDragon. If there are other dragon variables in the program, they do not fly as a result of this function call.

Objects You've Already Used

You might not know it, but you have already been using classes in your programs. It's true. At the beginning of every program, you've inserted the line

```
using System;
```

This statement tells the C# compiler that you're going to use something from the System namespace of the .NET Framework.

Part 5 presents the .NET Framework in greater detail. However, from your first C# program, you've been using objects in its namespace. The object you've used more than any other is the `Console` object.

Surprised? Probably not. It logically follows that if `Console` is an object, that `Read()`, `Write()`, and `WriteLine()` areits member functions. You've called these three functions in your programs repeatedly.

You've also been using another object in your programs. Listing 6.1 shows a program from Chapter 3. Can you find an object besides `Console`?

Listing 6.1   A Program That Uses Objects

```
1    using System;
2
3    namespace ConsoleApplication1
4    {
5        /// <summary>
6        /// Summary description for HelloCSharp class.
7        /// </summary>
8        class HelloCSharp
9        {
10           /// <summary>
11           /// The main entry point for the application.
12           /// </summary>
13           [STAThread]
14           static void Main(string[] args)
15           {
16               string inputString;
17
18               // Get the user's name.
19               System.Console.WriteLine("Please tell me your name.");
20               inputString = System.Console.ReadLine();
21
22               // Say hello.
23               System.Console.Write("Hello, ");
24               System.Console.WriteLine(inputString);
25               // All done.
26           }
27       }
28   }
```

If you look on line 8, you'll see the C# keyword `class`. Any time you see that keyword, it's a big red flag indicating that something's going on with an object. In this case, it defines `HelloCSharp` as the application class. The application class is an object. That object contains a member function called `Main()`.

So you see, C# is such an object-oriented programming language that even the program itself is an object.

The Least You Need to Know

- ◆ Software objects are types.
- ◆ Software objects enable programmers to create more complex types than the C# simple types.
- ◆ Software objects model or simulate something in software.
- ◆ C# objects are implemented using classes.
- ◆ Objects contain member data.
- ◆ Access to member data is provided through member functions.
- ◆ Programs call member functions using a class variable, followed by a period, followed by the function name.

7

Stringing Programs Along

In This Chapter

◆ Using character variables in programs.

◆ Escape sequences.

◆ Using strings in programs.

◆ Calling the string class member functions.

◆ Strings are parameters and return values.

Characters in C#

Previous chapters stated that characters in C# are really numbers. Using char variables tells the C# compiler to treat the number as a character rather than an integer. The compiler uses the Unicode character set to translate the numbers into characters. The first 127 characters in the Unicode set are the ASCII character set.

Previous chapters also demonstrated how to get input from the keyboard with the Read() function. They showed how to print characters to the screen with Write() and WriteLine().

Literal Characters

You've also probably noticed that I've been putting literal characters in single quotes. C# requires this when you use them in your code. Here's a few lines of example code that illustrate how character variables work.

```
1    char oneChar;      // Declares a variable.
2    oneChar = 'C';     // Stores a literal character.
3    oneChar = D;       // This will not compile!
4    oneChar = "C";     // Nope. "C" is a string.
```

The statement on line 1 of the example code declares a character variable named oneChar. Line 2 stores the character 'C' in oneChar. The statement on line 3 will not compile because it is missing the single quote marks around the D. In fact, the C# compiler will think that D is a variable.

> **CAUTION**
>
> **Programming Pitfalls**
>
> Literal characters in code must be preceded and followed by a single quote mark. If either quote mark is left off, the C# compiler generates an error.

Line 4 will also not compile. Anything in quote marks is considered a string. You cannot store a string in a character variable. Strings are groups of characters. A char variable stores one single character.

Escape Sequences

There are some literal characters that look like two characters but are really one. You've already seen one of these. It's the '\n' character. The newline is called an *escape sequence*. Table 7.1 contains the escape sequences supported by C#.

Table 7.1   The C# Escape Sequences

Escape Sequence	Sequence Name	Example
\'	Single Quote	'\''
\"	Quote	'\"'
\\	Backslash	'\\'
\0	Null Character	'\0'
\a	Alert	'\a'
\b	Backspace	'\b'
\f	Form Feed	'\f'
\n	Newline	'\n'
\r	Carriage Return	'\r'
\t	Horizontal Tab	'\t'
\v	Vertical Tab	'\v'

To use the escape sequences in your program code, you must put them in single quotes, as shown in the Example column of Table 7.1. Although sequences such as '\"' might look funny, they are very necessary. To see why, take a look at the code shown here.

```
char aCharVar = '''';    // This won't work!
```

This line of code attempts to store the single quote character in a character variable. However, C# sees anything between single quotes as a character. So it thinks the first two single quotes, which contain nothing, are surrounding the character to be assigned to aCharVar. That is definitely not what we're after. It doesn't know what to do with the third single quote mark.

Escape sequences fix this problem. They escape the normal meaning that the C# programming language uses for the character (hence the name escape sequence). To assign the single quote into the variable aCharVar, the line of code above would need to be changed to the following.

```
char aCharVar = '\'';    // This will work
```

Escape sequences serve a variety of purposes. The '\'', '\"', and '\\' characters enable the single quote, quote, and backslash characters to be assigned to char variables. The '\0' gives programs a way to set a char variable to nothing. That's important. It's often the case that you need to initialize a char variable to a value that says, "Nothing is stored here yet." and still have it be in a known state. That's exactly what '\0' is for.

The '\a' through '\v' characters are primarily holdovers from the days when a programmer's workstation consisted of a keyboard connected to a mainframe and a printer instead of a screen. But some of them still see quite a bit of use. This is especially true of '\n'. You'll use that one a lot.

Data Bit

If a character variable contains the '\0' character, it is empty. However, using '\0' keeps the variable in a known state.

Practice with Characters

Just for practice, let's write a C# program that enables the user to enter a character and get its Unicode value. This program is shown in Listing 7.1.

Listing 7.1   Getting Characters from the User

```
1     using System;
2
3     namespace prog7_1
4     {
5         /// <summary>
```

continues

Listing 7.1   Getting Characters from the User   (continued)

```
6        /// Summary description for ApplicationClass.
7        /// </summary>
8        class ApplicationClass
9        {
10           /// <summary>
11           /// The main entry point for the application.
12           /// </summary>
13           [STAThread]
14           static void Main(string[] args)
15           {
16               // Prompt the user for a character.
17               System.Console.WriteLine(
18                   "Please enter a character, then press Enter.");
19               System.Console.Write(">>>");
20
21               // Get the character.
22               char userInput = (char)System.Console.Read();
23
24               /* Convert the character to a Unicode value and
25               print it. */
26               System.Console.Write(
27                   "\nThe character {0} ",
28                   userInput);
29               System.Console.WriteLine(
30                   "has a Unicode value of {0}",
31                   (int)userInput);
32           }
33       }
34   }
```

I ran this program five times. The output looks like this. (As always, the characters I typed in on each run of this program are shown in bold.)

First run.

```
Please enter a character, then press Enter.
>>>d

The character d has a Unicode value of 100
```

Second run.

```
Please enter a character, then press Enter.
>>>A

The character A has a Unicode value of 65
```

Third run.

```
Please enter a character, then press Enter.
>>>%

The character % has a Unicode value of 37
```

Fourth run.

```
Please enter a character, then press Enter.
>>>'

The character ' has a Unicode value of 39
```

Fifth run.

```
Please enter a character, then press Enter.
>>>"
The character " has a Unicode value of 34
```

On lines 16–19, this program prints a prompt asking the user to enter a character. It reads the user's input as a character on line 22. Recall from the last chapter that (char) type casts the integer return value of Read() to a character.

Lines 26–28 print the character the user typed into the program. On lines 29–31, the program again uses a type cast to print the integer value of the character.

Strings in C#

Like the simple types shown in Chapter 4, the string type is built into the C# programming language. However, it is not one of the simple types. It is an object.

As an object, any variable of type string can be used to call string member functions. These functions enable your program to perform a wide variety of operations on string variables.

String Variables and String Literals

To declare strings in your programs, use the string type, as shown in this example.

```
string aStringVariable;
```

Data Bit _____

Reminder: Type casts change the type of a variable or a function return value for one statement only.

Data Bit _____

Remember objects? Chapter 6 introduced them. They are types defined by a programmer that contain member data and member functions.

As with other types of variables, your program can initialize variables of type string when it declares them. The following code snippet shows how.

```
string aStringVariable = "This is a string";
```

Techno Talk

A **literal string** is a string that you type into your program's source code as data.

Strings can contain any valid character from the Unicode character set. *Literal strings* must be in quote marks. The quotes must appear at the start and end of the string. Forgetting one or the other causes errors during compilation.

Your program can use a string variable almost anywhere it can use a literal string. The reverse is also true.

Using the string Class Member Functions

The string class contains more member functions than can be presented at this time. However, Table 7.2 shows the ones that programmers use most.

Table 7.2   Important String Functions

Name	Description
CompareTo	Compares the Unicode values of the individual characters in two strings.
Concat	Copies a string onto the end of the current string.
Equals	Evaluates to true if the two strings contain the same characters.
Insert	Inserts a string into the current string.
Remove	Deletes the specified characters from the string.
Substring	Retrieves a substring from the current string.
ToLower	Returns a copy of the string in lower case.
ToUpper	Returns a copy of the string in upper case.

Listing 7.2 shows a program that demonstrates how some of these functions work.

Listing 7.2   Using the string Class's Member Functions

```
1    using System;
2
3    namespace Prog7_2
4    {
5        /// <summary>
6        /// Summary description for ApplicationClass.
```

```
7          /// </summary>
8          class ApplicationClass
9          {
10             /// <summary>
11             /// The main entry point for the application.
12             /// </summary>
13             [STAThread]
14             static void Main(string[] args)
15             {
16                 // Declare a couple of strings.
17                 string stringOne,
18                     stringTwo = "A short string";
19
20                 // Grab a substring.
21                 stringOne = stringTwo.Substring(2,5);
22                 // Print it to the console.
23                 System.Console.WriteLine(
24                     "stringOne = {0}", stringOne);
25                 // Print the original for comparison.
26                 System.Console.WriteLine(
27                     "stringTwo = {0}\n", stringTwo);
28
29                 // Create a lowercase copy.
30                 stringOne = stringTwo.ToLower();
31                 // Print it to the console.
32                 System.Console.WriteLine(
33                     "stringOne = {0}", stringOne);
34                 // Print the original for comparison.
35                 System.Console.WriteLine(
36                     "stringTwo = {0}\n", stringTwo);
37
38                 // Create an uppercase copy.
39                 stringOne = stringTwo.ToUpper();
40                 // Print it to the console.
41                 System.Console.WriteLine(
42                     "stringOne = {0}", stringOne);
43                 // Print the original for comparison.
44                 System.Console.WriteLine(
45                     "stringTwo = {0}\n", stringTwo);
46
47                 // Delete some characters from the string.
48                 stringOne = stringTwo.Remove(2,6);
49                 // Print it to the console.
50                 System.Console.WriteLine(
51                     "stringOne = {0}", stringOne);
52                 // Print the original for comparison.
53                 System.Console.WriteLine(
```

continues

Listing 7.2 Using the string Class's Member Functions (continued)

```
54                    "stringTwo = {0}\n", stringTwo);
55
56            // Insert some characters into the string.
57            stringOne = stringOne.Insert(
58                2,
59                "long, long, long, long, long, long, ");
60            // Print it to the console.
61            System.Console.WriteLine(
62                "stringOne = {0}", stringOne);
63
64            int result = stringTwo.CompareTo(stringOne);
65            System.Console.WriteLine(
66                "\nresult = {0}",
67                result);
68        }
69    }
70 }
```

This is the output of the program.

```
stringOne = short
stringTwo = A short string

stringOne = a short string
stringTwo = A short string

stringOne = A SHORT STRING
stringTwo = A short string

stringOne = A string
stringTwo = A short string

stringOne = A long, long, long, long, long, long, string

result = 1
```

Data Bit

Variable declarations can span more than one line if each line except the last ends in a comma. The last line in a declaration should end with a semicolon (;).

This short program demonstrates the use of most of the functions in Table 7.2. It first declares two variables of type string, stringOne and stringTwo. Notice that there is a comma on the end of line 17. This indicates that more than one variable is being declared. The fact that the declaration stretches over two lines doesn't matter. As in previous instances, the compiler only sees whitespace when it occurs inside quote marks.

The program initializes stringTwo to "A short string" on line 18. The statement on line 21 calls the Substring() function. The Substring() function copies characters from a string. It returns the copied substring. This program assigns the return value to the variable stringOne.

The parameters to the Substring() function tell it which characters to copy. C# numbers the characters in a string object starting with 0. The next character is numbered 1, and so on. Figure 7.1 illustrates the numbering system.

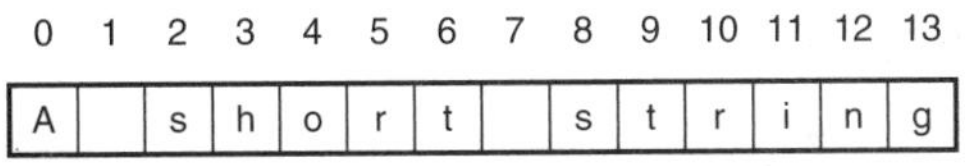

Figure 7.1

The characters in a string are always numbered beginning with 0.

The first parameter to the Substring() function on line 21 is a 2. This tells Substring() to begin copying at the *third* character in the string. Let me emphasize that. Character *numbered* 2 is the *third* character, not the second.

From the Knowledge Bank

A string is a collection of characters. Numbering collection items starting with 0 might not make sense when you first see it. The reason for this scheme is based in programming history. The C and C++ languages, from which C# is derived, both use 0-based numbering for very good reasons. These reasons primarily have to do with the way C and C++ use something called pointers. Pointers enable programs to manipulate directly. Therefore, they have a very strong influence on how compilers lay out programs in memory. In both C and C++, pointers are an extremely important language feature.

C# does not make as heavy use of pointers as C and C++ do. It uses more advanced techniques instead. Even so, C# uses the same 0-based numbering scheme as C and C++.

The second parameter to the Substring() function on line 21 tells the function to copy 5 characters. If it reaches the end of the string before it is able to copy 5 characters, it just returns the characters it could copy.

The call to Substring() does not change the contents of stringTwo in any way. Lines 23–27 demonstrate that clearly by printing the two strings to the screen.

Because stringTwo is intact, the program can use it again on line 30. It calls the ToLower() function on the stringTwo object. The ToLower() function creates a copy of stringTwo. The copy contains only lowercase characters. It assigns the lowercase string to the variable stringOne. On lines 32–36, the program prints the two strings again. As with Substring(), calling ToLower() on stringTwo does not change the contents of stringTwo.

Line 39 uses the ToUpper() function to create a copy of stringTwo that is all uppercase characters. It does not change the contents of stringTwo.

From the Knowledge Bank

Ever wonder why uppercase characters are called *uppercase* characters, and lowercase characters are called *lowercase* characters?

When printing presses were first invented, the person setting the type set each character for the page one at a time. Each character was a raised letter on the small end of a rectangle made of lead. The lead rectangles were about 3 inches by ½ inch by ½ inch.

Because all typesetters before them had done the same thing, every typesetter stored his lead rectangles in two boxes or cases attached to the printing press. The upper case contained the capital letters. The lower case contained what we now call the lowercase letters.

On line 48, the example program calls the Remove() function to delete some of the letters from stringTwo. However, it does not change stringTwo. It creates a copy with the specified characters removed. The program assigns the copy into the variable stringOne on line 48. As you can see from the program output, executing line 48 causes stringOne to contain the string "A string". It does not change stringTwo.

The first parameter to the Remove() function tells it to start with character number 2, which is the third character in the string (there's that 0-based numbering stuff again). The second parameter makes it remove 6 characters. As a result, it takes the string "short" out of a copy of stringTwo and returns the result.

Unlike the previous string member functions, calling the Insert() function on a string variable changes the contents of that variable. Lines 57–62 demonstrate what happens when the program calls Insert() on the variable stringOne. Before line 57 executes, stringOne contains "A string". The first parameter to Insert() tells the function to start with the third character (character number 2), and insert the string "long, long, long, long, long, long, " into stringOne.

The final string function called by the example program is CompareTo(). This function compares the characters in two strings. If the second string is less than the first, the function returns a number that is less than 0. If they are the same, it returns 0. If the second is greater than the first, CompareTo() returns a number that is greater than 0.

Data Bit

Reminder: The Unicode character set contains the ASCII character set as its first 127 characters.

The CompareTo() function enables programs to sort strings in Unicode order. This is almost, but not quite, alphabetical order. If you look at the ASCII table in Appendix C, you'll see why. In the table, the uppercase letters come before the lowercase letters. As a result, CompareTo() tells programs that the string "ABC" comes before the string "abc".

Strings and Functions

When your program passes simple data types to a function, it copies the values in the parameter list into the function's parameters. However, a string is a class, not a simple data type. It's reasonable to ask if it behaves any differently when passed to a function.

The best way to answer any question you have about the C# language is to ask the C# compiler itself. In other words, write a program to test it.

Listing 7.3 shows a test program that illustrates what happens when you pass a `string` variable to a function. It also demonstrates what happens when a function returns a `string`.

Data Bit

If you're unsure how a new technique you're using in a program will work, try writing a short "proof of concept" program to demonstrate the results.

Listing 7.3　Objects, Parameter Lists, and Return Values

```
1    using System;
2
3    namespace Prog7_3
4    {
5        /// <summary>
6        /// Summary description for ApplicationClass.
7        /// </summary>
8        class ApplicationClass
9        {
10            /// <summary>
```

continues

Listing 7.3   Objects, Parameter Lists, and Return Values   (continued)

```
11          /// The main entry point for the application.
12          /// </summary>
13          [STAThread]
14          static void Main(string[] args)
15          {
16              string theString = "This is a string.";
17              System.Console.WriteLine(theString);
18
19              WhatHappens(theString);
20              System.Console.WriteLine(theString);
21
22              theString = ChangesTheString();
23              System.Console.WriteLine(theString);
24
25          }
26
27          static void WhatHappens(string aString)
28          {
29              System.Console.WriteLine(
30                  "Enter WhatHappens()");
31              System.Console.WriteLine(aString);
32              aString = "Another string.";
33              System.Console.WriteLine(aString);
34              System.Console.WriteLine(
35                  "Exit WhatHappens()");
36          }
37
38          static string ChangesTheString()
39          {
40              return ("A different string.");
41          }
42      }
43  }
```

This program produces the output shown here.

```
This is a string.
Enter WhatHappens()
This is a string.
Another string.
Exit WhatHappens()
This is a string.
A different string.
```

As you can see, line 16 declares a string variable called theString. It initializes theString to "This is a string." Line 17 prints the contents of theString to the screen.

On line 19, the program calls the function `WhatHappens()`. It passes `theString` in through the parameter list. Of course, program execution jumps to line 27 when it calls `WhatHappens()` because that's how functions work. The question at this point is, what happens with `theString`?

Line 30 shows the first part of the answer. It prints the contents of the parameter `aString`. The output shows that the contents of the variable `theString` were copied into the parameter `aString`. So that demonstrates that, as far as passing values in, class variables in C# are treated the same as simple types.

Well then, what happens if the function changes the value of `aString`?

Line 32 answers this question by assigning the string `"Another string."` into the parameter `aString`. To prove that it gets changed, line 33 prints the contents of `aString`. The program's output demonstrates that it indeed is changed.

When the function ends, program execution returns to line 19. On line 20, the program prints the contents of `theString`. The program's output shows that it has not changed.

The answer to the question, then, is that C# treats class variables just the same as simple data types when it comes to passing them as parameters. It copies the data in the class variable into the function's parameter.

To demonstrate that strings can be returned just like any simple data type, the program calls the function `ChangesTheString()`. This function returns the string `"A different string."` to the program. The program uses an assignment operator to store the string into the variable `theString`. This changes the contents of the `theString`.

Data Bit

When programs pass variables to functions, the contents of the variables are copied into the function's parameters. The function can change the contents of its parameter. That does not change what's in the original variable. Why? Because what's in the parameters are copies, not the originals. You can change the copies without changing the originals.

This rule holds true whether the value being passed is a simple data type or a class.

Escape Sequences in Strings

Because strings are collections of characters, strings can contain escape sequences. You've already seen strings with escape sequences in them. Many of the programs presented in this book use literal strings that contain the `'\n'` character.

Programming Pitfalls

Watch out for accidental escape sequences in strings. If you intend to put a backslash into a string, you need to use the `'\\'` character.

It's sometimes the case that you unintentionally store escape sequences in strings. All programmers do this once in a while. This is especially true when we're working on computers running the Windows operating system. Look at this `string` variable, and see if you can spot the problems.

```
string filePath = "c:\ThisDir\ThatDir\AnotherDir\BluePic.bmp;
```

Look closely. There are four escape sequences in this string. There are two '\t' characters, one '\a', and one '\b'.

The intention here is to save a file's path name into the variable `filePath`. The path name contains the backslash character. If you need to put a backslash character into a string, you must use an escape sequence. In particular, you must use the '\\' character. So the previous literal string would need to change to …

```
string filePath = "c:\\ThisDir\\ThatDir\\AnotherDir\\BluePic.bmp;
```

The Least You Need to Know

- Characters are really stored in a computer's memory as numbers.
- The compiler uses the Unicode character set to translate the numbers into characters.
- Literal characters must be contained in single quote marks.
- C# supports a group of characters, called escape sequences, that serve special functions in the language.
- C# strings are classes.
- Literal strings must be preceded and followed by quote marks.
- To perform operations on strings, call the member functions of the string class.
- Even when passing class variables to functions, the values in the parameter list are copied into the parameters. A function can change the values in its parameters without affecting anything outside the function.
- Functions can return strings just the way they return simple data types.

Part 3

Beyond the Basics

Programs do more than just math. They do more than just print characters and string on the screen. If that were all programs could do, they'd be complete idiots.

This part describes how C# programs make decisions and how they perform tasks based on those decisions. In other words, you'll learn how to give your program some smarts. It also presents techniques for using files on disks to store information.

Making Choices

In This Chapter

- ◆ How programs make decisions
- ◆ Logical operators and data
- ◆ Conditional branching

Chapter 1 stated that computers cannot think. But, because they can follow instructions, they *can* make decisions. That is, if each individual decision is very, very simple. Programs can combine simple decisions in ways that enable them to deal with complex choices.

Computer programs make decisions by evaluating their data and executing (or not executing) blocks of code based on the results of the evaluation. They use the rules of classical logic to perform their evaluations. This chapter introduces the fundamentals of programming logic.

Decisions and Branching

Each day you make choices. Your day, and the rest of your life, becomes different as your choices accumulate. For instance, when you get up tomorrow, you might ask yourself, "Do I want to go to work today, or go fishing?" You can represent this choice in a diagram like the one shown in Figure 8.1.

Figure 8.1

The choice of whether to go fishing.

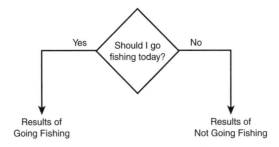

The choice in the diagram is actually simpler than the original question. The one in the diagram simply asks, "Should I go fishing today?" It says nothing about going to work. This is a very simple decision. The choices that computers make must be phrased this way. They must have simple, yes/no or true/false answers. You must be able to write them as a logical expression.

When you were in school, you probably had to learn some logic in your math classes. If you were like me when I was in school, you probably thought, "I'll never use this stuff." Well, now you actually get to use it. In fact, you might even want to go back and thank your math teacher for making you learn it.

From the Knowledge Bank

Certain techniques enable programs to deal with less absolute choices. To find out more about this, look in your local library for information on the topic of artificial intelligence. In particular, search for information on fuzzy logic (yes, it's really called that). The Internet is also an excellent source of information on artificial intelligence.

Programming Pitfalls

In C and C++, programs can use arithmetic expressions for Boolean expressions. As a result, anything with a numeric value can be treated as a Boolean value. In C and C++, any expression that evaluates to 0 is false; everything else is true.

C# is a more strongly typed language than C or C++. It does not allow numeric expressions to be used to make decisions unless you type cast the result.

Logical Data

Programs make decisions by evaluating their data. The C# language defines a special data type, called `bool`, just for making choices. The name `bool` is short for Boolean.

Variables of type `bool` can take on the values `true` and `false`. These are not strings. They are actual values defined by the C# language, just like the numeric values 1 and 2.

This code snippet demonstrates how your program declares Boolean variables.

```
bool aChoice = false;
```

From the Knowledge Bank

Boolean logic is named for George Boole, an English mathematician. Boole, born the son of a poor shoemaker, had very little formal education. However, he determined he would educate himself. By the time he was just 20, he was able to found his own school.

Boole wrote several significant papers that advanced the state of mathematics. These led to his appointment as a Professor of Mathematics at Queen's College in Cork, Ireland. He taught there the rest of his life, and continued to publish seminal works in mathematics and logic until his death from pneumonia in 1864.

Boole's work in symbolic logic is used today to teach mathematics, information theory, switching theory, graph theory, computer science, and artificial intelligence.

All logical expressions must evaluate to an answer that is of type `bool`. The answer to every expression must be `true` or `false`.

There are ways you can have your program make decisions based on the results of expressions that are not Boolean. One way is to type cast the results to type `bool`. Generally, I recommend against this.

A better way is to compare the results of the expression to a value using the logical operators.

Logical Operators

You're lucky. You probably know most of the logical operators already. Table 8.1 shows the list of logical operators.

Table 8.1   The C# Logical Operators

Operator	Description
<	Less than
<=	Less than or equal to
==	Equal to
!=	Not equal to
!	NOT
>=	Greater than or equal to
>	Greater than
&&	Logical AND
||	Logical OR

When you use these operators, you must type them exactly as you see here. For instance, changing >= to => causes a compiler error.

Programs use the operators in Table 8.1 to describe logical relationships between values. For example, consider the logical expressions shown in Listing 8.1.

Listing 8.1   Using the Logical Operators

```
1    thisInt < thatInt
2    thatLong <= theOtherLong
3    x >= screenLeftEdge
4    thisChar != thatChar
5    accountBalance + interestEarned == 1000000.00
```

As these expressions show, programs can use any of the simple data types in logical expressions. However, the expression on the left of the operator must be the same as the type of the item on the right.

The first expression compares the values in two integers. If the value in thisInt is less than the value in thatInt, the expression evaluates to true. Otherwise, it evaluates to false.

The expression on line 2 contains variables of type long. It evaluates to true when thatLong is less than or equal to theOtherLong. If the value in thatLong is greater than the value in theOtherLong, the expression is false.

In the expression on line 3, the data types are not clearly stated. However, because the variable names are x and screenLeftEdge, you can deduce that the statement most probably comes from a graphics application. Such programs often use expressions like this to determine whether something has gone off of the screen. You can assume that the type is probably int. Screen coordinates are usually expressed in terms of integer (x,y) locations. This expression tests an x location to see if it is still on the screen.

The expression on line 4 compares two character variables to determine whether they contain the same character. If they do not, then the expression evaluates to true. If they do contain the same character, the expression is false.

The final expression uses an addition on the left of the == sign. This is perfectly acceptable in C#. It tests if the account balance plus the interest earned is equal to 1000000.00. If so, the expression evaluates to true. If not, it evaluates to false.

One operator you might not be familiar with is the logical NOT, which is the exclamation point. This operator inverts the results of a Boolean expression. It turns true to false and false to true (if it were human, we'd call it a liar).

The last two operators in Table 8.1 are the logical AND and logical OR operators. These provide a way to create compound logical expressions.

Data Bit

Here's a bit of a brain teaser. After these two lines of code execute, what is the value in theAnswer?

```
1    int a = 5, b = -25, c = 6;
2    bool theAnswer = !((!(a >= b)) != (b < c));
```

To figure this out, look at it in parts. The expression a >= b is true because 5 is greater than −25. The ! makes it false. The expression b < c is true because −25 is less than 6. Since the expression on the left of the != is false, and the expression on the right of the != is true, and false is not equal to true, the result of the != is true. The ! on the far left makes it false, so that's the final answer.

Programming Pitfalls

It's important to get into the habit of calling these two operators logical AND and logical OR. Don't just call then AND and OR.

C# also offers bitwise operations. These are somewhat advanced and are not covered in this book. However, in the set of bitwise operators is another AND and OR.

If you call these operators AND and OR, it's easy to get confused between the logical and bitwise AND and OR operators.

The logical AND operator enables programs to combine two expressions into one. It requires that both of its conditions be true in order for the entire expression to be true. Listing 8.2 contains some conditions that use the logical AND.

Listing 8.2   Combining Conditions

```
1    (interestRate >= 0.005) && (interestRate < 0.10)
2    (x >=screenLeftColumn) && (x <= screenRightColumn)
3    (!doneReadingFile) && (andProgram == false)
```

Listing 8.2 shows three expressions that use the logical AND operator. The first tests to see if the value in interestRate is greater than or equal to 5 percent and less than 10 percent. If either of these two conditions in the first expression evaluates to false, the entire expression evaluates to false. They must both be true for the entire expression to be true.

Data Bit

Logical AND expressions combine two conditions. Both of the conditions must evaluate to true for the combined expression to be true.

Listing 8.3 illustrates the use of the logical OR operator. Like the logical AND, logical OR combines two conditions. Only one of the conditions in a logical OR must be `true` for the entire expression to be `true`.

Listing 8.3   Using Logical OR

```
1    (intetestRate >= 0.05) || (loanPaidOff == true)
2    (quitProgram == true) || (programError == true)
3    (!zapped) || (healthPoints > 0)
```

Line 1 of Listing 8.3 contains an expression that might be used in a financial application. It evaluates to `true` if either of its conditions is `true`. So if the interest rate is greater than or equal to 5 percent or the load is paid off, the expression is `true`. Both of those have to be `false` for the entire expression to be `false`.

You might use the expression on line 2 to exit a program. It becomes true if the variable `quitProgram` equals `true` or if `programError` equals `true`.

Line 3 shows a condition that might be used for a character in a computer game. To read the expression in English, you'd read it as, "If the character has not been zapped or its health points is greater than zero."

Branching Statements

Typically, logical expressions are not used by themselves. Programmers put them together with C# statements that control the flow of a program. There are two kinds of such statements. The first, called branching statements, are presented here. The second are called looping statements. These are discussed in the next chapter.

Let's revisit the example of deciding whether to go to work or go fishing. (This example assumes your job is not fishing.) If you choose to go to work, you will spend your day doing tasks associated with work. If you choose to go fishing, you'll do tasks associated with fishing. You can't do both.

Branching statements cause programs to conditionally execute blocks of code. C# has two branching statements: the `if-else` statement and the `switch` statement.

The branching statements have a condition associated with them. Every time the program executes the branching statement, it evaluates the branching statement's condition. If the condition is `true`, the block of code associated with the branching statement is executed. Otherwise, the code is skipped, and the program goes on to something else.

Data Bit

Those of you with a C or C++ background might be familiar with the conditional operator. The conditional operator is also sometimes grouped with the branching statement. To do so is really not accurate.

I don't present the conditional operator in this book because it is not that well used in C# programming, and because of space constraints. For more information on the conditional operator, see *The Complete Idiot's Guide to C++*, by Paul Snaith.

The if-else Statement

The if-else statement provides C# programs with a logical junction in program flow. When a program encounters an if-else statement, it selects one of two possible paths to follow. The if-else statement uses the C# keywords if and else (what a coincidence!). Listing 8.4 demonstrates their use.

Listing 8.4   A Simple if-else Statement

```
1    if (goFishing == true)
2    {
3        // Do fishing tasks.
4    }
5    else
6    {
7        // Do other tasks.
8    }
```

C# considers this a single statement. The condition on this statement is (goFishing == true). The conditions of if-else statements must appear in parentheses.

If the variable goFishing in this example contains the value true, then the program executes all of the C# statements between the opening and closing braces of the if portion of the statement. The braces for the if portion of the if-else statement are on lines 2 and 4. They may contain as many C# statements are needed. You can even put if-else statements inside this block of code.

If the variable goFishing contains false, the program executes the statements associated with the else portion of the if-else statement. Like the if portion, it has its own code block enclosed by braces. The braces for the else block are on lines 6 and 8 in Listing 8.4. This code block can also contain as many statements as needed.

CAUTION

Programming Pitfalls

The condition on an if-else statement must be in parentheses; otherwise, the C# compiler will generate an error.

Data Bit _____

To increase the readability of your program, indent to the right whenever you start a new code block with an opening brace. Indent to the left ("unindent") when you end the code block with a closing brace.

For simplicity, the two code blocks in Listing 8.4 just contain comments. An important thing to note, however, is that it is customary to indent the statements in a code block. Any time your program enters a code block, indent to the right. Whenever it leaves a code block, indent to the left (many would say, "unindent"). Formatting your source code in this way makes it much more readable.

To make the operation of if-else statements easier to visualize, programmers often diagram them. Figure 8.2 illustrates how the fishing example used in this chapter would look.

Figure 8.2

This is how the fishing example would look in an if-else *diagram.*

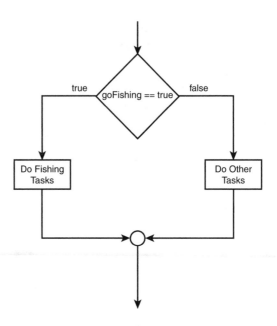

In the diagram, the diamond represents the if-else statement. It contains the if-else statement's conditional expression. The true branch indicates the code that gets executed when the condition evaluates to true. The false branch shows the if-else statement's code for the false condition.

Techno Talk _____

Diagrams like the one in the figure are called **flowcharts**. They have been used for many years to help design computer programs.

Variations on the if-else statement are allowed by the C# language. For instance, the else portion of the if-else statement is optional. You can leave it off, if need be. Listing 8.5 contains an example of how it works.

Listing 8.5   An `if` Statement Without an `else` Clause

```
1    if (anInt>10)
2    {
3        anInt = anotherInt + 100;
4        anotherInt++;
5    }
```

This code fragment shows an `if` statement with no `else`. If the value in the variable `anInt` is greater than 10, the program executes the code between the opening and closing braces. If the `anInt` is less than or equal to 10, the program does not execute the statements in the code block. Instead, program execution continues with the next statement after line 5.

Your program can nest `if-else` statements inside `if-else` statements. Listing 8.6 contains a code fragment, rather than entire program, that demonstrates nested `if-else` statements.

Data Bit

The `else` portion of an `if-else` statement is optional.

Listing 8.6   Nested `if-else` Statements

```
1    if (!fileName.Equals(""))
2    {
3        bool fileSaved = SaveTheFile(fileName);
4        if (fileSaved == true)
5        {
6            System.Console.WriteLine(
7                "Saved the file {0}",
8                fileName);
9        }
10       else
11       {
12           System.Console.WriteLine(
13               "Could not save the file {0}",
14               fileName);
15       }
16   }
17   else
18   {
19       System.Console.WriteLine(
20           "Please enter a file name.");
21   }
```

In this example, the variable `fileName` is assumed to be a string. The two `if-else` statements in this code fragment are nested one inside the other. The outer `if-else` begins on line 1. Its code block starts on line 2 and ends on line 16. The `else` that corresponds to the outer `if` is on line 17. The code block that goes with the `else` portion spans lines 18–21.

Data Bit _____

Looking at these nested `if`-`else` statements probably makes it clearer why indentation is so important for program readability.

Data Bit _____

You can indicate an empty string in your source code by placing a pair of quote marks together with nothing between them.

The condition on the outer `if`-`else` statement probably looks a bit unusual. It calls the `Equals()` function on the `fileName` variable. Recall from Chapter 7 that `Equals()` is a member function of the `string` class. It returns `true` if the string in its parameter list is equal to the current string. In this case, it compares the string `fileName` to an empty string. The empty string is indicated by two quote marks with nothing inside them.

If `fileName` is empty, the `Equals()` function returns `true`. However, the NOT operator (the exclamation point) inverts the condition. So if the `Equals()` function returns `true`, the `!` makes it `false`. In that case, the program does not execute the `if` portion of the outer `if`-`else` statement. Instead, it jumps to line 17 and executes the statements in the code block for the outer `else`.

On the other hand, if the `Equals()` function returns false, it means the variable `fileName` is not empty. The `!` turns the `false` to `true`. This causes the program to execute the code block for the outer `if`.

To summarize, if you were to read the condition on line 1 in English, it would be "If the filename is not empty."

If the filename is, in fact, not empty, the program executes the code block of the outer `if`. Inside that code block (lines 2–16) is another `if`-`else` statement. On line 3, the program calls a function named `SaveTheFile()`, and passes it the filename. `SaveTheFile()` is a function somewhere inside our imaginary example program. It is not provided in any library.

If `SaveTheFile()` is able to save the current file to the disk, it returns `true`. Otherwise, it returns `false`. The program saves its return value in the variable `fileSaved`. The condition for the inner `if`-`else` is on line 4. If `fileSaved` equals `true`, the program executes the code block on lines 5–9. If it is `false`, the program executes the code block on lines 11–15.

Programming Pitfalls _____

It is not a good idea to nest `if`-`else` statements more than 3 or 4 levels deep. If you nest them any deeper, your program can become unreadable.

A variation on the nested `if`-`else` is the chained `if`-`else` statement. Chained `if`-`else` statements are a series of `if`-`else` statements nested inside the `else` of the preceding `if`-`else`.

Boy, that was clear as mud. Let's try to unmuddy things with the sample code in Listing 8.7.

Listing 8.7   Chained `if`-`else` Statements

```
1    if (inputChar=='S')
2    {
3        SaveTheFile();
4    }
5    else
6    {
7        if (inputChar == 'L')
8        {
9            LoadTheFile();
10       }
11       else
12       {
13           if (inputChar == 'X')
14           {
15               quitProgram = true;
16           }
17           else
18           {
19               System.Console.WriteLine(
20                   "That is not a valid menu selection.");
21           }
22       }
23   }
```

The `if` on line 1 tests the variable `inputChar`. If it equals `'S'`, the program in Listing 8.7 calls `SaveTheFile()`. Else, if it equals `'L'`, then call `LoadTheFile()`. Else if it is equal to `'X'` set the variable `quitProgram` equal to `true`. Else if `inputChar` does not equal any of these values, print a message to the user.

Although this indentation style for chained `if`-`else` statements is correct, it is not the convention. Listing 8.8 shows how most programmers would write the same chained `if`-`else`.

Listing 8.8   The Common Indentation Style for Chained `if`-`else` Statements

```
1    if (inputChar=='S')
2    {
3        SaveTheFile();
4    }
5    else if (inputChar == 'L')
6    {
7        LoadTheFile();
8    }
```

continues

Listing 8.8   The Common Indentation Style for Chained `if`-`else` Statements   (continued)

```
9     else if (inputChar == 'X')
10    {
11        quitProgram = true;
12    }
13    else
14    {
15        System.Console.WriteLine(
16            "That is not a valid menu selection.");
17    }
```

If you read this closely, you'll find it does the same thing as the previous version. However, it doesn't drift as far to the right, so most programmers prefer it.

If an `if`-`else` contains only one statement, you can omit the opening and closing braces.

Data Bit

When formatting code, many style issues are a matter of convention. In general, it's best to follow the convention unless you have a compelling reason not to.

```
1     if (x < 100)
2         x++;
```

This `if` statement tests the variable x to see if it is less than 100. If so, it increments x. The C# compiler has no problems with this style. You can use it with `if` statements that have `else` statements, as well. This is illustrated in Listing 8.9.

Listing 8.9   An `if` with Only One Line of Code

```
1     if (x < 100)
2         x++;
3     else
4     {
5         x=0;
6         y=0;
7     }
```

On this `if`-`else` statement, the `if` portion has only one statement in its code block, so the braces are omitted. You can just as easily leave them off the `else`, if needed.

Although this style is common among programmers, I advise against using it. Listing 8.10 demonstrates why.

Listing 8.10   If the Braces Are Left Off ...

```
1     if (x < 100)
2         x++;
3         y=0;
```

The indentation in this example shows that the programmer who wrote it intended for the statements on lines 2 and 3 to be in the same code block. However, that is not the case. Because the braces were left off, only the increment statement on line 2 is in the if statement's code block. The program will *always* execute the statement on line 3.

The way to solve this problem is to use braces, even if there is only one statement in the code block. It might seem like more trouble than it's worth. However, my experience is that the opposite is true. It saves us from having to track down this type of error.

Data Bit

I know I've said it several times before, but to avoid mistakes, it bears repeating. The C# compiler does not care about whitespace such as indentation. The only time it matters to the compiler is when it occurs between quote marks.

The switch Statement

C# provides another branching statement, called the switch statement. Unlike if statements, switch statements provide more than two possible code blocks to execute. Listing 8.11 demonstrates how programs use the switch statement.

Listing 8.11   Using the switch Statement

```
1    switch (inputChar)
2    {
3        case 'S':
4            SaveTheFile();
5        break;
6
7        case 'L':
8            LoadTheFile();
9        break;
10
11        case 'X':
12            quitProgram = true;
13        break;
14
15        default:
16            System.Console.WriteLine(
17                "That is not a valid menu selection.");
18        break;
19    }
```

As you can see, a `switch` statement is very much like a group of `if-else` statements chained together, one after the other. Figure 8.3 shows a flowchart of a generic `switch` statement.

Figure 8.3

The program flow of a generic `switch` statement.

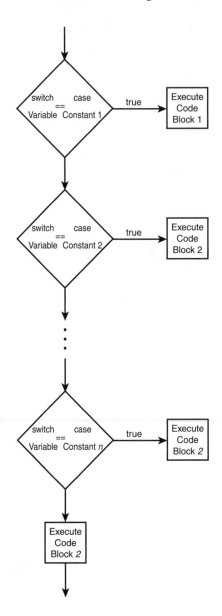

A `switch` statement contains one or more `case` statements. Each `case` statement has a block of code associated with it. The code blocks are not marked by braces. Instead, the code block for each `case` is contained between the `case` and `break` statements.

A literal value must be associated with every case statement. The program compares the literal value to the value of the switch variable. The switch variable is in parentheses the beginning of the switch statement. If the case statement's literal value equals the value in the switch variable, the program executes the case statement's code block.

That's a bit of a mouthful. To get an idea of what it means, take a look back at Listing 8.11. Of course line 1 contains the switch keyword that marks the beginning of the switch statement. The switch statement's code block begins on line 2 and ends on line 19.

See the variable inputChar in parentheses on line 1? That's the value being tested. The program tests it against the literal value associated with each case statement, starting from the first case.

The default statement at the end is executed if inputChar is not equal to any of the case values. Like an else in an if-else statement, the default is optional. If the switch variable is not equal to any of the case values and there is no default, the switch statement does nothing. Program execution continues with the next statement after the switch statement's code block.

You can read the switch statement in the example like this, "If inputChar equals 'S', then call SaveTheFile(). Otherwise, if it equals 'L', then call LoadTheFile(). Else if it is equal to 'X' set the variable quitProgram equal to true. Else if inputChar does not equal any of these values, print a message to the user."

The Least You Need to Know

- Programs make decisions by evaluating logical expressions.
- Logical expressions must have a true or false answer.
- All logical expressions in C# must be of type bool.
- Expressions using the logical operators evaluate to a bool value.
- C# provides branching statements to conditionally execute blocks of code.
- The if-else statement offers a choice between executing, at most, one of two possible blocks of code.
- The switch statement enables programs to select, at most, one of several blocks of code.

Chapter 9

Getting a Bit Loopy

In This Chapter

- ◆ Performing loops in programs
- ◆ Using pretest and post-test loops
- ◆ The `while`, `do-while`, and `for` loops

In Chapter 8 you saw how programmers control the flow of programs with branching statements. C# also offers looping statements for controlling program flow.

What's the difference?

Branching statements execute blocks of code based on the evaluation of conditions. They execute their code blocks just once. Looping statements also execute code based on the evaluation of conditions. But they execute their code blocks over and over until their conditions evaluate to `false`.

This chapter discusses how to use looping statements in your programs. It's important to note, however, that I do not present all of C# looping statements in this chapter. The `foreach` loop, which is used with collections such as arrays, is discussed in Chapter 10.

Testy Start, Testy End

All loops have a condition. If the condition evaluates to `true`, the program executes the loop's code block. If the loop's condition evaluates to `false`, the program doesn't execute the code block.

Data Bit _____

The code block of a loop (and of a branching statement) is also called its body.

Techno Talk _____

Loops whose conditions are tested at the beginning are called **pretest loops**. If a loop's condition is tested at the end, it is a **post-test loop**.

A loop's condition can occur at the beginning of a loop, or at its end. If the program evaluates a loop's condition at the beginning of the loop, it is a *pretest loop*. If the program evaluates the condition at the end, it is a *post-test loop*.

The pretest loops in C# are the `while` and `for` loops. C# only has one post-test loop, the `do-while` loop.

The while Loop

Probably the easiest looping statement in C# is the `while` loop. It is a pretest loop, so its condition is tested before its code block is executed. Figure 9.1 shows a diagram of a `while` loop.

Figure 9.1

Generically, this is how a `while` *loop operates.*

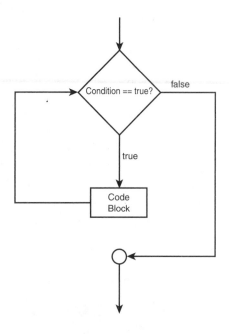

Like `if` statements, the condition of a `while` loop must be in parentheses. Its code block can contain zero or more statements. The statements should be inside opening and closing braces.

I'm going to change the subject just a bit. I remember watching the moon launches when I was a boy. One of the most memorable events of my life was the first moon landing. I used to love to sit in front of the TV and watch the rockets blast off. During the final countdown of the last ten seconds before the launch, adrenalin would pump through me as I wished it was me riding that rocket into space.

Listing 9.1 shows an example of a `while` loop that simulates the final ten seconds of rocket launch.

Programming Pitfalls

It is possible to create `while` loops that do everything inside their conditions. These loops have no statements in their code blocks. Loops like this are very efficient, but they're tricky. I generally advise against writing them until you are very familiar with C#.

Listing 9.1   T Minus Ten Seconds and Counting

```
1     using System;
2
3     namespace Prog9_1
4     {
5     /// <summary>
6     /// Summary description for ApplicationClass.
7     /// </summary>
8     class ApplicationClass
9     {
10        /// <summary>
11        /// The main entry point for the application.
12        /// </summary>
13        [STAThread]
14        static void Main(string[] args)
15        {
16            int loopCounter = 9;
17
18            System.Console.WriteLine(
19                "10 seconds to liftoff");
20
21            while (loopCounter >= 0)
22            {
23                System.Console.WriteLine(
24                    "T Minus: {0}",
25                    loopCounter--);
26            }
27
```

continues

Listing 9.1 T Minus Ten Seconds and Counting (continued)

```
28                    System.Console.WriteLine(
29                        "Liftoff!");
30                }
31           }
32      }
```

The output of the program looks like this.

```
10 seconds to liftoff
T Minus: 9
T Minus: 8
T Minus: 7
T Minus: 6
T Minus: 5
T Minus: 4
T Minus: 3
T Minus: 2
T Minus: 1
T Minus: 0
Liftoff!
```

Can't you just hear the thunder of the rockets? No? Oh, well. I guess you had to be there.

The program in Listing 9.1 declares an integer variable called loopCounter on line 16 and initializes it to 9. It enters a while loop on line 18. The program tests the loop's condition. If it evaluates to true, the program executes the loop's code block. If it does not, the program jumps to the next statement after the loop.

The first time through the loop, the value of loopCounter is 9. As a result, the condition evaluates to true. The program executes the loop's code block, which spans lines 22–26.

Notice on line 25, the program decrements loopCounter with a postdecrement. This decreases the value in loopCounter by 1 each time the program executes the loop's code block. On the loop's first pass, the value is decremented from 9 to 8. The program reaches the end of the loop's code block. It goes back to the beginning of the loop and performs the test. Because loopCounter is 8, the condition evaluates to true and the program executes the code block.

Data Bit _____

The increment and decrement operators introduced in Chapter 5 are often used with loops.

This continues until the value of loopCounter reaches -1. When it does, the test evaluates to false. The program does not execute the loop's code block. Instead, it continues on with the next statement after line 26. The next statement appears on lines 28-29. It prints the string "Liftoff!" to the screen.

What would happen if the program in Listing 9.1 used a predecrement instead? Listing 9.2 demonstrates this.

Listing 9.2 Using the Predecrement Operator with a `while` Loop ...

```
1    using System;
2
3    namespace Prog9_2
4    {
5        /// <summary>
6        /// Summary description for ApplicationClass.
7        /// </summary>
8        class ApplicationClass
9        {
10           /// <summary>
11           /// The main entry point for the application.
12           /// </summary>
13           [STAThread]
14           static void Main(string[] args)
15           {
16               int loopCounter = 9;
17
18               System.Console.WriteLine(
19                   "10 seconds to liftoff");
20
21               while (loopCounter >= 0)
22               {
23                   System.Console.WriteLine(
24                       "T Minus: {0}",
25                       --loopCounter);
26               }
27
28               System.Console.WriteLine(
29                   "Liftoff!");
30           }
31       }
32   }
```

Here's the program output. See the difference? NASA wouldn't like this countdown very much.

```
10 seconds to liftoff
T Minus: 8
T Minus: 7
T Minus: 6
T Minus: 5
T Minus: 4
T Minus: 3
T Minus: 2
T Minus: 1
T Minus: 0
T Minus: -1
Liftoff!
```

The postdecrement operator in Listing 9.1 told the program to use the value in the variable first, then decrement it. The predecrement performed on line 25 of Listing 9.2 says decrement the value in the variable first, then use it.

Data Bit _____

If you want to, you can increment or decrement variables in a loop's condition. Just be sure you understand *exactly* what's going on.

Listing 9.3 shows another variation on this. It uses a postdecrement *in the condition*. That's right. You can actually perform an increment or decrement in the condition of a `while` loop. This program uses a postincrement. What will be the output of the program?

Listing 9.3   A Postdecrement in the Condition of a `while` Loop

```
1      using System;
2
3      namespace Prog9_3
4      {
5          /// <summary>
6          /// Summary description for ApplicationClass.
7          /// </summary>
8          class ApplicationClass
9          {
10             /// <summary>
11             /// The main entry point for the application.
12             /// </summary>
13             [STAThread]
14             static void Main(string[] args)
15             {
16                 int loopCounter = 10;
17
18                 System.Console.WriteLine(
19                     "10 seconds to liftoff");
20
21                 while (loopCounter-- > 0)
22                 {
23                     System.Console.WriteLine(
24                         "T Minus: {0}",
25                         loopCounter);
26                 }
27
28                 System.Console.WriteLine(
29                     "Liftoff!");
30             }
31         }
32     }
```

Here's the output.

```
10 seconds to liftoff
T Minus: 9
T Minus: 8
T Minus: 7
T Minus: 6
T Minus: 5
T Minus: 4
T Minus: 3
T Minus: 2
T Minus: 1
T Minus: 0
Liftoff!
```

Notice that I had to make some changes to the program to get a proper countdown. On line 16, the variable `loopCounter` is now initialized to 10, rather than 9. The loop's condition now tests to see if the value in `loopCounter` is greater than 0. In the previous two versions, it tested whether `loopCounter` was greater than or equal to 0.

The first time through the loop, `loopCounter` is 10. The condition evaluates to `true`. Before anything else happens, the postdecrement operator decrements `loopCounter` to 9. Inside the body of the loop, the call to `WriteLine()` prints the value in `loopCounter`. Next, the program returns to the beginning of the loop where it tests the condition again.

Let's think a moment about what happens when the program executes the loop with the value of 1 in `loopCounter`. It performs the test, which evaluates to `true`. The program then decrements `loopCounter` to 0. It prints the 0 and reaches the end of the loop. Jumping back to the beginning of the loop, the program performs the test again. This time, the value in `loopCounter` is 0. Because the condition tests whether `loopCounter` is greater than 0, the test evaluates to `false`.

If this program used the same condition as the previous two versions (`loopCounter-- >= 0`), it would execute the loop's code block again. However, it would also perform the decrement. So the value it would print would be –1. That's why the loop's condition is different this time.

What would happen if we changed line 21 to use a predecrement? The easiest way to answer that question is to try it and see. Listing 9.4 shows the code.

Listing 9.4   A Predecrement in a `while` Loop

```
1    using System;
2
3    namespace Prog9_4
4    {
```

```
5          /// <summary>
6          /// Summary description for ApplicationClass.
7          /// </summary>
8          class ApplicationClass
9          {
10             /// <summary>
11             /// The main entry point for the application.
12             /// </summary>
13             [STAThread]
14             static void Main(string[] args)
15             {
16                 int loopCounter = 10;
17
18                 System.Console.WriteLine(
19                     "10 seconds to liftoff");
20
21                 while (--loopCounter > 0)
22                 {
23                     System.Console.WriteLine(
24                         "T Minus: {0}",
25                         loopCounter);
26                 }
27
28                 System.Console.WriteLine(
29                     "Liftoff!");
30             }
31         }
32     }
```

Here's the output.

```
10 seconds to liftoff
T Minus: 9
T Minus: 8
T Minus: 7
T Minus: 6
T Minus: 5
T Minus: 4
T Minus: 3
T Minus: 2
T Minus: 1
Liftoff!
```

Why the difference?

Because the loop now uses a predecrement, it does the decrement *before* it tests the condition. On the first pass through the loop, the value of loopCounter decreases to 9 before the program performs the test. It continues like this through each pass of the loop until it reaches 1. At that point, it decrements the variable to 0, and the test evaluates to false. The program skips the loop's code block and continues with the next statement after line 26.

The do-while Loop

C# gives us a post-test variation of the while loop. It's called the do-while loop. Because do-while is a post-test loop, programs do not check its condition until they reach the end of the loop. In all other respects, the do-while loop works just like the while loop.

Figure 9.2 illustrates the execution of the do-while loop.

Data Bit _____

If you use a preincrement to increment a variable in a condition, the program performs the increment *before* it tests the condition. If you use a postincrement, it performs the increment *after* it does the test.

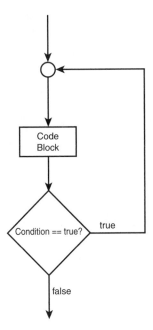

Figure 9.2

The flow of execution for a do-while loop.

Even though it probably wasn't very thrilling, let's use the countdown program from the previous looping examples. We'll rewrite it to use the do-while loop. Listing 9.5 contains the resulting program.

Listing 9.5   Blasting off with the `do-while` loop

```
1     using System;
2
3     namespace Prog9_5
4     {
5         /// <summary>
6         /// Summary description for ApplicationClass.
7         /// </summary>
8         class ApplicationClass
9         {
10            /// <summary>
11            /// The main entry point for the application.
12            /// </summary>
13            [STAThread]
14            static void Main(string[] args)
15            {
16                int loopCounter = 9;
17
18                System.Console.WriteLine(
19                    "10 seconds to liftoff");
20
21                do
22                {
23                    System.Console.WriteLine(
24                        "T Minus: {0}",
25                        loopCounter--);
26                } while (--loopCounter >= 0);
27
28                System.Console.WriteLine(
29                    "Liftoff!");
30            }
31        }
32    }
```

This is the output from Listing 9.5.

```
10 seconds to liftoff
T Minus: 9
T Minus: 8
T Minus: 7
T Minus: 6
T Minus: 5
T Minus: 4
T Minus: 3
T Minus: 2
T Minus: 1
T Minus: 0
Liftoff!
```

The output of this program is the same as the output of the program in Listing 9.1. That's not always the case. Because a do-while loop performs its test at the end of the loop, it will *iterate* at least once. Pretest loops such as the while loop might not iterate at all.

The best way to understand the difference between pretest and posttest loops is to walk through the program in Listing 9.5 step by step. On line 16, the program sets `loopCounter` to 9. It enters the `do-while` loop on line 21. Because the test of a `do-while` loop is not done until the end of the code block, the program will always execute the loop's code block at least once.

Techno Talk

When speaking of loops in programs, the term **iterate** is used to indicate a pass through the loop's code block.

Data Bit

The code block of a pretest loop may never execute. If the loop's condition evaluates to `false` the first time it is tested, the program will never execute the loop's code block.

The code block of a post-test loop always executes at least once. The test is done after the first iteration. Even if the test evaluates to `false` on the first iteration, the loop will execute at least once.

After executing the loop's code block, the program performs the test on line 26. The test says that the loop will continue while `loopCounter` is greater than or equal to 0. On the first pass, it contains 9, but the predecrement makes it 8 before the program performs the test. Because 8 is greater than 0, the test evaluates to `true` and the loop continues.

Let's imagine that the loop keeps going until the point that `loopCounter` is decremented to 0. At that point, the program has executed the loop 10 times. Now step through the program again in your imagination. The integer variable `loopCounter` contains 0, but the predecrement operator decrements to –1. So the test on line 26 results in a value of `false`, and the loop ends.

What happens when you use a postdecrement instead? I think you can already predict the result, but Listing 9.6 demonstrates it anyway.

Listing 9.6   Postdecrement in a do-while Loop

```
1     using System;
2
3     namespace Prog9_6
4     {
```

continues

Listing 9.6   Postdecrement in a do-while Loop   (continued)

```
5       /// <summary>
6       /// Summary description for ApplicationClass.
7       /// </summary>
8       class ApplicationClass
9       {
10          /// <summary>
11          /// The main entry point for the application.
12          /// </summary>
13          [STAThread]
14          static void Main(string[] args)
15          {
16              int loopCounter = 9;
17
18              System.Console.WriteLine(
19                  "10 seconds to liftoff");
20
21              do
22              {
23                  System.Console.WriteLine(
24                      "T Minus: {0}",
25                      loopCounter);
26              } while (loopCounter-- >= 0);
27
28              System.Console.WriteLine(
29                  "Liftoff!");
30          }
31      }
32  }
```

Here's the output. Did it do what you thought it would?

```
10 seconds to liftoff
T Minus: 9
T Minus: 8
T Minus: 7
T Minus: 6
T Minus: 5
T Minus: 4
T Minus: 3
T Minus: 2
T Minus: 1
T Minus: 0
T Minus: -1
Liftoff!
```

In this version, the program decrements loopCounter after it performs the loop's test. As a result, the loop executes 11, rather than 10, times.

The for Loop

The `while` and `do-while` loops both generally require that you initialize some sort of loop control variable. They also need that variable to change over time. This is typically done by incrementing or decrementing it. In addition, they both require that a test be performed to determine whether the loop should continue.

The C# language's `for` loop brings all three of those tasks into one place. Figure 9.3 shows a flowchart of how it works.

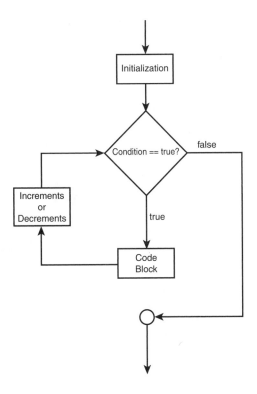

Figure 9.3

The `for` loop performs an initialization, test, and increment/decrement in one place.

Whenever a program executes the `for` statement, it performs the instructions in the parentheses after the keyword `for`. The parentheses contain three expressions separated by two semicolons. There must never be more or less than two semicolons in the parentheses of a `for` loop.

The first expression in the parentheses is an initialization. It is performed once. Usually, you will initialize a loop control variable in this expression.

The second expression in a `for` loop's parentheses is the loop's condition. The `for` loop is a pretest loop, so the program performs the test before it executes the code block.

The third and final expression in the parentheses is the loop's increment or decrement. The program performs the statement in this section only if it executed the code block.

Let's do an example to see how these different pieces of the for loop work. Listing 9.7 uses the rocket countdown program to demonstrate a simple for loop.

Listing 9.7   The Rocket Countdown for Loop

```
1      using System;
2
3      namespace Prog9_7
4      {
5          /// <summary>
6          /// Summary description for Class1.
7          /// </summary>
8          class Class1
9          {
10             /// <summary>
11             /// The main entry point for the application.
12             /// </summary>
13             [STAThread]
14             static void Main(string[] args)
15             {
16                 int loopCounter;
17
18                 System.Console.WriteLine(
19                     "10 seconds to liftoff");
20
21                 for (loopCounter = 9; loopCounter >=0; loopCounter--)
22                 {
23                     System.Console.WriteLine(
24                         "T Minus: {0}",
25                         loopCounter);
26                 }
27
28                 System.Console.WriteLine(
29                     "Liftoff!");
30             }
31         }
32     }
```

The output from the program looks like this.

```
10 seconds to liftoff
T Minus: 9
T Minus: 8
T Minus: 7
```

```
T Minus: 6
T Minus: 5
T Minus: 4
T Minus: 3
T Minus: 2
T Minus: 1
T Minus: 0
Liftoff!
```

Try walking through the execution of a for loop by using your imagination, or by stepping through it with Visual Studio's debugger. The program in Listing 9.7 begins the loop on line 21 by performing the loop's initialization. It sets loopCounter to 9. After that, the program evaluates the test. In this case, it checks to see whether the value in loopCounter is greater than or equal to 0. As long as that is true, the loop continues. If it does, the program executes the loop's code block. In Listing 9.7, the for loop's code block appears on lines 22–26. After it completes the code block, the program performs the decrement (or increment) in the third expression in the for loop's parentheses.

Programs always execute the parts of a for loop in this order.

The Least You Need to Know

- ◆ Looping statements enable programs to execute blocks of code repeatedly.
- ◆ Every looping statement has a conditional expression.
- ◆ The conditional expression of a pretest loop is evaluated at the beginning of the loop. Pretest loops execute zero or more times.
- ◆ The while and for loops are pretest loops.
- ◆ The conditional expression of a post-test loop is evaluated at the end of the loop. Post-test loops execute one or more times.
- ◆ The do-while loop is a post-test loop.

Arrays: More Fun Than a Stamp Collection

In This Chapter

- ◆ Arrays are data collections
- ◆ Declaring and initializing arrays
- ◆ Accessing array elements
- ◆ Single- and multidimensional arrays

Programs store data in variables. The variables presented so far each hold one piece of data. In C#, you can also create variables that hold collections of data items. These are called *arrays*.

What Is an Array?

An array is a group or collection of data items. The entire collection goes by one name. Every item is the same type as all the others in the collection. Your program can access any individual item.

The items can be any valid C# type. So, for instance, your program can declare arrays whose items are the simple types you saw in previous chapters. They can also be strings, or other objects.

A Different Kind of Animal

Because it is a collection, an array is different than a variable of the same type. Your program declares it differently than variables.

To declare an array, you must state the type first. Like this:

```
int
```

Next is a pair of square brackets with nothing inside. This tells the C# compiler that the variable is an array.

```
int []
```

The square brackets are followed by the variable name.

```
int [] anIntArray
```

Techno Talk _____

Dedicating memory for use by a variable is called **allocating** memory.

At this point, you've created an array, but you haven't set aside any memory for it. The result isn't very useful.

When programs declare arrays, they almost always *allocate* some memory to the array with the new keyword. It works like this.

```
int [] anIntArray = new int[10];
```

From the Knowledge Bank

The array allocation size that your program specifies does not have to be a literal number. It can be a variable. As a result, it is possible for your program to calculate the amount of memory it needs and allocate arrays accordingly.

This code snippet shows the declaration of the array variable on the left of the assignment operator. It uses the new keyword on the right to allocate memory. When you use new, you must specify the type of the data the memory will hold, and the number of items to allocate. The type that you allocate on the right of the assignment should be the same as the type of the array variable on the left.

Using Arrays

Arrays, like most types of collections in C#, use a 0-based numbering system.

Data Bit _____

All arrays use 0-based item numbering. The first item in the array is item number 0. The second is item number 1, and so on.

To access individual array items, your program must state the name of the array variable. The array name must be followed by the item number in square brackets, like so.

```
anIntArray[3] = -85;
```

This statement stores the value –85 into the fourth location in the array variable anIntArray.

Listing 10.1 contains a program that combines arrays with loops.

Listing 10.1   Arrays and Loops

```
1     using System;
2
3     namespace Prog10_1
4     {
5         /// <summary>
6         /// Summary description for ApplicationClass.
7         /// </summary>
8         class ApplicationClass
9         {
10            /// <summary>
11            /// The main entry point for the application.
12            /// </summary>
13            [STAThread]
14            static void Main(string[] args)
15            {
16                int []anIntArray = new int[10];
17                int i,j;
18
19                for (i=0,j=10;i<10;i++,j—)
20                {
21                    anIntArray[i]=j;
22                }
23
24                for (i=0;i<10;i++)
25                {
26                    System.Console.WriteLine(
27                        "i={0}",
28                        anIntArray[i]);
29                }
30            }
31        }
32    }
```

The program output looks like this:

```
i=10
i=9
i=8
i=7
i=6
i=5
```

```
i=4
i=3
i=2
i=1
```

Line 16 of Listing 10.1 demonstrates how to declare an array, and how to allocate memory for it. Line 17 declares two integer variables. The really interesting part starts on line 19.

When the program enters the `for` loop on line 19, it executes what it finds in the loop's initialization section. But wait. There's something new going on here. The initialization section looks like this.

```
i=0,j=10
```

This is actually a correct initialization. It initializes multiple variables. C# allows this if a comma separates the initializations. The initialization on line 19 sets the variable `i` to 0. It also sets the variable `j` to 10.

After it does the initialization, the program tests the `for` loop's condition. The loop continues while `i` is less than 10.

> **Data Bit**
>
> Your program can do multiple initializations in a `for` loop. The initializations must be separated by commas.

If the condition evaluates to `true`, the program executes the statements in the loop's code block. The statement on line 21 copies the value in `j` into an array location. The first time through the loop, the value of `i` is 0. As a result, the value in `j`, which is 10, gets copied into `anIntArray[0]`. The location `anIntArray[0]` is the first location in the array.

After code block is done, the program executes whatever it finds in the increment/decrement section of the parentheses. On line 19, the `for` loop's increment/decrement section looks like this.

> **Techno Talk**
>
> A single item in an array is often called an **array element**.

```
i++,j--
```

You've probably already figured out that this statement performs both an increment and a decrement. It increments `i` and decrements `j`. C# allows multiple increments and decrements in this section of the `for` loop. They must be separated by commas.

You cannot use a comma to create multiple conditions in the test portion of a `for` loop. Instead, you must use the logical AND or logical OR operator.

The second loop in Listing 10.1 iterates through the array again. As it does, it prints the values copied into the array.

As you can see from Listing 10.1, array items are like variables. Your program can use them anywhere they would use a variable of the same type. The program in Listing 10.1

is perfectly happy to use an array element on the left of an equal sign (line 21). It is also pleased to use the array element as a parameter to the `WriteLine()` function (line 28).

Initializing Arrays

Like other types of variables, programs can initialize arrays. By default, the C# compiler generates code that stores the value 0 in all memory allocated to arrays.

If you don't want an array to contain zeros when it's created, you can initialize it yourself. To do so, specify the initial values in braces. Here's an example:

Data Bit

To initialize a variable means to store an initial value in it. Initializing variables is always a good idea. It helps keep them in a known state. When variables contain unknown or random values, it's a sure sign of a program error.

```
int [] anIntArray = new int[] {1, 3, 5, 7, 9};
```

This statement creates an array variable called `anIntArray`. It allocates 5 integers for the array. The 5 integers contain the values shown in the braces: 1, 3, 5, 7, and 9.

Notice that there is no number in the square brackets on the right of the equal sign. That number is the array declaration's size specifier. It tells the program how many items to allocate for the array. But it's missing from this example declaration. How does the program know to allocate 5 integers for this array? When you leave off the size specifier (the number in the square brackets), it counts the number of items in the braces.

Programming Pitfalls

If you don't put in a size specifier when you use **new** to allocate an array, you must put in a list of initial values. If you do not, the compiler will generate an error.

If you want to, you can put both a size specifier and a list of initial values into the array declaration, like this.

```
int [] anIntArray = new int[10] {1, 3, 5, 7, 9};
```

This declaration allocates ten integers for the array. It sets the first five to the values 1, 3, 5, 7, and 9. The other five contain zeros.

Wish Upon a Star

It's time practice using arrays. The program in Listing 10.2 demonstrates many of the C# language elements presented so far.

Listing 10.2   Learning About Arrays and Stars

```
1    using System;
2
3    namespace prog10_2
4    {
5        /// <summary>
6        /// Summary description for Class1.
7        /// </summary>
8        class ApplicationClass
9        {
10            /// <summary>
11            /// The main entry point for the application.
12            /// </summary>
13            [STAThread]
14            static void Main(string[] args)
15            {
16                string [] starName = new string [10]
17                    {
18                        "Sun", "Alpha Centauri A",
19                        "Alpha Centauri B", "Alpha Centauri C",
20                        "Barnard's Star", "Wolf 359",
21                        "Lalande 21185", "Sirius A",
22                        "Sirius B", "Luyten 726-8 A"
23                    };
24
25                double [] starDistance = new double [10]
26                    {
27                        0.0, 4.35, 4.35, 4.25, 5.96,
28                        7.8, 8.25, 8.6, 8.6, 8.8
29                    };
30
31                string userInput;
32
33                // The primary program loop.
34                do
35                {
36                    // Clear the screen (more or less).
37                    ClearScreen();
38
39                    // Print a menu on the screen.
40                    DisplayMenu(starName);
41
42                    // Get the user's choice
43                    userInput = System.Console.ReadLine();
44
45                    // If the user does not want to quit...
46                    if ((userInput.CompareTo("q")!=0) &&
```

```
47                          (userInput.CompareTo("Q")!=0))
48                      {
49                          // Conver the input to an integer.
50                          int itemNumber = Convert.ToInt16(userInput);
51
52                          // If the input value was in range...
53                          if ((itemNumber >= 1) && (itemNumber <= 10))
54                          {
55                              // Array index numbers start with 0.
56                              itemNumber—;
57
58                              // Display the information about the star.
59                              DisplayStarInfo(
60                                  starName[itemNumber],
61                                  starDistance[itemNumber]);
62                          }
63                      }
64                  } while ((userInput.CompareTo("q") != 0) &&
65                          (userInput.CompareTo("Q") != 0));
66              }
67
68              static void ClearScreen()
69              {
70                  int i;
71
72                  for (i=0; i<25; i++)
73                  {
74                      System.Console.Write("\n");
75                  }
76              }
77
78              static void DisplayMenu(string [] starName)
79              {
80                  System.Console.WriteLine(
81                      "Select a Star From the List.");
82                  int i;
83                  for (i=0; i<10; i++)
84                  {
85                      System.Console.WriteLine(
86                          "{0} {1}",
87                          i+1,
88                          starName[i]);
89                  }
90
91                  System.Console.Write("Enter an Item Number: ");
92              }
93
```

continues

Listing 10.2   Learning About Arrays and Stars   (continued)

```
94              static void DisplayStarInfo(
95                  string starName,
96                  double starDistance)
97          {
98              System.Console.WriteLine(
99                  "\n\nStar Name: {0}",
100                 starName);
101             System.Console.WriteLine(
102                 "Distance in Light Years: {0}",
103                 starDistance);
104
105             System.Console.WriteLine(
106                 "\nPress Enter to Continue...");
107
108             // Throw away the carriage return and line feed.
109             System.Console.Read();
110             System.Console.Read();
111         }
112     }
113 }
```

The program in Listing 10.2 uses two arrays. The first contains items of type string. The declaration of the string array begins on line 16. This declaration allocates memory for 10 strings. It initializes them to names of the stars that are nearest to Earth.

The second array contains double values. These are the distances in light years (the distance light travels in a year) to the stars named in the first array.

Data Bit

The ClearScreen() function shown in Listing 10.2 works on most displays because most displays have fewer than 25 lines of text. However, it's not a method you would want to use in a professional program. It's slow, it wastes CPU time, and you can see the text scroll up the screen as it executes. Professional programs clear the screen using methods that blank the entire screen at once.

On line 34, the program enters a do-while loop. Recall that the do-while loop is a post-test loop, so the program executes its code block at least once.

The first thing the program does inside the loop is to call the ClearScreen() function. This function begins on line 68. It uses a for loop to write a newline to the screen 25 times. This is an extremely simple-minded way to clear a screen. It is not at all efficient. However, it demonstrates how to use a for loop, so it is included here.

When the ClearScreen() function ends, program execution umps back to line 37. Next, the program calls the DisplayMenu() function on line 40. It passes the array of strings in the parameter list. The DisplayMenu() function appears on lines 78–92. It prints a prompt for the user on lines 80–81. Using a `for` loop, it prints a number followed by a string from the array of strings. Each string in the array is a star name. When the loop finishes, the program prints another prompt for the user and returns to `Main()`.

On line 43, the program gets a string from the user. The `if` statement beginning on lines 46–47 tests to see whether the user typed in the characters 'q' or 'Q'. It performs the test using the `CompareTo()` function from the string class. As a result, the letters q and Q are in quote marks, not single quotes. This condition

```
userInput.CompareTo("q")!=0
```

tests whether the `string` variable `userInput` is not equal to the string `"q"`, not the character `'q'`. `"q"` and `'q'` are not the same thing. The first is a string that happens to contain one character. The second is a character. Those are two different data types.

If the user does not want to quit, the program executes the `if` statement's code block. Inside the code block, the program calls the `Convert.ToInt16()` function. The .NET Framework, which is explained more fully in Part 5, provides the `Convert.ToInt16()` function, which can convert a variety of data types to a 16-bit integer.

The `Convert.ToInt16()` function converts the user's input into an integer menu selection. On line 53, the program tests to see if the integer it got from `Convert.ToInt32()` is valid input. If it is not, `itemNumber` contains 0.

From the Knowledge Bank

Notice that there is no `else` for the `if` statement that begins on line 53 of Listing 10.2. There should be.

Try adding one yourself. The program should output an error message (a polite error message!) so that the user knows when the input is invalid.

If the user's input is valid, the program calls `DisplayStarInfo()` on lines 59–61. The program passes in the items corresponding to the star the user selected from each of the three arrays. The `DisplayStarInfo()` appears on lines 94–111. It prints labels for the star data, and the star data itself. At the end of the function, program execution jumps back to lines 59–61.

Data Bit

Like me, you might wonder if there is any intelligent life on any planets that might be around these stars. A friend of mine says that Title 14, Section 1211 of the Code of Federal Regulations, implemented on July 16, 1969, makes it illegal for U.S. citizens to have any contact with extraterrestrials or their vehicles.

I've never looked this up to find out if it's true. But if it is, I have to wonder if anyone has been convicted of this crime.

The do-while loop continues while userInput does not contain the string "q" and it does not contain the string "Q". If userInput contains either one of those values, the loop ends. When the loop is finished, the program ends.

Meanwhile, Back on Earth ...

One of my favorite features of C# is its ability to iterate easily through arrays. In fact, it provides a special looping statement for arrays and similar collections. It's called the foreach statement.

Programming Pitfalls

Starting and ending loops correctly can be a source of problems in programs. If your program encounters an error in a loop, check your loop control variables first.

The foreach statement iterates once for each item in an array. One of the reasons I like it so much is that it knows where to start and stop automatically. Starting and stopping a loop can be a source of program errors. This is especially true when you're using arrays. It's nice that C# can handle it for you.

Listing 10.3 contains a short program that uses the foreach loop.

Listing 10.3   Looping with the foreach Statement

```
1     using System;
2
3     namespace Prog10_3
4     {
5         /// <summary>
6         /// Summary description for Class1.
7         /// </summary>
8         class Class1
9         {
10            /// <summary>
11            /// The main entry point for the application.
12            /// </summary>
13            [STAThread]
14            static void Main(string[] args)
15            {
16                string [] starName = new string [10]
17                    {
18                        "Sun", "Alpha Centauri A",
19                        "Alpha Centauri B", "Alpha Centauri C",
20                        "Barnard's Star", "Wolf 359",
21                        "Lalande 21185", "Sirius A",
22                        "Sirius B", "Luyten 726-8 A"
```

```
23                        };
24
25                   System.Console.WriteLine(
26                        "I'm from one of these stars.");
27
28                   foreach (string star in starName)
29                   {
30                        System.Console.WriteLine(star);
31                   }
32                   System.Console.WriteLine(
33                        "I'm not saying which one.");
34               }
35          }
36     }
```

This program uses the array of star names from Listing 10.2. It iterates through the array, printing each star name. Here's the output.

```
I'm from one of these stars.
Sun
Alpha Centauri A
Alpha Centauri B
Alpha Centauri C
Barnard's Star
Wolf 359
Lalande 21185
Sirius A
Sirius B
Luyten 726-8 A
I'm not saying which one.
```

Lines 28–31 show how the program uses the foreach loop. Like other loops, the foreach loop has a statement in parentheses that controls loop iteration. But that statement isn't the kind of condition the other loops use. Instead, it declares a variable. Each time through the loop, the program copies the value in one array item into the variable.

If you step through the loop on lines 28–31 with Visual Studio's debugger, it copies the string in starName[0] into star on the first iteration. The second time through, it copies starName[1] into star, and so on. When it reaches the end of the array, it stops.

An important thing to know about the foreach loop is that the loop variable (star, in this case) is read-only. That means you can read the value from it, but you can't store values into it in the loop's code block.

Programming Pitfalls

The loop control variable in a foreach loop is read-only. You cannot assign a value to it.

To test this, try changing the `foreach` loop in Listing 10.3 to look like this.

```
foreach (string star in starName)
{
    System.Console.WriteLine(star);
    star = "Bobstar";
}
```

When you compile this version of the program, Visual Studio generates an error. But in spite of this limitation, the `foreach` loop is a handy tool.

Multidimensional Arrays

Your program can create arrays of nearly any data type. That includes simple types, like `int` or `double`, and more complex types, such as `string`. Programs can even declare arrays of arrays. We call them *multidimensional arrays*.

Techno Talk _____

Arrays that contain elements that are also arrays are called **multidimensional arrays**.

From the Knowledge Bank

A 2-D array is not really a table. It doesn't have rows and columns. It's an array of arrays. As a result, it is possible to create an array of different-sized arrays. It's like having a table with rows that are different lengths.

Most programmers call an array of arrays a two-dimensional array (or a 2-D array). It's declared somewhat differently than a single-dimensional array.

```
int [,] myData = new int[10,20];
```

This statement declares a variable called `myData`. The comma in the leftmost set of square brackets says that `myData` is a 2-D array. It's often helpful to think of it as a table with rows and columns. This declaration allocates 10 rows of integers to `myData`. Each row contains 20 columns.

Using a 2-D array requires that you specify both the row and column number of the element you want to access. To store a value in the first column of the second row of the array `myData`, your program would use a statement like this.

```
myData[1,0] = 10;
```

Iterating through a multidimensional array generally requires one loop for each dimension.

Listing 10.4 shows a short program that illustrates the use of multidimensional arrays.

Programming Pitfalls

This style of array indexing is different from C and C++. In C and C++, the array row and column numbers are each put into their own set of square brackets. So instead of ...

```
MyData[1,0] = 10;  // C# style
```

...they access array elements like this:

```
myData[1][0] = 10;  // C and C++ style
```

If you've got a background in C or C++, you'll need to be sure you use the C# style of array indexing.

Listing 10.4   Iterating Through a 2-D Array

```
1    using System;
2
3    namespace Prog10_4
4    {
5        /// <summary>
6        /// Summary description for Class1.
7        /// </summary>
8        class ApplicationClass
9        {
10           /// <summary>
11           /// The main entry point for the application.
12           /// </summary>
13           [STAThread]
14           static void Main(string[] args)
15       {
16               int [,] timesTable = new int [10,10];
17               int i,j;
18
19               for (i=0; i<10; i++)
20               {
21                   for (j=0; j<10; j++)
22                   {
23                       timesTable[i,j] = (i+1)*(j+1);
24                   }
25               }
26
```

continues

Listing 10.4 Iterating Through a 2-D Array (continued)

```
27              for (i=0; i<10; i++)
28              {
29                  for (j=0; j<10; j++)
30                  {
31                      if (timesTable[i,j] < 10)
32                      {
33                          System.Console.Write(
34                              "{0}  ",timesTable[i,j]);
35                      }
36                      else
37                      {
38                          System.Console.Write(
39                              "{0} ",timesTable[i,j]);
40                      }
41                  }
42                  System.Console.Write("\n");
43              }
44          }
45      }
46  }
```

The program in Listing 10.4 uses an array, some loops, and an `if-else` statement to print a multiplication table. Here's the output.

```
1   2   3   4   5   6   7   8   9   10
2   4   6   8   10  12  14  16  18  20
3   6   9   12  15  18  21  24  27  30
4   8   12  16  20  24  28  32  36  40
5   10  15  20  25  30  35  40  45  50
6   12  18  24  30  36  42  48  54  60
7   14  21  28  35  42  49  56  63  70
8   16  24  32  40  48  56  64  72  80
9   18  27  36  45  54  63  72  81  90
10  20  30  40  50  60  70  80  90  100
```

Data Bit

It's important to remember that 2-D arrays don't really have rows and columns. It's just convenient to think of them as if they do.

On line 16, the program in Listing 10.4 declares a 2-D array called `timesTable`. It allocates 10 rows and 10 columns of integers for the array.

After declaring two loop control variables (`i` and `j`), the program enters a pair of nested `for` loops. A loop's code block can contain any valid C# statement. That includes other loops. The outer loop begins on line 19. It iterates once for each row in the array, for a total of 10 iterations. The inner loop starts on line 21. It iterates once for each column in a row. So it iterates 10 times for every row. Because there are 10 rows, the inner loop iterates a total of 100 times.

The pair of loops on lines 19–25 goes through every row in the array. In each row, it stores a value in each column.

After storing the values into timesTable, the program in Listing 10.4 again enters another pair of nested for loops. These loops print out the values in the array. They contain an if-else statement that controls the alignment of the printed table. If the value in the array is less than 10, the program prints the value followed by two spaces. If it is 10 or greater, the program prints the value followed by one space. This gives the column alignment shown in the program output.

Data Bit

The parentheses in the statement

`(i+1)*(j+1)`

on line 23 are not needed for precedence. They are there for clarity.

Data Bit

It's always a good idea to "pretty up" your output as this example program does. Doing something as simple as aligning output into columns goes a long way toward making your users happy.

It's possible to declare arrays of even higher dimensions. For instance, your program could create a 3-D or 4-D array like this.

```
int [,,] threeDArray = new int[4,5,6];
int [,,]fourDArray = new int[4,5,6,10];
```

The first declaration creates an array with 4 rows, 5 columns, and a depth of 6. The second creates an array that is 4x5x6x10.

Business programs typically only use 1-D or 2-D arrays. 3-D arrays are very common in computer graphics applications. Creating arrays with more than three dimensions is rare.

The Least You Need to Know

- An array is a variable that holds a collection of data items rather than just one data item.
- All of the items in an array must be of the same data type.
- Your program must declare and allocate memory for the array.
- Arrays use a 0-based numbering system for their items.
- Arrays can be initialized when they are declared.
- Programs often use the foreach loop with arrays.
- Multidimensional arrays are arrays of arrays.

Chapter 11

Being Persistent: Storing Information in Files

In This Chapter

- ◆ Storing information in files
- ◆ Buffered and unbuffered I/O
- ◆ Text and binary files
- ◆ Files, streams, binary readers, and binary writers

In the previous chapters, all data input came from the keyboard. All data output went to the screen. As you've used your computer, you've undoubtedly noticed that almost all programs output data to devices such as disks and printers. They read data from disks, scanners, modems, and so on. Your C# programs can work the same way.

To introduce how programs perform data I/O, this chapter explains *file handling*. File handling is the technique of reading data from files and writing it to files. The files exist on external devices such as disks.

Data held in memory goes away when the computer is turned off. In programmer jargon, we say the data in memory (RAM) does not persist. Data stored on disks persists when the computer is off. So basically, file handling is all about how to help your data be persistent.

Buffered Input and Output

I've shown example programs in previous chapters that got single characters from the keyboard. After they did, they had to read a carriage return and line feed from the keyboard, as well, and throw them away. I said that I'd explain the reason later. Well, now's the time for that explanation.

Techno Talk _____

Programmers often abbreviate the term "input and output" as I/O.

Data Bit _____

Buffered I/O improves the efficiency of I/O operations.

Computers perform two kinds of input and output. Some do unbuffered *I/O*. Most use buffered I/O. A *buffer* is a small area of memory dedicated to holding I/O data for a while.

At certain times, the buffers are flushed. If they are line buffers, they are flushed when a newline character comes into the buffer. Most operating systems have keyboard buffers. Keyboard buffers are line buffers.

Most operating systems use buffers for disk I/O. It makes the I/O operations more efficient. Disk buffers are flushed when they are full, when a program closes their associated file, or when a program sends them a flush command.

For the most part, C# handles the issues associated with buffered I/O. This is an improvement over C and C++. About the only time you need to deal with buffers is when you use the Read() function to read a single character from the keyboard. This is actually not a very common task. Part 5 introduces Windows GUI programming using the .NET Framework. In it, you'll see that there are better ways of getting input and output that don't involve dealing with I/O buffers.

From the Knowledge Bank

Be thankful that C# handles most I/O issues as buffers for you. When I started programming in C, the C Standard Library (which actually wasn't called that yet) had very little support for such operations. At the time, the college class I was taking was writing our programs on a minicomputer. (In case you're not familiar with them, minicomputers support several users at once.) We sat at terminals writing and debugging our programs, all using the same computer.

You could always tell when the C students got to the section on file I/O by the occasional wails of all of the students in the lab. It was not uncommon for someone to write a program that trashed the entire hard disk due to incorrect file handling.

The version of C we were using was a rather obscure one. Fortunately, I haven't had to deal with it since. Today's compilers for C, C++, and C# don't give you those kind of problems.

The Nuts of Bolts of Files

How does C# file handling work?

Your program uses functions in the System.IO namespace to access a file on a disk. In particular, there's a class in the System.IO namespace called `File`. The namespace also contains the `StreamReader`, `StreamWriter`, `BinaryReader`, and `BinaryWriter` classes. Programs perform file I/O using these classes.

The `File` object in the System.IO namespace is a software representation of a file on the disk. However, to use it, you must connect a `File` object to a stream.

A stream?

Picture a pool of water. For the water in that pool to get to the sea, it must flow in a stream. Imagine that the data in your program is like that pool of water. The file on the disk is the sea. To get from your program to the disk, your data must flow through a data stream.

To write data to disks, your program attaches a `File` object to a stream. The stream manages the process of getting the data to the disk so you don't have to worry about it. You just drop your data into the stream, and it flows automatically to its destination.

C# provides two kinds of files: text file and binary files. Text files contain text (surprise!); and binary files can hold any valid binary number. Most programs store their data in binary files because it's a more flexible format. But the default file type is text, so that's where we'll start.

Writing Data to Text Files

To write text to a file on a disk you must

1. Open a file.
2. Attach it to a stream.
3. Write text.
4. Close the file.

Listing 11.1 contains a program that illustrates these steps.

Listing 11.1   Sending Text to a Text File

```
1    using System;
2    using System.IO;
3
4    namespace Prog11_1
```

continues

Listing 11.1   Sending Text to a Text File   (continued)

```
5    {
6        /// <summary>
7        /// Summary description for ApplicationClass.
8        /// </summary>
9        class ApplicationClass
10       {
11           /// <summary>
12           /// The main entry point for the application.
13           /// </summary>
14           [STAThread]
15           static void Main(string[] args)
16           {
17               string [] poem = new string[]
18                   {
19                       "Now Beowulf bode in the burg of the Scyldings,",
20                       "leader beloved, and long he ruled",
21                       "in fame with all folk, since his father had gone",
22                       "away from the world, till awoke an heir,",
23                       "haughty Healfdene, who held through life,",
24                       "sage and sturdy, the Scyldings glad.",
25                       "Then, one after one, there woke to him,",
26                       "to the chieftain of clansmen, children four:",
27                       "Heorogar, then Hrothgar, then Halga brave;",
28                       "and I heard that was his queen,",
29                       "the Heathoscylfing's helpmate dear.",
30                   };
31
32               StreamWriter outputFile = File.CreateText("Beowulf.txt");
33
34               foreach (string oneLine in poem)
35               {
36                   outputFile.WriteLine(oneLine);
37               }
38
39               outputFile.Close();
40           }
41       }
42   }
```

This program creates a file on the disk. If you look in the file, this is how it appears:

```
Now Beowulf bode in the burg of the Scyldings,
leader beloved, and long he ruled
in fame with all folk, since his father had gone
away from the world, till awoke an heir,
haughty Healfdene, who held through life,
```

```
sage and sturdy, the Scyldings glad.
Then, one after one, there woke to him,
to the chieftain of clansmen, children four:
Heorogar, then Hrothgar, then Halga brave;
and I heard that was his queen,
the Heathoscylfing's helpmate dear.
```

From the Knowledge Bank

One of the first things that my students used to ask me when they ran a program like this was, "Where's my file? I can't find it."

The program in Listing 11.1 opens a file in the default directory on the default disk. Those are determined by the operating system. Most probably, the default disk and directory are the disk and directory where the executable version of this program resides.

If you're having trouble finding your program, the easiest thing to do is to save it to a floppy in the A drive. To do so, change the statement on line 32 of the program to the following.

```
StreamWriter outputFile = File.CreateText("a:\Beowulf.txt");
```

This writes the output file to the A drive. Be sure to put a floppy disk in the drive before you run the program.

Because the program in Listing 11.1 uses objects in the System.IO namespace, the statement ...

```
using System.IO;
```

... appears on line 2.

On line 17, the program declares a string array. It initializes the array on lines 18–30. On line 32, the program opens the output file and attaches it to a stream.

Output files require the use of a `StreamWriter` object. The `File` class member function `CreateText()` opens a file and creates a `StreamWriter`. It opens the file whose name is in the string in its parameter list. You can have the program open the file in the current directory, as this one does, or specify a full path name (the disk and directory name).

On lines 34–37, the program uses a `foreach` loop to write each string in the array to the output file. The program closes the file on line 39.

CAUTION **Programming Pitfalls**

Be sure and close your files! Remember file buffers? Closing a file flushes its buffer. To be sure that all of your data gets written to the disk, close your files before exiting the program.

When you're working with files, you use the functions from the `File` class to create, open, copy, move, and delete files. Use the stream classes to read data, write data, and flush a stream's buffers.

From the Knowledge Bank

It's time for a flashback. Some of the programs in previous chapters used the `Read()` function to read characters from the keyboard. The programs used a type cast to change them to characters. I said then that there was a good reason for that, and here it is.

Your program sees the keyboard essentially as a text file. Every text file has an end of file marker at the end. You can type an end of file marker on the keyboard. On Windows-based computers, it's Ctrl+Z. The `Read()` function must be able to return a value that indicates the end of the file. That value is −1. So `Read()` must return integers to be able to return the −1.

Reading Data from Text Files

Reading from a file follows almost exactly the same steps as writing a file. The only difference is the direction of the flow of the data. The steps for reading are

1. Open a file.
2. Attach it to a stream.
3. Read text.
4. Close the file.

The program in Listing 11.2, which reads the data file created in Listing 11.1, shows these steps.

Listing 11.2   Reading Text from a Text File

```
1    using System;
2    using System.IO;
3
4    namespace Prog11_1
5    {
6        /// <summary>
7        /// Summary description for ApplicationClass.
8        /// </summary>
9        class ApplicationClass
10        {
11            /// <summary>
12            /// The main entry point for the application.
```

```
13                    /// </summary>
14                    [STAThread]
15                    static void Main(string[] args)
16                    {
17                         string oneLine;
18
19                         StreamReader inputFile = File.OpenText("Beowulf.txt");
20
21                         while ((oneLine = inputFile.ReadLine()) != null)
22                         {
23                              System.Console.WriteLine(oneLine);
24                         }
25
26                         inputFile.Close();
27                    }
28               }
29          }
```

Before you run this program, *be sure* to copy the file Beowulf.txt to the directory that contains this program. If you do not, the program will generate an error. If the program runs correctly, you'll see the following output on your screen.

```
Now Beowulf bode in the burg of the Scyldings,
leader beloved, and long he ruled
in fame with all folk, since his father had gone
away from the world, till awoke an heir,
haughty Healfdene, who held through life,
sage and sturdy, the Scyldings glad.
Then, one after one, there woke to him,
to the chieftain of clansmen, children four:
Heorogar, then Hrothgar, then Halga brave;
and I heard that was his queen,
the Heathoscylfing's helpmate dear.
```

There are some differences between this program and the one in Listing 11.1. The first is that this program is shorter because it does not need a large array to hold the strings. This program reads each string from the file, one at a time, and prints it.

Another difference is that this program opens an input stream rather than an output stream. The variable `inputFile` is of type `StreamReader` instead of `StreamWriter`.

Also, this program uses the `File` member function `OpenText()` rather than `CreateText()`.

Data Bit _____

If you took my advice earlier and changed Listing 11.1 to save your data file to the A drive, you can have the program in Listing 11.2 read it from the A drive. Simply change line 19 to read as follows.

```
StreamReader inputFile =
File.OpenText("a:\Beowulf.
txt");
```

The `OpenText()` function opens an existing file. If the file does not exist, the program generates an error. On the other hand, `CreateFile()` creates a new file from scratch. If the file already exists, `CreateFile()` overwrites it and starts a new one with the same name.

Writing Data to Binary Files

As mentioned previously, binary files contain any valid binary number. Most programs keep their data in binary format.

Writing data to binary files follows the similar steps as writing to text files. One difference is the type of stream your program uses to write the data. For binary files, the program creates a FileStream rather than a StreamWriter. It also must attach a BinaryWriter to the stream. The following steps show you how to write to a binary file:

1. Open a file and a stream.
2. Open a binary writer.
3. Attach the file and stream to the writer.
4. Write binary data.
5. Close the writer.
6. Close the file and stream.

Listing 11.3 shows a short sample program to demonstrate a binary file.

Listing 11.3   Writing to a Binary File

```
1    using System;
2    using System.IO;
3
4    namespace Prog11_3
5    {
6        /// <summary>
7        /// Summary description for ApplicationClass.
8        /// </summary>
9        class ApplicationClass
10        {
11            /// <summary>
12            /// The main entry point for the application.
13            /// </summary>
14            [STAThread]
15            static void Main(string[] args)
16            {
17                FileStream fileStream = new FileStream(
18                                            "numbers.dat",
19                                            FileMode.CreateNew);
```

```
20              BinaryWriter outputFile =
21                  new BinaryWriter(fileStream);
22
23              for (int i=0; i<100; i++)
24              {
25                  outputFile.Write(i);
26              }
27
28              outputFile.Close();
29              fileStream.Close();
30          }
31      }
32  }
```

The program in Listing 11.3 writes integers to a binary file. To do so, it creates a file and a stream on lines 17–19 using the new keyword. The name of the file is numbers.dat. To create a new file from scratch, you pass the value `FileMode.CreateNew`. This is a special value defined in the System.IO namespace.

On lines 20–21, the program creates a binary writer and attaches it to the stream. The binary writer is like a translator. It translates the stream's data into binary format. The program uses a `for` loop on lines 23–26 to write integers to the output file. It's the job of the `BinaryWriter` object to translate the integers that flow down the stream into binary.

Data Bit

Did you notice that the program declares the integer variable i on line 23 inside the `for` loop's parentheses? You did? I guess I'll have to explain it, then.

This is not a mistake, it's yet another feature of the `for` loop. You can declare variables inside the initialization section of a `for` loop. If you do, they are only visible within the `for` loop's code block. They cannot be used anywhere else.

Line 25 of the program uses the `Write()` function to write the integers to the file. In binary mode, you must always use `Write()` rather than `WriteLine()`. The `WriteLine()` function is for strings, and should only be used for text files.

On lines 28–29, the program closes the `BinaryWriter` and the `FileStream`. To avoid errors, programs must close these object in the order shown on lines 28–29.

Reading Data from Binary Files

By now, using files should be easy for you. You can probably guess the steps needed to read data from a binary file. They are …

1. Open a file and a stream.

2. Open a binary reader.

3. Attach the file and stream to the reader.

4. Read binary data.

5. Close the reader.

6. Close the file and stream.

The program in Listing 11.4 reads the data file created by the program in Listing 11.3.

Listing 11.4 Reading a Binary File

```
1    using System;
2    using System.IO;
3
4    namespace Prog11_4
5    {
6        /// <summary>
7        /// Summary description for ApplicationClass.
8        /// </summary>
9        class ApplicationClass
10         {
11            /// <summary>
12            /// The main entry point for the application.
13            /// </summary>
14            [STAThread]
15            static void Main(string[] args)
16            {
17                FileStream fileStream =
18                    new FileStream("numbers.dat",FileMode.Open);
19                BinaryReader inputFile =
20                    new BinaryReader(fileStream);
21
22                int inputData,i;
23                bool atEndOfFile;
24                for (atEndOfFile = false, i = 0;
25                     !atEndOfFile;
26                    i++)
27                {
28                    if (inputFile.PeekChar() != -1)
29                    {
30                        inputData = inputFile.ReadInt32();
31
32                        if (inputData < 10)
```

```
33                                  {
34                                      System.Console.Write("{0}    ",inputData);
35                                  }
36                                  else
37                                  {
38                                      System.Console.Write("{0}   ",inputData);
39                                  }
40                                  if ((i != 0) && (i % 10 == 0))
41                                  {
42                                      System.Console.Write("\n");
43                                  }
44                              }
45                              else
46                              {
47                                  atEndOfFile = true;
48                              }
49                          }
50
51                      inputFile.Close();
52                      fileStream.Close();
53                  }
54              }
55          }
```

Lines 17–18 of this program create a `FileStream`. On lines 19–20, the program creates a `BinaryReader` and attaches the `FileStream` to it. The program declares some variables it needs on lines 22–23. It then enters a `for` loop.

The initialization section of the `for` loop initializes the variables `atEndOfFile` and `i`. The loop's condition appears on line 25. It states that the loop will continue while the program is not at the end of the file.

Each time through the loop, the program executes the `if-else` statement that begins on line 28. In its condition, the `if` statement calls the `PeekChar()` function. `PeekChar()` is a member of the `BinaryReader` class. It looks ahead at the next character in the stream. However, it does not remove the character from the stream like `Read()` does.

 **Data Bit**

You can initialize anything you need to in the initialization section of a `for` loop. It doesn't have to be the loop control variable.

If the next character in the stream is not equal to –1, the program executes the code block for the `if` statement. Inside the `if` statement, the program calls the `ReadInt32()` function (a member of the `BinaryReader` class) to read the next integer from the stream. It assigns the integer to `inputData`.

Data Bit

The `BinaryReader` class contains member functions to read each of the simple data types. In Visual Studio's online documentation (press F1) for the `BinaryReader` class are functions such as `ReadChar()`, `ReadDouble()`, and `ReadByte()`.

If the integer in `inputData` is less than 10, the `if` statement beginning on line 34 prints the number to the screen, followed by three spaces. If it is greater than or equal to 10, the `else` statement prints the number followed by two spaces.

Another `if` statement begins on line 40. It tests to see whether `i` is not equal to 0. It also uses the modulus operator to see whether `i` is divisible by 10. If both of those conditions are true, it prints a newline to the display.

Back on line 28, the program used `PeekChar()` to see whether the next value in the stream was a –1. When the program reaches the end of the file, `PeekChar()` returns a –1. That makes the condition `false`. As a result, the program executes the `else` statement beginning on line 45. The else statement sets the variable `atEndOfFile` to `true`. This ends the `for` loop that begins on line 24.

The output of the program loops like this.

```
0    1    2    3    4    5    6    7    8    9    10
11   12   13   14   15   16   17   18   19   20
21   22   23   24   25   26   27   28   29   30
31   32   33   34   35   36   37   38   39   40
41   42   43   44   45   46   47   48   49   50
51   52   53   54   55   56   57   58   59   60
61   62   63   64   65   66   67   68   69   70
71   72   73   74   75   76   77   78   79   80
81   82   83   84   85   86   87   88   89   90
91   92   93   94   95   96   97   98   99
```

The Least You Need to Know

- Storing information on disks saves it in a persistent format. Information in a persistent format is not lost when the computer is turned off.
- I/O can be buffered or unbuffered. Most computers use buffered I/O.
- File operations use classes from the System.IO namespace.
- Programs make information flow to and from files by using streams.
- C# programs can create and use two types of files: text and binary.
- To read from and write to files, programs must open the appropriate type of stream.

Part 4

Object-Oriented Programming

Right now, you've very much like Columbus. He set out knowing much about the territories familiar to explorers for centuries. What you've learned in Parts 1, 2, and 3 of this book are the territories familiar to programmers for decades.

At this point, you're about to embark on something new. It's called object-oriented programming (OOP). OOP is a fairly new development in computer programming. As you set sail in Part 4, you will learn the intricacies of creating your own classes. You'll see new and powerful ways to create simple and intuitive types. As you learn to navigate the waters of OOP, you'll use your types to build professional and robust programs.

Bon voyage!

Under Construction: Building Classes

In This Chapter

◆ Defining classes

◆ Classes as data types

◆ Adding member data and functions

◆ Using constants in classes

Back in Chapter 6 you got your first look at classes. You saw that classes implement software objects. Since then, you've used classes from the System and System.IO namespaces. You already know that classes have member data and member functions. The member data stores the object's information. The member functions define the list of operations that program can perform on the object.

In this chapter, you'll create your own classes. To create classes, you:

1. Define the class, with its class name.
2. Specify the member data.
3. Add the member functions.

When you've completed these steps, you've got an object you can use in your programs.

Defining C# Classes

When you sit down to design your program, you must pick the classes it needs. To illustrate what I mean, let's design a game. The name of this game is Gobbler.

In this game, the player controls the yellow Gobbler. The Gobbler moves through the maze eating green power pills. When all of the power pills are gone, the player moves to the next level of the game. The Gobbler can also eat the red hearts. If it does, it gets another life. In the center of the maze, evil, mean, foul, and bad-smelling Purple Nasties appear. They chase the yellow Gobbler. If a Purple Nasty touches the Gobbler, the Gobbler loses a life.

If you're writing this game, you need to ask yourself, "What objects does my program need?" When you figure out the answer, you define a class for each object. The objects required for the Gobbler program are …

- The Gobbler.
- The walls.
- The power pills.
- Power-ups, such as the hearts.
- The Purple Nasties.

There will likely be other objects needed as well, but this will do for the purposes of this example. To demonstrate the definition of a C# class, let's define a class called `gobbler`. Listing 12.1 contains its definition.

Listing 12.1   The Bare-Bones gobbler Class

```
1    class gobbler
2    {
3    };
```

Well, that sure doesn't look like much. However, it does show the general form of a class definition. Every class definition uses the keyword `class`, followed by the class's name. The contents of the class are inside its opening and closing braces.

It's important to know that, when you define a class, you do not allocate memory for it.

Data Bit

Allocating memory for a class variable creates an **instance** of the class. Creating a class definition does not create an instance of the class.

Let me repeat that. When you define a class, you do not allocate memory for it. All you do is specify what information it contains (member data) and what you can do with it (member functions). To actually allocate memory for a `gobbler`, you must declare a variable of type `gobbler` in a program.

The next thing to do is add member data.

Member Data

A class's member data stores information for the object. Member data is essentially a group of variables that you define inside the class.

Looking back at the example of the Gobbler game clarifies this. The software for the game needs a `gobbler` class. The `gobbler` class must keep track of the Gobbler's position in the maze. Most games of this type use a simple (x,y) positioning system for things on the screen. Listing 12.2 contains the `gobbler` class with data members for tracking the Gobbler's (x,y) position.

Listing 12.2   Adding Member Data to the `gobbler` Class

```
1    class gobbler
2    {
3        private int x,y;
4    };
```

In classes, you declare member data in almost the same way you declare variables. You must state the member's type, and its name. In addition, you should put the keyword `private` at the beginning of the member declaration. This tells the compiler that only the `gobbler` member functions can access x and y.

I cannot overstress that declaring member data in a class does not allocate memory for them. It tells the compiler what to create whenever a program creates an instance of the `gobbler` class. Programs create instances of the `gobbler` class by declaring variables of type `gobbler`.

Data Bit _____

The keyword **private** is an access modifier. The other two access modifiers discussed in this book are the keywords **public** and **protected**. The use of **public** is presented in this chapter. Chapter 15 describes the **protected** keyword.

Selecting Appropriate Member Data

As shown in Listing 12.2, the `gobbler` class is useless. One reason is because it does not have all of the member data it needs. A Gobbler moves around the screen, so it must keep track of its (x,y) position. Okay, the class does that much. However, a Gobbler must also know whether it's moving, and in what direction. In addition, it must display an animated image. It has to keep track of whether it's alive or dead. Listing 12.3 shows a version of the `gobbler` class that has member data to store this information.

Listing 12.3   More Member Data for the gobbler Class

```
1    class gobbler
2    {
3        private int x,y;
4
5        // 0 = not moving, -1 = moving left
6        // 1 = moving right, 2 = moving down
7        // -2 = moving up
8        private int movementDirection;
9
10       private byte [] imageBitmap;
11
12       private bool isAlive;
13   };
```

This version of the gobbler class is beginning to actually look useful. Is this enough information to begin writing the game? Probably not. According to the rules of the game, the Gobbler must eat all of the power pills before the player can move on to the next level. So it should keep track of how many it's eaten (in other words, it must know how full it is). It must also keep track of any power-ups or bonuses it ate (could those be considered dessert?), and how many lives it has left. Listing 12.4 has one more attempt at a gobbler class.

Listing 12.4   A More Realistic gobbler Class

```
1    class gobbler
2    {
3        private int x,y;
4
5        // 0 = not moving, -1 = moving left
6        // 1 = moving right, 2 = moving down
7        // -2 = moving up
8        private int movementDirection;
9
10       private byte [] imageBitmap;
11
12       private bool isAlive;
13
14       private int powerPillsEaten, bonusesEaten;
15
16       private int livesLeft;
17   };
```

Is this, at last, enough information to begin writing the game? Maybe. It depends on how you want to design the software. But it's likely that the final version of the class would be very similar to this.

Creating objects for programs means becoming familiar with the context in which the objects are used. You have to know at least a little about how the class will be used. For instance, if you are writing a customer database program for a software store, you would create a `customer` class. You probably would not include the user's eyeglass prescription in the class. However, if you were writing the customer database program for a store that sells eyeglasses, you would. The context in which the class will be used usually dictates the information to be included.

Data Bit

How do you know when you've got enough information in a class? Primarily by experience. There's no real substitute for it. When you're learning, you might have a tendency to put too many data members in your classes. So, as you write your classes, make yourself justify each data member that you put in.

Data Bit

There are a lot of database programs in use today. In most of them, the customer information contains the customer's name, address, and phone number. That's something that the programs have in common. It would be nice if C# provided a way to make generic objects that you could specialize for use in your applications. In fact, it does. The technique is called inheritance, and it's presented in Chapter 15.

Because you can enhance or specialize generic classes, classes you create do not have to contain every possible data member you can think of to put in them. As much as possible, you should think "lean and mean" when it comes to member data.

So selecting the appropriate member data comes down to this:

♦ Ensuring you have enough information

♦ Ensuring you do not have too much information

♦ Ensuring the information fits the context of the program

Private and Public

Before learning to create member functions, you need to know a few things about access modifiers. Access modifiers control the visibility, or *scope*, of items in your program. They specify where an item can be "seen."

Simply put, the keyword `private` in front of a member data declaration means that only members of the class can access the data item.

Techno Talk

The technical term for the visibility is **scope**. In the some-times-incongruous language of Programmerese, access modifiers are keywords that control the scope of program elements such as classes, member data, and member functions.

In English, access modifiers tell the compiler what portions of the program can see things like classes, member data, and member functions.

Programming Pitfalls

Member data should nearly always be **private**. There is almost no reason to have **public** member data in your classes.

Techno Talk

In programming, **encapsulation** means to hide something and strictly control access to it. Encapsulation is a major goal of object-oriented programming.

This is exactly what you want. One of the goals of object-oriented programming is *encapsulation*. By encapsulating, or hiding, the data inside the class, you control which functions can directly access the data. Member data with `private` access can only be seen by member functions in the same class. No other functions in the program can get access to the data.

This means that the rest of the program *must* use the class's member functions to change or read the data in the class. The member functions can validate that the data is being accessed correctly. This technique helps keep the data in a known and valid state for as long as the program runs.

Access modifiers aren't just for member data. C# programs need them on member functions, as well. Most member functions use the `public` access modifier. The `public` keyword tells the C# compiler that the program item can be seen by any other function in the program. So if you apply `public` to a member function, any function in the namespace can call the member function.

If you write a member function that you don't want called by functions outside the class, you can make the member function `private`. This is not uncommon at all. In fact, with nearly every class you write, there will be a few member functions that you won't want non-member functions to call.

You can also use access modifiers on your classes. It is very common to do so. Specifying `public` on your class declaration makes the class usable by functions outside the current namespace. This is another form of encapsulation. It helps hide the implementation of a library of functions.

For example, the .NET Framework provides the System and System.IO namespaces. It also provides many others. Inside these namespaces are classes that should not be used by functions outside the namespace. These classes do not have the `public` access modifier on them.

So before we jump into member functions, let's summarize:

◆ The keywords `public` and `private` are access modifiers.

◆ Access modifiers specify the scope, or visibility, of a program item.

◆ Member data should have `private` scope. This means that they can only be seen by the class's member functions.

◆ Most member functions you write will have `public` scope. This means they can be called by any function that can see the class.

◆ Some member functions you write will use `private` scope. These functions can only be called by other member functions in the same class.

◆ Classes can have `public` scope. If they do, they can be seen outside the namespace. If they do not, they cannot be seen outside the namespace in which they are defined.

Member Functions—Oops! I Mean Methods

In C++ terminology, functions that are members of a class are called member functions (go figure). Other object-oriented programming languages use the term *method* instead of member function. The Microsoft documentation for the C# language uses method rather than member function. Most C# programmers are former C++ programmers. They are just as likely to say "member function" as they are to say "method."

Because both terms are widely used in the industry, I've presented both. I used the term member functions first because my teaching experience has shown me that students understand the term better. However, to help you get used to the term methods, I'll use that term in preference to member function for the rest of the book.

Methods are actually very easy to learn. In fact, you've already learned them. All of the functions presented in the sample programs are methods. They are the methods of their application classes.

Listing 12.5 shows a version of the `gobbler` class with some methods.

Data Bit _____

Any class can have methods, including a program's application class.

Listing 12.5   The `gobbler` Class with Methods

```
1    public class gobbler
2    {
3        //
4        // Private Data
5        //
6
7        private int x,y;
8
9        // 0 = not moving, -1 = moving left
10       // 1 = moving right, 2 = moving down
```

continues

Listing 12.5 The gobbler Class with Methods (continued)

```
11          // -2 = moving up
12          private int movementDirection;
13
14          private byte [] imageBitmap;
15
16          private bool isAlive;
17
18          private int powerPillsEaten, bonusesEaten;
19
20          private int livesLeft;
21
22          //
23          // Public methods
24          //
25
26          public void SetX(int newX)
27          {
28              x=newX;
29          }
30
31          public int GetX()
32          {
33              return (x);
34          }
35
36          public void SetY(int newY)
37          {
38              y=newY;
39          }
40
41          public int GetY()
42          {
43              return (y);
44          }
45
46          public bool IsMoving()
47          {
48              return (movementDirection != 0));
49          }
50
51          public void SetMovementDirection(int newDirection)
52          {
53              // If the direction is valid...
54              if ((newDirection >= -2) && (newDirection <= 2))
55              {
```

```
56                // Set the direction.
57                movementDirection = newDirection;
58          }
59       }
60
61       public void Dead()
62       {
63          if (isAlive)
64          {
65              isAlive = false;
66              livesLeft--;
67          }
68       }
69
70       public bool IsAlive()
71       {
72          return (isAlive);
73       }
74
75       public void AtePowerPill()
76       {
77          powerPillsEaten++;
78       }
79
80       public int GetPowerPillsEaten()
81       {
82          return (powerPillsEaten);
83       }
84
85       public void AteBonus()
86       {
87          bonusesEaten++;
88       }
89
90       public int GetBonusesEaten()
91       {
92          return (bonusesEaten);
93       }
94
95       public int GetLivesLeft()
96       {
97          return (livesLeft);
98       }
99    };
```

Like the version of the gobbler class from Listing 12.4, this version declares the required
member data. It also contains a section for methods. The SetX() and GetX() functions set

and get the x value of the Gobbler's (x,y) location. The SetY() and GetY() functions do the same for the y value. In a class for a real game, the SetX() and SetY() functions would probably contain if statements to check whether the Gobbler was about to move off the screen.

The IsMoving() function, which begins on line 46, compares the value of movementDirection to 0. If they are not equal, the comparison returns true. This indicates that the Gobbler is moving. If the Gobbler is not moving, the value of movementDirection is 0, so the comparison on line 48 evaluates to false.

Data Bit _____

Game programming is about the only situation I know of where you can ask someone if they're dead, get "Yes" for an answer, and have it be correct.

A program would call the SetMovementDirection() function on lines 51–59 to change the Gobbler's direction of movement. Notice that it contains an if statement that validates the value of the parameter.

When one of the Purple Nasties touches the Gobbler, the game calls Dead(). This kills the Gobbler, and decrements its remaining lives. The if statement on lines 63–67 determines whether the Gobbler is alive. If not, it does not kill the Gobbler again. That wouldn't be nice.

Data Bit _____

For simplicity, I deliberately left out anything to do with the Gobbler's animated image in Listing 12.5. Bet you thought I forgot it.

The AtePowerPill() and AteBonus() functions both tell the Gobbler that it ate something good. The GetPowerPill() and GetBonusesEaten() return the number of power pills and bonuses the Gobbler ate, respectively.

And, of course, GetLivesLeft() returns the number of lives the Gobbler has left.

Your program calls a class's methods by stating the class variable name, followed by a period, followed by the function name. Suppose, for instance, your program contains the declaration

```
gobbler theGobbler;
```

In that case, it calls gobbler methods like this

```
theGobbler.SetX(10);
```

or this

```
if (theGobbler.IsAlive())
{
    // Eat and run away.
}
```

Constructors

Any C# class can have a special type of method called a constructor. C# programs automatically call constructors whenever they create an object. *Constructors* set objects into a known state. To see how this is done, take a look at the version of the gobbler class in Listing 12.6.

Listing 12.6   Adding a Constructor to the gobbler Class

```
1    public class gobbler
2    {
3        //
4        // Private Data
5        //
6
7        private int x,y;
8
9        // 0 = not moving, -1 = moving left
10       // 1 = moving right, 2 = moving down
11       // -2 = moving up
12       private int movementDirection;
13
14       private byte [] imageBitmap;
15
16       private bool isAlive;
17
18       private int powerPillsEaten, bonusesEaten;
19
20       private int livesLeft;
21
22       //
23       // Public methods
24       //
25
26       public gobbler(int initialX,int initialY)
27       {
28           x = initialX;
29           y = initialY;
30
31           isAlive = true;
32           livesLeft = 3;
33
34           movementDirection = 0;
35
36           powerPillsEaten = 0;
37           bonusesEaten = 0;
38       }
```

To save space, Listing 12.6 does not include the entire gobbler class. If you want to see the rest of the gobbler methods, please refer back to Listing 12.5.

The gobbler constructor appears on lines 26–38. Notice that the name of the method is the same as the name of the class. This is required for constructors. Notice also that the gobbler() constructor does not have a return type. That's because it returns a gobbler object.

Data Bit

Technically speaking, constructors do not really return anything. When a program declares a class variable, it allocates the memory for the variable and calls the constructor. The constructor initializes the memory that the program already allocated. So it doesn't need to return anything.

Constructors, like any other class method, can have parameters. The gobbler class is an example. Whenever a program allocates a gobbler variable, it must pass the initial (x,y) values to the gobbler() constructor.

```
gobbler theGobbler = new gobbler(50,100);
```

You can also create constructors with no parameters. Listing 12.7 shows a version of the gobbler constructor without parameters.

Listing 12.7   A gobbler Constructor with No Parameters

```
1          public gobbler()
2          {
3              x = 0;
4              y = 0;
5
6              isAlive = true;
7              livesLeft = 3;
8
9              movementDirection = 0;
10
11             powerPillsEaten = 0;
12             bonusesEaten = 0;
13         }
```

Programming Pitfalls

If you write a class that has a constructor with parameters, you cannot allocate an array of that object. However, there is a way around that. It is called overloading, which is the subject of the next chapter.

If a program were to use the gobbler class with this constructor, it would not pass any values to the constructor when it allocated the variable.

```
gobbler theGobbler = new gobbler();
```

Selecting Appropriate Methods

It's easy to get carried away when you're writing methods for your class, especially when you first start writing classes. You want to cover every possible situation in which the class might be used. Don't try. As mentioned previously, C# gives you a simple technique called inheritance that you can use to enhance any class. Inheritance is the subject of Chapter 15.

Because you don't have to provide methods for every possible use of your classes, you should instead focus on the most likely uses. If you write methods for the most common uses of a class, that's enough.

How do you select the most likely uses to write method for? You guessed it. Time and experience. There's no teacher like them.

Until you have some experience under your belt, you'll have to use the same technique you use for member data. That is ...

From the Knowledge Bank

If time is a great teacher, why does it kill off all of its students?

♦ Ensure you have enough methods.

♦ Ensure you do not have too many methods.

♦ Ensure the methods fit the context of the program.

As you create each method, make it justify its existence. Ask yourself if it's really necessary. One of the main purposes of methods is to provide code that the program calls repeatedly. Would leaving it out make you write the same code several times throughout your program? If so, add it in. If not, think about leaving it out.

Also, if you use the class in another program, would the method be useful there, as well? If so, you should definitely write the method. If not, it might not be needed.

Constants—the Cure for Magic Numbers

Although it's not absolutely essential for understanding classes, there's one more topic I like to introduce whenever I talk about C# classes. That is constants.

A *constant* is more or less the opposite of a variable. A variable changes values as a program runs. A constant does not. It keeps the same value for as long as the program runs.

Why do you need constants? To get rid of *magic numbers*.

A magic number is a number in a program that does not explain itself. For example, look at this short program fragment.

```
1    for (int i=0; i<25; i++)
2    {
3        // Do something in this loop.
4    }
```

Try this. Turn to the person next to you and explain what the 25 in this program fragment means. Okay, so it means that the loop executes 25 times, but why 25? Why not 24 or 26?

Now take a look at this version.

```
1    for (int i=0; i<STUDENTS_PER_CLASS; i++)
2    {
3        // Do something in this loop.
4    }
```

See the difference? This version uses a constant. The constant has a name. The name tells what the loop does. If the person next to you has not looked at you funny and changed seats, turn to him or her and explain that the loop does some processing on information about one classroom of students.

Constants help document programs. They describe what their values mean. By C# convention, the names of constants are usually in uppercase. This is not required by the C# programming language. However, if you follow the convention, all other programmers will know the constants when they see them in your program.

Techno Talk

Constants do not change their value while the program runs. Their names help explain what their values mean.

You declare constants in your program in almost the same way you declare variables. Here's an example.

```
const float PI = 3.14159;
```

The only real difference is the addition of the keyword const. Listing 12.8 shows some handy ways to use constants.

Listing 12.8   Using a Constant in a Program

```
1    using System;
2
3    namespace Prog12_8
4    {
5        /// <summary>
6        /// Summary description for ApplicationClass.
7        /// </summary>
8        class ApplicationClass
9        {
10           class classwitharray
11           {
12               public const int ARRAY_SIZE = 10;
13
14               private int [] anArray = new int [ARRAY_SIZE];
15
16               public classwitharray()
17               {
```

```
18                      for (int i=0; i<ARRAY_SIZE; i++)
19                      {
20                          anArray[i] = 0;
21                      }
22                  }
23
24              public void SetItem(int itemNumber, int itemValue)
25              {
26                  if ((itemNumber >= 0) &&
27                      (itemNumber < ARRAY_SIZE))
28                  {
29                      anArray[itemNumber] = itemValue;
30                  }
31              }
32
33              public int GetItem(int itemNumber)
34              {
35                  int itemValue = 0;
36
37                  if ((itemNumber >= 0) &&
38                      (itemNumber < ARRAY_SIZE))
39                  {
40                      itemValue = anArray[itemNumber];
41                  }
42
43                  return (itemValue);
44              }
45          };
46
47          /// <summary>
48          /// The main entry point for the application.
49          /// </summary>
50          [STAThread]
51          static void Main(string[] args)
52          {
53              classwitharray arrayClass = new classwitharray();
54              int i;
55
56              for (i=0; i<classwitharray.ARRAY_SIZE; i++)
57              {
58                  System.Console.WriteLine(
59                      "{0}",
60                      arrayClass.GetItem(i));
61              }
62
63              System.Console.WriteLine("");
64
```

continues

Listing 12.8 Using a Constant in a Program (continued)

```
65              for (i=0; i<classwitharray.ARRAY_SIZE; i++)
66              {
67                  arrayClass.SetItem(i,i*i);
68              }
69
70              for (i=0; i<classwitharray.ARRAY_SIZE; i++)
71              {
72                  System.Console.WriteLine(
73                      "{0}",
74                      arrayClass.GetItem(i));
75              }
76          }
77      }
78  }
```

This program defines a class that contains an array. Each time an instance of the class (a class variable) is created, the array is also allocated. The program uses the class's methods to store values into the array. It also uses them to get values from the array, which it prints. Here's the output.

```
0
0
0
0
0
0
0
0
0
0

0
1
4
9
16
25
36
49
64
81
```

The definition of the classwitharray class begins on line 8. Line 12 defines an integer constant called ARRAY_SIZE. The program uses that constant on line 14. The constant specifies the size of the array that is created when the program declares a classwitharray variable.

The constructor for the classwitharray class appears on lines 16–22. It uses a for loop to initialize each of the values in anArray to 0. This is not strictly necessary. By default, C# programs automatically initialize memory they allocate to 0. However, I recommend that you get into the habit of initializing all memory your programs allocate. It makes sure that the memory is in a known state.

The SetItem() and GetItem() functions (lines 24–31 and 33–44, respectively) enable programs to access the values in the array. Notice that they both use if statements to validate the index number of the array element that is being accessed.

When you run the program, it begins with Main() on line 51. On line 53, the program declares the variable arrayClass, which is of type classwitharray. That declaration causes the program to execute the statement on line 14. The statement allocates memory for the private array anArray.

Next, the program enters a for loop on line 56. Inside the loop, it calls the GetItem() method to get the current contents of each array element. It passes that value to the WriteLine() function so that it is printed on the screen.

After printing a blank line on the screen (line 63), the program enters another for loop. This loop, which spans lines 65–68, calls the SetItem() method to store values into the array. The first parameter to SetItem() is the index number of the item. The second parameter is the value being stored into the array.

On lines 70–75, the program uses another for loop to print the contents of the array.

Notice that the program in Listing 12.8 repeatedly uses the value ARRAY_SIZE. This is a public constant, so it may be used both inside and outside the class.

Class methods can use the constant by name. The methods of the classwitharray class use ARRAY_SIZE on lines 14, 18, 27, and 37.

From the Knowledge Bank

Experience has taught me that it is best to initialize all memory you allocate. That's true even if the program automatically initializes memory to 0. Automatic initialization is often a compiler option. It's likely that you'll work on project teams for most of your career, and you never know when someone else in your project group will turn off automatic initialization.

 Data Bit

See how often the constant is used in this program? If you suddenly decide that the value of ARRAY_SIZE should be 100 rather than 10, you can change it on line 12, and the entire program continues to work properly. It just prints more output.

Constants enable you to make large changes to your program with little effort. Little effort = large results. That's a formula I like.

Functions outside the class, such as Main(), can also use the constant. However, because they are not members of the classwitharray class, they must specify the scope of the constant. They do that by naming the class that contains it. In the program in Listing 12.8, Main() uses the constant on lines 56, 65, and 70. On each of these lines, it accesses the constant by the name classwitharray.ARRAY_SIZE.

The Least You Need to Know

- When you define a class, you define its member data and its methods (member functions).
- Member data should be private. If it is, only a class's methods can access it.
- Never define public member data.
- Most methods should be public. They can be accessed by functions outside the class.
- Some methods might be private.
- Defining a class does not allocate memory for it. To do that, you must create an instance of the class.
- Magic numbers in programs are numbers that do not explain themselves. Most numbers do not explain themselves.
- It is wise to use constants in your class rather than magic numbers.

Chapter 5

Overloading (Heavy, Dude!)

In This Chapter

◆ Polymorphism through overloading

◆ Overloading constructors, methods, and operators

◆ Using overloaded constructors, methods, and operators

Ready to learn a big word for a pretty simple concept? The word is polymorphism. The concept is simply this: making two or more things with the same name. Most C# programmers use the term *overloading* instead of polymorphism. But for some reason that no one seems to be able to explain, we all have to know the word polymorphism as well.

The word polymorphism is made up of two components. The prefix *poly-* means many. To morph something is to map or change it from one thing to another. So polymorphism is a one-to-many mapping.

In the case of C# overloading, it means that you can write more than one method or operator with the same name. Essentially, you're mapping one name to many methods.

Overloading (a.k.a. polymorphism) enables you to write more than one function with the same name. You might wonder why you would want to write two functions with the same name. You might also wonder how the compiler tells them apart. For the answer to both questions, read on.

Overloading Constructors

Remember me introducing constructors back in Chapter 12? I wrote the `gobbler` class for a hypothetical game called Gobbler. Recall that I showed two versions of its constructor. One had parameters, and the other didn't. One reason you might want to use overloading is to overload a class's constructions.

To show what this looks like in a program, Listing 13.1 contains a version of the `gobbler` class from Chapter 12. This version has both constructors in the same class.

Listing 13.1   Overloading the `gobbler` Constructor

```
1    public class gobbler
2    {
3        //
4        // Private Data
5        //
6
7        private int x,y;
8
9        // 0 = not moving, -1 = moving left
10       // 1 = moving right, 2 = moving down
11       // -2 = moving up
12       private int movementDirection;
13
14       private byte [] imageBitmap;
15
16       private bool isAlive;
17
18       private int powerPillsEaten, bonusesEaten;
19
20       private int livesLeft;
21
22       //
23       // Public methods
24       //
25       public gobbler()
26       {
27           x = 0;
28           y = 0;
29
30           isAlive = true;
31           livesLeft = 3;
32
33           movementDirection = 0;
34
```

```
35              powerPillsEaten = 0;
36              bonusesEaten = 0;
37          }
38
39      public gobbler(int initialX,int initialY)
40          {
41              x = initialX;
42              y = initialY;
43
44              isAlive = true;
45              livesLeft = 3;
46
47              movementDirection = 0;
48
49              powerPillsEaten = 0;
50              bonusesEaten = 0;
51          }
52
53      // Other methods go here.
```

As in the last chapter, I haven't shown the entire class in this listing. I've omitted all of the methods except the constructors.

Because there are two constructors in this class, the game can declare gobbler variables in two ways. First, it can declare gobbler variables with no parameters, as shown here.

```
gobbler aGobbler = new gobbler();
```

Second, the game can declare gobbler variables and set the Gobbler to an initial position, like this.

```
gobbler aGobbler = new gobbler(24,34);
```

It is important to note that the game must call either the constructor with no parameters or the one with two parameters. That means that statements like the following are not allowed.

```
gobbler aGobbler = new gobbler(10);
```

If it saw a statement like that in a program, the C# compiler would have no idea what to do. It would generate an error message.

As you can see from this example, overloading constructors can give you very intuitive ways of declaring class variables. In the Gobbler program, it is very normal for programmers to want to declare gobbler variables with no parameters. It is also common to want to set the Gobbler to an initial (x,y) location when it is declared. Constructor overloading makes sure you can do both.

Data Bit _____

In C and C++, a function's parameters are also called its arguments. Because C was originally written for computers with very limited memory (by today's standards), the keywords and function names were very terse. That same terseness carried over, to a more limited extent, into C++ and C#. Programmers even picked it up in the way they speak. So many long-time C and C++ programmers refer to parameters as args, rather than arguments. If you hear them talking about a "no-arg constructor," they mean a constructor with no parameters. Similarly, one-arg and two-arg constructors are constructors with one and two parameters, respectively.

You've probably guessed by now that the C# compiler knows which version of the constructor to call by looking at the parameter list. You're right. But to be picky, it looks at the function's _signature_, or _prototype_. A function's signature is made up of its name, return type, and parameter list.

Data Bit _____

For our purposes, a function's signature and prototype are the same thing. That's really not quite true, but many C, C++, and C# programmers use the terms interchangeably. The term _signature_ is more accurate than prototype in this context.

Each version of an overloaded constructor must have a different signature than all others in the class. They don't have to differ in the number of parameters. They can differ in the parameters' types.

For instance, you might write a class where every version of the constructor has one parameter. The type of the parameter in the first constructor might be int. They type of the second might be double, and so on. They can all have one parameter as long as the parameter is a different type in each version.

Overloading Methods

In addition to overloading constructors, you can overload any method in a given class. Each version of the method must have a signature. The difference must occur in the parameter list. C# does not allow you to create two methods that differ in only their return types.

Once again, let's use the Gobbler game as an example. Listing 13.2 contains yet another version of the gobbler class. In this version, notice the overloaded X() and Y() methods.

Listing 13.2 Overloading Methods in a Class

```
1    using System;
2
3    namespace Prog13_2
4    {
```

```
5        public class gobbler
6
7        {
8            //
9            // Private Data
10           //
11
12           private int x,y;
13
14           // 0 = not moving, -1 = moving left
15           // 1 = moving right, 2 = moving down
16           // -2 = moving up
17           private int movementDirection;
18
19           private byte [] imageBitmap;
20
21           private bool isAlive;
22
23           private int powerPillsEaten, bonusesEaten;
24
25           private int livesLeft;
26
27           //
28           // Public methods
29           //
30           public gobbler()
31           {
32               x = 0;
33               y = 0;
34
35               isAlive = true;
36               livesLeft = 3;
37
38               movementDirection = 0;
39
40               powerPillsEaten = 0;
41               bonusesEaten = 0;
42           }
43
44           public gobbler(int initialX,int initialY)
45           {
46               x = initialX;
47               y = initialY;
48
49               isAlive = true;
50               livesLeft = 3;
51
```

continues

Listing 13.2   Overloading Methods in a Class   (continued)

```
52                      movementDirection = 0;
53
54                      powerPillsEaten = 0;
55                      bonusesEaten = 0;
56              }
57
58              // Other methods go here.
59
60              public void X(int newX)
61              {
62                  x=newX;
63              }
64
65              public int X()
66              {
67                  return (x);
68              }
69
70              public void Y(int newY)
71              {
72                  y=newY;
73              }
74
75              public int Y()
76              {
77                  return (y);
78              }
79
80              public bool IsMoving()
81              {
82                  return (movementDirection != 0);
83              }
84
85              public void SetMovementDirection(int newDirection)
86              {
87                  // If the direction is valid...
88                  if ((newDirection >= -2) && (newDirection <= 2))
89                  {
90                      // Set the direction.
91                      movementDirection = newDirection;
92                  }
93              }
94
95              public void Dead()
96              {
97                  if (isAlive)
```

```
98                    {
99                        isAlive = false;
100                       livesLeft--;
101                   }
102           }
103
104           public bool IsAlive()
105           {
106               return (isAlive);
107           }
108
109           public void AtePowerPill()
110           {
111               powerPillsEaten++;
112           }
113
114           public int GetPowerPillsEaten()
115           {
116               return (powerPillsEaten);
117           }
118
119           public void AteBonus()
120           {
121               bonusesEaten++;
122           }
123
124           public int GetBonusesEaten()
125           {
126               return (bonusesEaten);
127           }
128
129           public int GetLivesLeft()
130           {
131               return (livesLeft);
132           }
133       };
134
135       /// <summary>
136       /// Summary description for Class1.
137       /// </summary>
138       class ApplicationClass
139       {
140           /// <summary>
141           /// The main entry point for the application.
142           /// </summary>
143           [STAThread]
144           static void Main(string[] args)
```

continues

Listing 13.2   Overloading Methods in a Class   (continued)

```
145            {
146                 gobbler theGobbler = new gobbler();
147
148                 theGobbler.X(10);
149                 int currentX = theGobbler.X();
150
151            }
152
153        };
154    }
```

Although it's a bit long, I've shown the entire class here to more clearly demonstrate over-loading. This version of the gobbler class overloads the constructors and some methods. The Main() function (lines 144–151) declares a gobbler variable on line 146. The com-piler routes the call to the version of the constructor with no parameters.

On line 148, it uses a version of the X() method to set the x value of the object's (x,y) location on the screen. Because it finds the value 10 in the call to X(), it calls the version of X() with one parameter. This version of the X() function replaces the SetX() function used in previous versions of the gobbler class.

On line 149, it calls the version of X() with no parameters. This version of the X() func-tion replaces the GetX() function that appeared in previous versions of the gobbler class.

Overloading provides use with a way of creating very easy and intuitive interfaces for our classes. With overloading, we can decrease the number of method names programmers need to remember when using our classes. In this version of the gobbler class, a programmer only has to remember one method name to set or get the x value of the Gobbler's location. The same is true for getting and setting the y value.

In addition, overloading enables use to create a group of methods that all do the same task in slightly different ways. All of these methods can have the same name. Again, this version of the gobbler class provides a ready example. The gobbler class's constructors both accomplish the same task. They both set a gobbler object into a known state. They accomplish the task slightly different ways. However, because they both do essentially the same thing, it makes sense to give them the same name.

Overloading Operators

You can make your classes even more intuitive to use by overloading operators as well as constructors and methods. Some of the operators presented so far include +, -, >=, and !=. You can write your own methods that implement these operators for your classes. Listing 13.3 shows a short program that uses the + operator from the string class.

Listing 13.3   Using the + Operator

```
1    using System;
2
3    namespace Prog13_3
4    {
5        /// <summary>
6        /// Summary description for ApplicationClass.
7        /// </summary>
8        class ApplicationClass
9        {
10           /// <summary>
11           /// The main entry point for the application.
12           /// </summary>
13           [STAThread]
14           static void Main(string[] args)
15           {
16               string s1, s2 = "A string";
17               string s3 = " is a nice thing.";
18
19               s1 = s2 + s3;
20               System.Console.WriteLine(s1);
21           }
22       }
23   }
24
```

You know what the + operator does for integers and floating point numbers. It adds two numbers together. You would expect it to do something similar for strings. So this program should add the two strings together. In fact, it does. Here's what is printed by the statement on line 20.

```
A string is a nice thing.
```

Your program can use the + operator on strings because someone overloaded + operator for the string class.

If you're thinking, "Wow! I'd really like to be able to do that for my classes," then you're in luck. Listing 13.4 shows you how. If you're not thinking that, well … Listing 13.4 shows you how anyway.

Listing 13.4   Overloading Operators in a Class

```
1    using System;
2
3    namespace Prog13_4
4    {
```

continues

Listing 13.4   Overloading Operators in a Class   (continued)

```
5        /// <summary>
6        /// Summary description for ApplicationClass.
7        /// </summary>
8        class ApplicationClass
9        {
10           class simple_vector
11           {
12               double x,y;
13
14               public simple_vector()
15               {
16                   x = y = 0;
17               }
18
19               public simple_vector(
20                   double newX,
21                   double newY)
22               {
23                   x = newX;
24                   y = newY;
25               }
26
27               public void X(double newX)
28               {
29                   x = newX;
30               }
31
32               public double X()
33               {
34                   return (x);
35               }
36
37               public void Y(double newY)
38               {
39                   y = newY;
40               }
41
42               public double Y()
43               {
44                   return (y);
45               }
46
47               static public simple_vector operator +(
48                   simple_vector vLeft,
```

```
49                        simple_vector vRight)
50              {
51                      return (new simple_vector(
52                                  vLeft.x + vRight.x,
53                                  vLeft.y + vRight.y));
54              }
55          };
56
57          /// <summary>
58          /// The main entry point for the application.
59          /// </summary>
60          [STAThread]
61          static void Main(string[] args)
62          {
63                  simple_vector v1 = new simple_vector(1.1,2.2);
64                  simple_vector v2 = new simple_vector(3.3,4.4);
65                  simple_vector v3 = new simple_vector();
66
67                  v3 = v1 + v2;
68                  System.Console.WriteLine(
69                      "({0},{1})",
70                      v3.X(),
71                      v3.Y());
72          }
73      }
74  }
```

This program defines a class that implements a simplified 2-D vector object. A vector has a magnitude and a direction. However, it can be described in terms of a set of x and y components. You can add vectors together to get a resulting vector. There are other operations you can do on vectors, but just doing addition is enough for this example. When you add two vectors together, you add the x components to get x component of the resulting vector. You do the same for the y components.

In Listing 13.4, the class definition begins on line 10. It defines the private data members x and y on line 12. The class contains two constructors. One has no parameters and the other has two. In addition, the simple_vector class overloads its X() and Y() functions. The program uses these to get and set the x and y components of the vector.

Data Bit

The keyword static in front of a method means that it can be called without an object of that type. Using the keyword static leads into some rather advanced topics that would make it difficult to clearly explain operator overloading. So, once again, I'll ask your patience and wave my hands at the whole question. For now, just know that static is required at the beginning of overloaded operator methods.

Lines 47–54 is where things really start to get interesting. That's where the simple_vector class defines its addition operator. The first thing to notice is that the operator method has the keyword static at the beginning. This is required; if you forget it, the C# compiler will give you all sorts of errors when you compile.

Next in the operator +() method is the keyword public (of course, we want this function publicly available), and the return type simple_vector. Addition operators almost always return their class type. The keyword operator follows the type name. This is always required on overloaded operator methods. The last thing on line 47 is the operator the class is overloading, which is the + operator, and the beginning of the method's parameter list.

At this point, let's jump down to line 67 of the program. Line 67 is inside Main(). It shows where the operator +() method is actually called. As you can see, the operator is used just like the + operator with any other data type (integers, for instance).

Data Bit

Overloaded binary operators require two parameters. The value on the left of the operator in the method call is passed to the operator method as its first parameter. The value on the right of the operator in the method call is passed to the operator method as its second parameter.

Now look back at lines 48–49. The operator +() method requires two parameters because it's a binary operator. The first parameter is the simple_vector variable on the left of the + operator. The second is the simple_vector variable on the right of the + operator. On line 67 of the program, the variable v1 gets passed as the first parameter. The variable v2 gets passed as the second parameter.

Inside the method, there is only one statement, and it's definitely odd-looking the first time you see it. This return statement builds a vector containing the answer and returns it to the method that called the overloaded + operator. It builds a vector using the new keyword and the simple_vector constructor. The new simple_vector object will not have a name. It exists only in the return statement. The operator +() method creates it expressly so it will have a simple_vector to return. After it finishes the return statement, the operator +() method releases the memory used by the nameless temporary variable.

Data Bit

Using a nameless temporary variable in a return statement is a common technique in C# programs.

The new statement on line 51 calls the simple_vector constructor that takes two parameters. The first parameter is the x component, and the second is the y component. The statement on lines 52 and 53 calculate the values of the vector's x and y components, respectively. The operator +() method passes these calculated values to the two-arg constructor. (Oops! I'm doing it, too. Like so many C# programmers, I find it easier to say "two-arg constructor" rather than "constructor with two arguments" or "constructor with two parameters." Oh, well. Hope you like speaking Programmerese.) The result is a simple_vector object that contains the answer to the addition operation.

Now that you have a class with an overloaded operator, take a look at `Main()` to see how it all works.

Lines 63–64 of `Main()` declare the `simple_vector` variables v1 and v2. They both call the `simple_vector` class's two-arg constructor. Line 65 creates the variable v3. It calls the no-arg constructor.

As mentioned before, the statement on line 67 calls the `operator +()` method. It passes v1 as the first parameter, and v2 as the second. The `operator +()` method calculates the x and y components of the answer and puts them into the nameless temporary variable. It returns the answer to line 67. `Main()` assigns the answer into the variable v3. Lines 68–71 use the `simple_vector` class's `X()` and `Y()` methods to retrieve and print the resulting vector's x and y components.

Data Bit

The `operator +()` method is a member of the `simple_vector` class. As a result, it can directly access the private member data of all `simple_vector` objects it knows about. All of a class's member functions have direct access to its private data.

You can use the techniques shown here to overload other binary operators. Table 13.1 contains the list of operators you can overload.

Table 13.1   Overload-able Operators

Operators	Description
+	Addition. Binary operator.
-	Subtraction. Binary operator.
*	Multiplication. Binary operator.
/	Division. Binary operator.
%	Modulus. Binary operator.
&	Bitwise AND. Binary operator.
|	Bitwise OR. Binary operator.
^	Bitwise exclusive OR. Binary operator.
<<	Left shift. Binary operator.
>>	Right shift. Binary operator.
==	Equal to. Binary operator. Classes that overload this operator must also overload !=.
!=	Not equal to. Binary operator. Classes that overload this operator must also overload ==.
>	Greater than. Binary operator. Classes that overload this operator must also overload <.

continues

Table 13.1 Overload-able Operators (continued)

Operators	Description
<	Less than. Binary operator. Classes that overload this operator must also overload >.
>=	Greater than or equal to. Binary operator. Classes that over-load this operator must also overload <=.
<=	Less than or equal to. Binary operator. Classes that overload this operator must also overload <=.
+	Positive. Unary operator.
-	Negative. Unary operator.
!	Logical NOT. Unary operator.
~	Bitwise negation. Unary operator.
++	Increment. Unary operator.
--	Decrement. Unary operator.

Note that some of the operators must be overloaded in pairs. For example, if you overload the == operator for a class, you must also overload the != operator. If you do not, the C# compiler generates an error message when you compile.

The Least You Need to Know

♦ Programs use polymorphism, also called overloading, to create multiple methods with the same name.

♦ You can overload constructors, methods, and operators in your programs.

♦ The parameter lists of every overloaded constructor, method, or operator must be different than all other overloaded versions.

♦ Overloaded operator methods require the use of the keywords `static` and `operator`.

Properties: Nothing to Do with Acreage

In This Chapter

◆ Providing encapsulated and validated access to member data with properties

◆ How to create properties

◆ How to use properties

◆ When to write properties, and when to write methods

The last couple of chapters demonstrated different aspects of how to create and use classes. This chapter continues that theme. It shows how C# simplifies the process of getting and setting member data. It does this through the use of properties.

What Do You Get When You Cross Member Data with Methods?

Properties combine the information storage of member data with the processing ability of methods. Remember that member data stores the information that a class contains. You could also say that member data describes a class's characteristics, attributes, or properties. In C#, properties formalize the notion of member data as a class's attributes. They also simplify and standardize the task of getting and setting member data.

Let's move forward by looking back. Listing 13.2 in Chapter 13 contains a version of the gobbler class. It has functions that get and set member data. In particular, it uses the overloaded X() and Y() functions to get and set the values of the Gobbler's x and y locations on the screen.

When programs call these functions, they are getting and setting the state of Gobbler objects, rather than performing actions on them. If the Gobbler object's member data were public (that would be bad), programs would not have to use function notation. They could contain statements like these:

```
gobbler aGobbler;
aGobbler.x = 10;
aGobbler.y = 20;
```

Statements like these could go anywhere in the program. These statements clearly set the object's attributes, rather than perform an action on it. However, if a function that is not a member of the gobbler class could contain statements such as these, the whole purpose of object oriented programming would be defeated.

C# provides a way to *look* like you're providing direct access to a class's member data, without providing direct access to member data. This language feature is called properties.

Properties are a special type of method. The primary purpose of a property is to set or get a class's member data. However, because it is a method, a property also enables you to validate the data it receives. In a very real way, properties are a cross between member data and methods.

To see how properties work, I'll rewrite the gobbler class from Listing 13.2 so that it uses properties. Listing 14.1 contains the new version of the class. To save a bit of space (my editors like to get after me about that sort of thing), I've omitted some of the member functions from Listing 14.1. However, I've indicated where they go with the comment on lines 82–83.

Listing 14.1   The gobbler Class with Properties

```
1       using System;
2
3       namespace Prog14_2
4       {
5           public class gobbler
6
7           {
8                   //
```

```
9           // Private Data
10          //
11
12          private int x,y;
13
14          // 0 = not moving, -1 = moving left
15          // 1 = moving right, 2 = moving down
16          // -2 = moving up
17          private int movementDirection;
18
19          private byte [] imageBitmap;
20
21          private bool isAlive;
22
23          private int powerPillsEaten, bonusesEaten;
24
25          private int livesLeft;
26
27          //
28          // Public methods
29          //
30          public gobbler()
31          {
32              x = 0;
33              y = 0;
34
35              isAlive = true;
36              livesLeft = 3;
37
38              movementDirection = 0;
39
40              powerPillsEaten = 0;
41              bonusesEaten = 0;
42          }
43
44          public gobbler(int initialX,int initialY)
45          {
46              x = initialX;
47              y = initialY;
48
49              isAlive = true;
50              livesLeft = 3;
51
52              movementDirection = 0;
53
54              powerPillsEaten = 0;
55              bonusesEaten = 0;
```

continues

Listing 14.1   The gobbler Class with Properties   (continued)

```
56          }
57
58          public int X
59          {
60              get
61              {
62                  return (x);
63              }
64              set
65              {
66                  x = value;
67              }
68          }
69
70          public int Y
71          {
72              get
73              {
74                  return (y);
75              }
76              set
77              {
78                  y = value;
79              }
80          }
81
82      // The rest of the member functions are omitted to save space.
83      // If you want to see them, please look in Listing 13.2.
84
85          /// <summary>
86          /// Summary description for ApplicationClass.
87          /// </summary>
88          class ClassApplication
89          {
90              /// <summary>
91              /// The main entry point for the application.
92              /// </summary>
93              [STAThread]
94              static void Main(string[] args)
95              {
96                  gobbler theGobbler = new gobbler();
97
98                  theGobbler.X = 50;
99                  theGobbler.Y = 20;
100
101                  int currentX = theGobbler.X;
```

```
102                   int currentY = theGobbler.Y;
103             }
104       }
105   }
```

In Listing 14.1, the overloaded X() and Y() methods are gone. They are replaced by the methods on lines 58–68 and 70–80. However, these methods don't look like typical methods.

One reason properties are different than methods is that they have no parameters. You can pass values to properties. It's just done differently than with methods.

When a program uses the gobbler class from Listing 14.1, it sets the values of the X and Y properties with the assignment operator, as shown on lines 98–99. The statements on lines 101–102 get the property values. These statements look very much like the program is setting and getting the values of member data. That is exactly the point of properties. From the point of view of a programmer using the class, it looks like you're setting and getting the attributes of the object. It's very intuitive to use properties in this way.

Data Bit

When you compile this program, you get a warning telling you that the private data member imageBitmap is not used. Usually, you need to pay attention to that warning. In this sample program, however, it is safe to ignore it.

The properties shown in Listing 14.1 contain get and set statements. Both of these statements have a block of code associated with them. Whenever the program sets or gets the values of the properties, it calls the property just like a method. If, for example, the call is to the right of an assignment operator, then the program gets the value of the property. In the case of the X property of the gobbler class, it executes the code block associated with the get statement beginning on line 60. That code block just returns the value of the private data member x.

Data Bit

Properties enable programmers to set the value of member data as if they had direct access to it. However, because access to the data is provided through properties, the class can perform checking to ensure the data is correct.

If, on the other hand, the property is to the left of an assignment, the C# compiler knows that the program is setting the property value. It calls the property just like a method and executes the code block associated with the set statement on line 64. Even though there is no parameter list, the C# compiler knows to pass a value to the set portion of the property. For every property that contains the set statement, the C# compiler creates a parameter called value. The type of value is the same as the type of the private data member being set. So in the case of the gobbler class in Listing 14.1, the statement …

```
theGobbler.X = 50;
```

... calls the X property and executes the code block for the set statement. It automatically generates the value parameter and sets it to 50. On line 66, it assigns the value in value into the private data member x.

Techno Talk _____

Properties are also called **accessor methods**.

The properties in Listing 14.1 just get and set the values of the private data members x and y. However, you can put any C# statements into the get and set code blocks that you can put in methods.

For instance, you could modify the X and Y properties so that they validate their input values. Listing 14.2 shows what X and Y might look like if you did.

Listing 14.2   Properties That Perform Data Validation

```
1      public int X
2      {
3          get
4          {
5              return (x);
6          }
7          set
8          {
9              if ((value >= 0) && (value < 800))
10             {
11                 x = value;
12             }
13         }
14     }
15
16     public int Y
17     {
18         get
19         {
20             return (y);
21         }
22         set
23         {
24             if ((value >= 0) && (value < 600))
25             {
26                 y = value;
27             }
28         }
29     }
```

This version of the properties X and Y contain `if` statements that check whether `value` is within a valid range. The properties in your programs will almost always perform validation such as this. In general, they should not set the values of the private data members without checking the input values first.

Read-Only Properties

Sometimes you need properties in your classes that should not be set. You want programs to read their values, but not modify them.

As an example, suppose you are writing your own string class. Imagine that your string class has a property called `Length`. Programs should not set the length of a string. That should be calculated when it is needed. Listing 14.3 demonstrates how this might look.

Listing 14.3   A Read-Only Property

```
1    class my_string
2    {
3        private char [] theString;
4
5        public int Length
6        {
7            get
8            {
9                int i;
10               for (i=0;theString[i]!='\0';i++)
11               {
12                   // Nothing happens in here.
13               }
14               return (i);
15           }
16       }
17   };
```

The class in Listing 14.3 only contains enough code to demonstrate the idea of read-only properties. I've omitted all the other code that would be needed for a real class that implemented strings.

The `Length` property calculates the length of a string whenever a program contains a statement such as

```
int stringLength = thisString.Length;
```

Data Bit _____

The `for` loop on lines 10–13 of Listing 14.3 does nothing in its code block. It accomplishes all of its work (counting characters) in its control portion (in the parentheses). Although this code is a bit tricky, it's not unusual in C# programming.

This statement calls the `Length` property. It executes the code block for the `get` statement. Inside the code block, the `Length` property uses a `for` loop to count the number of characters in the string. Strings in C# end with a `'\0'` character (a null character).

Any program can use the `my_string` class. If we were writing for real-world use, we would provide a way to set the characters in the string. This would enable programs to use statements like this:

```
my_string thisString = "A short string.";
```

In that case, you could then use the `Length` property to find out how many characters the string contains, as we saw earlier in the statement,

```
int stringLength = thisString.Length;
```

Use read-only properties whenever you need a property that should not be set by method outside the class in question.

Write-Only Properties

In addition to read-only properties, C# also enables you to create write-only properties. With read-only properties, you omit the `set` statement. To create a write-only property, you leave out the `get` statement and include only a `set`.

When you create a write-only property, the property must still have a type. The reason is because the C# compiler uses the property type as the type of the `value` parameter it generates.

Listing 14.4 demonstrates a class with a write-only property.

Listing 14.4   A Write-Only Property

```
1     using System;
2
3     namespace WriteOnlyPropertyDemo
4     {
5         class write_only
6         {
7             private int anInt;
8
9             public int IntValue
10            {
```

```
11              set
12              {
13                  anInt = value;
14              }
15          }
16      };
17
18      /// <summary>
19      /// Summary description for Class1.
20      /// </summary>
21      class Class1
22      {
23          /// <summary>
24          /// The main entry point for the application.
25          /// </summary>
26          [STAThread]
27          static void Main(string[] args)
28          {
29              write_only writeOnlyValue = new write_only();
30
31              writeOnlyValue.IntValue = 5;
32          }
33      }
34  }
```

Write-only properties are not very common. The properties of most classes are either read/write or read-only.

Properties and Methods

When you create your classes, you have to decide whether to write your functions as methods or properties. It's not always clear which to use, but there are some guidelines.

If a function's main purpose is to query or set the state of an object, it should be a property. In the gobbler class, for instance, the function IsAlive should be a property.

Another way to tell whether a function should be a method or a property is to ask yourself, "If I wrote this as a method, what would I call it?" Does the name you would want to use contain the word "get" or "set"? If so, it should be a property and not a method. If the name contains a verb (other than "get" or "set"), you should probably write it as a method. If the name contains a verb and an object, then it is definitely a method and not a property.

For example, a function with the name MoveGobbler should never be a property. Make it a method. Never write a method with a name like SetMovementDirection. Instead, it should be a property called MovementDirection.

Programming Pitfalls _____

Watch out for misnamed functions! They can mislead you into writing properties instead of methods.

For instance, the `gobbler` class in Listing 14.1 contains a method called `Dead()` on lines 97–104. That name sounds like it's setting the state of the object. At first glance, you might want to implement it as a property. However, if you look at the code you'll see that what the function really does is tell the Gobbler to die. It's performing an action. As such, it should be written as a method, not a property. The method should be named `Die()` or `KillGobbler()` rather than `Dead()`.

In addition, look at the parameter list and return type of the function you are writing. Functions that do not return values and do not take parameters should never be properties. They should always be methods.

Also, functions that do not change the state of the object probably should not be properties. Another way to say this is, if a function doesn't change an object's member data, it should usually not be a property; write it as a method.

The Least You Need to Know

◆ Properties make it look like programs can get and set member data directly. However, like methods, they provide a way to encapsulate and validate data.

◆ Properties can have a `get` statement, a `set` statement, or both.

◆ Properties have no parameter lists. If the property contains a set statement, the C# compiler automatically generates a parameter call value.

◆ All properties have a type. The `get` statement uses it as the return type. The `set` statement uses it as the type of the value parameter.

Laziness Is a Virtue: Reusing Code with Inheritance

In This Chapter

- ◆ Enhancing and reusing classes through inheritance
- ◆ Adding characteristics to derived classes
- ◆ Adding functionality to derived classes
- ◆ Creating specific derived classes from generic base classes

Do you want to get something for nothing? Do you want to get a lot of results from a little work? Would you like to be successfully lazy? If so, inheritance is for you.

When I teach classes on object-oriented programming, I tell my students that they should not be hardworking programmers. They should be successfully lazy. Surprised? So are they.

If a hardworking programmer is told by his boss to write some software, he goes straight to his keyboard and starts banging it out. On the other hand, if a successfully lazy programmer gets the same assignment, she sits down and designs her objects. Her first step is to look through objects she's already created for other programs. As much as possible, she grabs generic objects that she's already written, and reuses them in her new software. That's just sheer successful laziness. It's also called working smarter instead of working harder.

Inheritance enables us to be like the successfully lazy programmer. It enables us to be lazy by not having to rewrite objects we've already written. Being successfully lazy helps us get the maximum mileage from our efforts.

The Same Thing, Only Different

Think of a car. How many different types of cars are there? I don't know either. But there are lots of them. Suppose you're writing software for the automobile industry. Wouldn't it be great to write a generic automobile object and use it over and over in all of your programs? Well, that's exactly what inheritance is about.

> **Data Bit**
>
> Inheritance enables you to create specialized objects from generic classes. Another way of saying that is that, through inheritance, you can derive a specialized class from a generic base class.

Classes give programmers a way to create generic objects. Through inheritance, we can specialize those objects for particular programs.

If, for example, you're writing software for the automobile industry, the first class to write is the `automobile` class. From the `automobile` class, you can derive more specific classes, as shown in Figure 15.1.

Figure 15.1

The `car` and `truck` classes are derived from `automobile`. They are specific types of automobiles.

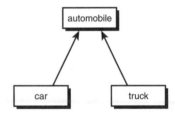

The diagram shows that the `car` and `truck` classes are derived from `automobile`. Cars and trucks both share characteristics common to all automobiles. They both have four wheels, an engine, a gas tank, and so on. The `car` and `truck` classes also have characteristics that are unique to those classes. For instance, trucks have a bed for carrying loads, cars do not.

> **Techno Talk**
>
> A **base class** is a class from which other classes are derived. It is also called the **parent class**. The derived class is also called the **child class**.

When a class is derived from another, the class being derived from is called the *base class* or the *parent class*. The derived class is called the *derived class* or the *child class*.

Listing 15.1 demonstrates how to derive a class from another class.

Listing 15.1   Deriving the `point_3d` Class from the `point_2d` Class

```
1      using System;
2
3      namespace Prog15_1
4      {
5          /// <summary>
6          /// Summary description for ApplicationClass.
7          /// </summary>
8          class ApplicationClass
9          {
10             class point_2d
11             {
12                 private int x,y;
13
14                 public point_2d()
15                 {
16                     x = y = 0;
17                 }
18
19                 public point_2d(int newX, int newY)
20                 {
21                     x = newX;
22                     y = newY;
23                 }
24
25                 public int X
26                 {
27                     get
28                     {
29                         return (x);
30                     }
31                     set
32                     {
33                         x = value;
34                     }
35                 }
36
37                 public int Y
38                 {
39                     get
40                     {
41                         return (y);
42                     }
43                     set
44                     {
```

continues

Listing 15.1 Deriving the `point_3d` Class from the `point_2d` Class (continued)

```
45                         y = value;
46                     }
47                 }
48             }
49
50         class point_3d : point_2d
51         {
52             private int z;
53
54             public point_3d() : base()
55             {
56                 z = 0;
57             }
58
59             public point_3d(int newX,
60                 int newY,
61                 int newZ) : base(newX,newY)
62             {
63                 z = newZ;
64             }
65
66             public int Z
67             {
68                 get
69                 {
70                     return (z);
71                 }
72                 set
73                 {
74                     z = value;
75                 }
76             }
77         }
78
79         /// <summary>
80         /// The main entry point for the application.
81         /// </summary>
82         [STAThread]
83         static void Main(string[] args)
84         {
85             point_2d a2DPoint = new point_2d();
86
87             a2DPoint.X = 5;
```

```
88                    a2DPoint.Y = 10;
89
90                    System.Console.WriteLine(
91                        "({0},{1})",
92                        a2DPoint.X,
93                        a2DPoint.Y);
94
95                    point_2d another2DPoint = new point_2d(10,20);
96
97                    System.Console.WriteLine(
98                        "({0},{1})",
99                        another2DPoint.X,
100                       another2DPoint.Y);
101
102                   point_3d a3DPoint = new point_3d();
103
104                   a3DPoint.X = 20;
105                   a3DPoint.Y = 30;
106                   a3DPoint.Z = 40;
107
108                   System.Console.WriteLine(
109                       "({0},{1},{2})",
110                       a3DPoint.X,
111                       a3DPoint.Y,
112                       a3DPoint.Z);
113
114                   point_3d another3DPoint =
115                       new point_3d(40,50,60);
116
117                   System.Console.WriteLine(
118                       "({0},{1},{2})",
119                       another3DPoint.X,
120                       another3DPoint.Y,
121                       another3DPoint.Z);
122               }
123           }
124       }
```

Lines 10–48 of Listing 15.1 define the point_2d class. The point_2d class is a software implementation of a point in a two-dimensional space. It contains the private data members x and y. It has two constructors, and properties for setting the member data.

This class is just the sort of class you would create for a graphics program. It also provides an excellent base class for a three-dimensional point class, which is implemented as the point_3d class.

The point_3d class begins on line 50. A colon appears after the name of the class. It is followed by the name point_2d. This specifies that the point_3d class derives from the point_2d class.

The point_3d class contains the private data member z. However, because it is derived from point_2d, the point_3d class contains all of the characteristics of the point_2d class. This means that a variable of type point_3d contains three private data members, not one. In addition to z, it has the members x and y in it, as shown in the Figure 15.2.

Figure 15.2

A derived class always contains a copy of its parent object.

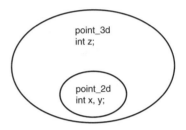

A point_3d object contains the private data member z. It also contains a point_2d object through inheritance. The point_2d object contains the private data members x and y.

Examining the Main() function also shows that the point_3d class inherits the methods of the point_2d class. For instance, line 102 contains the declaration of a point_3d variable called a3DPoint. Lines 104–106 show that the program can use the X and Y properties of the point_2d class on a point_3d variable. It can also invoke the Z property from the point_3d class.

Data Bit

Derived classes contain all of the characteristics of their base class. This includes the base class's member data and methods.

Stepping through the program demonstrates how inheritance works. On lines 85–100, the program shows the use of the point_2d object. Main() calls both of the class's constructors (lines 85 and 95). It uses the get and set portions of the X and Y properties (lines 87–88 and 92–93).

The program also creates instances of the point_3d class on lines 102 and 114–115. It invokes the get and set portions of the X, Y, and Z properties (lines 108–112 and 117–121). The X and Y properties are provided by the point_2d class. The point_3d class provides the Z property. Here is the output of the program.

```
(5,10)
(10,20)
(20,30,40)
(40,50,60)
```

Through inheritance, a `point_3d` object contains a `point_2d` object. So when the program calls a `point_3d` constructor, it must also call a `point_2d` constructor. The technique for doing this is shown on lines 54 and 61. The parameter lists of the two `point_3d` constructors are each followed by a colon. The colon, in turn, is followed by what looks like a call to a method named `base()`. This is actually a call to the constructor of the base class. The C# compiler translates the call to `base()` on line 54 to a call to the no-arg constructor in the `point_2d` class. It translates the call on line 61 to a call to the two-arg constructor in `point_2d`.

Using this technique, derived classes can automatically call the appropriate constructors in their base classes. They can also pass parameter values to the base class constructors. On lines 59–61, the `point_3d` class declares a three–arg constructor. It passes the first two parameters to the two-arg constructor of the `point_2d` class. This enables the `point_2d` constructor to initialize its x and y data members.

This example demonstrates that you can use inheritance to get more mileage out of your efforts. Because it inherits from the `point_2d` class, the `point_3d` class contains very little code.

Not Just Public and Private

If you're a parent, you're used to your kids asking to borrow your stuff. (Example: "Dad, can I borrow the car?") If they don't do it yet, they will when they get older.

Recall that base classes are also called parent classes, and derived classes are also called child classes. Like any parents, base classes can choose whether to allow their children (derived classes) to use their stuff. Specifically, they can let their derived classes have access to their member data.

Most classes declare their data to be `private`. If you want, your parent classes can grant special access to their children. To do this, use the keyword `protected` where you would normally use `private`. Data declared with the protected keyword can be accessed directly by a class's children. Classes that are "outside the family," so to speak, cannot access the data. The keyword `protected` only grants access to a class's methods and its children.

Overriding Base Class Methods

Remember overloading from Chapter 13? You can use method overloading with inheritance. Derived classes inherit all of the methods of their base classes. If you want to, you can overload the functions a child class inherits from its parent. Overloading a method in a parent class is called *overriding* it.

Why might you want to do this?

To answer this question, let's revisit the automobile example. Previous sections in this chapter presented a generic automobile class. Suppose the automobile class has a method called Accelerate() that makes the car go faster. If you derive a class called car and one called truck from automobile, you need to change the Accelerate() method. Cars accelerate faster than trucks. Taking the example a bit further, suppose you derive a sports_car class from car. Sports cars accelerate faster than regular cars (that, in fact, is the point of a sports car). Listing 15.2 shows simplified versions of these classes.

> **Techno Talk** _____
>
> Overloading a method inherited from a base class is called **overriding** it.

Listing 15.2 Overriding Methods in Base Classes

```
1     using System;
2
3     namespace Prog15_2
4     {
5         class automobile
6         {
7             protected int currentSpeed;
8
9             public automobile()
10            {
11                currentSpeed = 0;
12            }
13
14            public void Accelerate()
15            {
16                currentSpeed += 5;
17            }
18        }
19
20        class truck : automobile
21        {
22            public void Accelerate()
23            {
24                currentSpeed += 3;
25            }
26        }
27
28        class car : automobile
29        {
30            public void Accelerate()
```

```
31                  {
32                      currentSpeed += 7;
33                  }
34          }
35
36      class sports_car : car
37      {
38          public void Accelerate()
39          {
40              currentSpeed += 10;
41          }
42      }
43
44
45      /// <summary>
46      /// Summary description for ApplicationClass.
47      /// </summary>
48      class ApplicationClass
49      {
50          /// <summary>
51          /// The main entry point for the application.
52          /// </summary>
53          [STAThread]
54          static void Main(string[] args)
55          {
56              automobile anAuto = new automobile();
57              anAuto.Accelerate();
58
59              truck aTruck = new truck();
60              aTruck.Accelerate();
61
62              car aCar = new car();
63              aCar.Accelerate();
64
65              sports_car aFastCar= new sports_car();
66              aFastCar.Accelerate();
67          }
68      }
69  }
```

In Listing 15.2, I've only shown the methods needed to demonstrate how to override base class methods. All of the classes in this example are ultimately derived from automobile. They each have methods named Accelerate(). Notice that the Accelerate() method in each of the child classes accesses the data member currentSpeed. Because currentSpeed is declared in the automobile class with protected access, methods in the child classes can access it directly.

CAUTION

Programming Pitfalls

Be aware that a lot of object-oriented programming literature recommends against using **protected** access for data members. It decreases a class's encapsulation.

A better approach is to make the data member **private** and to write a property that can get and set it. You can make the property **protected** rather than **public**. That way, the **private** data member can only be accessed by methods in the base class. Because the property is **protected**, only methods in derived classes can call it. Therefore, they are the only methods that can set or get the property.

If you use your debugger to step through this program, you'll see that the C# compiler can figure out the appropriate version of the Accelerate() method call.

Data Bit

If you do not provide a constructor for a class you define, the C# compiler generates one automatically. The constructor it generates initializes all memory used by the object to zero.

On line 56, Main() calls the automobile constructor to create a variable called anAuto. It uses the variable on line 57 to call the Accelerate() method. The C# compiler knows that program is invoking the Accelerate() method in the automobile class because that is the type of the variable anAuto.

Main() creates a variable of type truck on line 59. Looking at the truck class shows that it does not have a constructor. That's okay. If you do not provide a constructor for a class, the C# compiler automatically generates one that initializes all memory used by the object to zero.

Data Bit

If a child class overrides a parent method, the C# compiler uses the type of the variable to determine which version of the method to call.

Line 60 of the program uses the variable aTruck to call the Accelerate() method. As before, the program calls the correct version of the method. The C# compiler connects this call to the Accelerate() method in the truck class because it knows that aTruck is of type truck. The same is true for each of the other variables in the program. In each case, the C# compiler selects the appropriate version of the Accelerate() method by using the type of the variable.

It is possible to call the base version of a function from the overridden version in the derived class. For instance, if you wanted the Accelerate() method in the car class to call the one in the automobile class, you would call the base version of Accelerate() as shown in Listing 15.3.

Listing 15.3   Calling the Overridden Base Class Method

```
1    class car : automobile
2    {
3        public void Accelerate()
4        {
5            base.Accelerate();
6        }
7    }
```

This version of the `Accelerate()` method uses the `base` keyword to call `Accelerate()` in the `automobile` class.

The techniques demonstrated here work for nearly any type of method. In addition to normal methods, you can override properties and operators. You cannot override constructors.

The Least You Need to Know

♦ Inheritance enables you to get more benefits for your efforts.

♦ Inheritance is based on the idea of creating generic classes, and extending their functionality for specific programming situations.

♦ You specify inheritance in a derived class definition. To do so, put a colon after the name of the class on the first line of the definition. Follow the colon with the name of the base class.

♦ Derived classes contain all of the characteristics of their base classes. They can also add additional characteristics and functionality.

♦ Constructors in derived classes call constructors in base classes by using the `base` keyword.

♦ Methods in derived classes can override methods in base classes.

♦ Methods in derived classes that override base class methods can call the overridden base class method using the `base` keyword.

Part 5

Programming in the Real World

Congratulations! You now have a pretty solid understanding of the C# language. However, the language itself is part of a development environment. It's just one tool in a set of tools. Microsoft calls that set of tools the .NET Framework.

You've already used some of the classes and methods in the .NET Framework. With those classes, you've created a variety of console programs. However, the .NET Framework also contains classes called Windows Forms. With Windows Forms, you can rapidly build C# programs that look as professional as anything on the market today. This part introduces you to how that's done.

Net Gain

In This Chapter

♦ The context for the C# programming language

♦ The relationship between C#, the .NET Framework, and the .NET development platform

♦ What's in the .NET Framework?

♦ Windows Forms

This chapter gives an introduction to the .NET Framework and Windows Forms. You'll use Windows Forms to build high-quality GUI-based Windows applications.

Introducing the .NET Framework

The .NET Framework contains components and tools that you can use in your C# programs. There are literally thousands of components and tools available to you. In that respect, the .NET Framework is a code library (a very large one).

But thinking of the .NET Framework as a library is a little like thinking of a Swiss army knife as a good potato peeler. It's correct as far as it goes, but it's a lot more than that.

Techno Talk

Microsoft's **Common Language Specification** defines an intermediate language and the ways that intermediate language is converted to executable binary.

Data Bit

C# uses tools provided by the .NET Framework. Both C# and the .NET Framework are part of the .NET development platform.

C# and the .NET Framework are part of the .NET development platform. The components and tools in the .NET Framework, and C# itself, are written with the *Common Language Specification* (CLS) in mind. The CLS defines Intermediate Language (IL), which is similar to object code.

Potentially, programs written in many different source languages can be compiled to the intermediate language defined by the CLS. These programs can run on the Common Language Runtime (CLR).

To understand what's going on here, it's helpful to go back and examine the way source code is converted into executable code. Take a look at Figure 16.1. You first saw this back in Chapter 1. It illustrates the traditional model for compiling and linking programs.

Figure 16.1

The traditional model for compiling and linking programs.

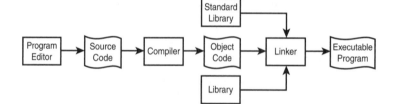

This isn't quite how the .NET platform handles programs written in C#. Instead, it uses the process shown in Figure 16.2.

This figure shows the important differences between the traditional model and the model used by the .NET development platform. Instead of compiling C# source code into object code, Visual Studio compiles it to Intermediate Language (IL). The IL program can be linked to other components. These components don't have to be written in C#. They can be written in any language that compiles to IL.

Data Bit

As of this writing, Microsoft is the only compiler vendor that is producing languages that can be compiled into IL. So far, they've implemented two such languages: Visual C# and Visual Basic.

To make the .NET platform more accessible, Microsoft has set things up such that other compiler vendors can potentially write compilers for the CLS.

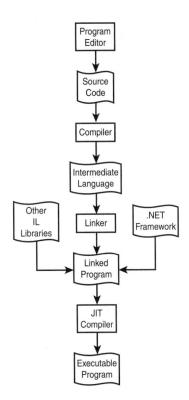

Figure 16.2

A simplified version of the .NET model for compiling and linking programs.

The linker does not convert the IL code into an executable program. Instead, it creates linked IL code. The program stays in this form on the disk until you are ready to run it. When the IL program runs, the CLR compiles it again using its Just in Time (JIT) compiler. The JIT compiler translates linked IL into an executable binary program.

Data Bit _____

By defining IL, the CLS essentially defines a computer that doesn't exist. It defines an idealized or generic computer. A computer that is implemented in software like this is called a virtual machine (VM). All CLS-compliant compilers (right now there's only one) can compile programs for this VM. The CLR's Just in Time (JIT) compiler translates programs for the VM into programs for the actual hardware it's running on.

Java and Python are other programming languages that use VMs.

After a program has been compiled by the JIT compiler, the CLR stores it in its final compiled form. The CLR does not recompile the program each time you run it.

But What Does It Do?

All of this seems like a lot of trouble to go to (it is). It might also seem a bit pointless at first. What's the sense of compiling a program twice?

The answer has to do with Microsoft's goals, and those of the rest of the computer industry. Microsoft wants everything it produces to work together nicely. All other companies have that same goal for their products. Unfortunately, it's difficult to achieve in practice. It's a complex problem that's been worked on by very smart people for years.

Data Bit

The Java programming language uses a compilation model that is similar to that of the .NET platform and .NET Framework.

Compiling a program twice enables programs and components written in different languages to work together properly. Any component written in a language that conforms to the CLS can be compiled into IL. Any IL component can be linked to any other IL component or program.

That's the theory, anyway. If it all works as it should, we'll see some important advances in the computer industry.

The second reason for compiling a program twice is portability. Remember portability? That's the ability to take a program written for one computer or operating system and run it on another. I said earlier that portability is a kind of "holy grail" for programmers.

Intermediate Language is completely independent of any operating system or hardware. In theory, it is possible to write a JIT compiler for any operating system or hardware. The JIT compiler should be able to take any IL program created on any operating system or computer and compile it to a program that runs on the current hardware and operating system.

Microsoft has announced plans to implement the CLR, which contains the JIT compiler, for some versions of Unix. It will include part, but not all, of the .NET Framework. Many in the industry are skeptical about how dedicated Microsoft is to portability. I guess only time will tell on this issue.

Tools to Use and Reuse

As previously stated, the .NET Framework provides us with tools we can use in many programs. What kind of tools?

You've already used components for helping your programs do math, read from and write to files, read from the keyboard, and write to the screen. In addition, the .NET Framework contains components that enable programs to easily get access to databases. Others help with drawing graphics. All of these tools (and others that have not been presented) perform tasks that programs commonly need. This saves you and me a lot of work.

WinForms for Easy Windows Programming

Nearly every program uses menus, dialog boxes, and other GUI elements. It would be silly for each of us to have to write our own code to display them. Fortunately, we don't have to. The .NET Framework provides them in the System.Windows.Forms namespace.

What kind of tools does System.Windows.Forms contain? In a word, Windows Forms controls (three words, actually). Windows Forms controls are objects that implement graphical user interface elements. With these controls, you can rapidly design and develop the user interface for your program. In fact, you can develop most of it interactively in Visual Studio by dragging controls from the Toolbox onto the design palette. The Toolbox is shown in Figure 16.3.

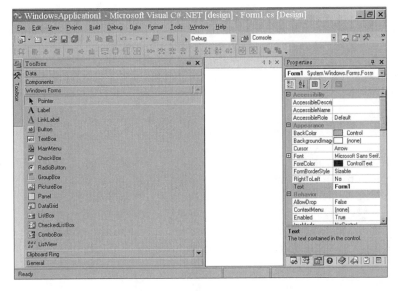

Figure 16.3

The Toolbox is at the left of the Visual Studio's program window.

After designing the user interface, you can add your C# code to the controls to make them do whatever you want. The code resides in a file called the code-behind page. It's called that because it holds the code "behind" the control.

Rapid Application Development

The intent of the .NET Framework is to provide you with classes that do most of the common tasks your programs need to handle. This saves you from having to write these classes yourself. It decreases the time required to develop your applications. For this reason, Microsoft advertises the .NET development platform as a rapid application development (RAD) tool.

A variety of RAD tools are currently on the market. Like other RAD tools, the .NET development platform enables you to quickly construct the user interface of your program. Making a user interface that does nothing but display menus, dialog boxes, and so forth is called *prototyping* your application.

Techno Talk

RAD tools enable you to **prototype** your program's user interface. They do this by providing tools to create a user interface that does nothing but display menus, dialog boxes, and so forth.

RAD is about more than just prototyping program interfaces. RAD tools also provide support for common programming tasks such as accessing files and directories, accessing networks, and connecting to databases. The .NET Framework assists you in all of these tasks and more.

An Assortment of Building Blocks

Windows Forms are a collection of controls. A control is a software object that implements a user interface element. Controls can be forms, buttons, dialog boxes, menus, and so forth.

Each type of control has methods, properties, and events.

A control's methods are just the same as a class's methods; so are its properties. Events are discussed in Chapter 17.

The remaining chapters of this book provide an overview of the more commonly used controls. Before going on to the next chapter, I strongly suggest that you take some time to look at the controls in the Visual Studio Toolbox. If you click a control, Visual Studio displays a list of help topics about it in the Dynamic Help window. It's a good idea to read through these help topics.

Data Bit

Controls are not the same as classes. However, the controls are made with classes. This enables you to use inheritance to derive new controls from existing controls.

In addition to the controls, the .NET Framework provides dialog boxes for common tasks. They are called the Common Dialog Boxes. They are in the namespace System.Windows.Forms.CommonDialog. You'll read about the Common Dialog Boxes in Chapter 26.

The Least You Need to Know

◆ The C# programming language is part of the .NET development platform.

◆ The .NET Framework is also part of the .NET platform.

◆ The .NET Framework contains components that make it easier and faster for you and me to write programs.

◆ Among the components available in the .NET Framework are the Windows Forms controls.

◆ The Windows Forms controls provide the ability to rapidly create user interfaces for Windows programs.

Chapter 17

Properties, Events, and Methods

In This Chapter

◆ Adding controls to Windows Forms

◆ Using the Visual Studio designer

◆ Setting a control's properties

◆ Getting controls to respond to input and other events

Windows Forms controls give you an easy way to build programs. The question is, how do they work?

The answer can be summed up in four words: properties, methods, and events.

Like classes, controls hold information. And like classes, they have properties. They also have methods. Your programs perform operations on controls by calling their methods. In addition, controls have something that classes do not have—events. Their events tell your programs when it's time to do something.

This chapter describes how to use the properties, methods, and events of Windows Forms controls.

Controls Have Properties, Too

Every Windows Forms control has properties. Because the .NET Framework implements controls using classes, it uses class properties to implement the properties of controls. As your program executes, it can set a control's properties just the way it would set a class's properties.

Visual Studio provides a Properties window you can use to interactively view and set a control's properties. Figure 17.1 shows a picture of the Properties window. It's in the pane on the right side of Visual Studio's main window.

Figure 17.1

Visual Studio's Properties window displays the properties of the currently selected control.

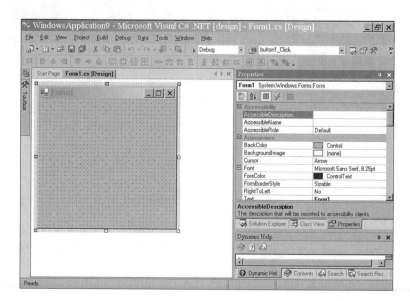

Designer Defaults

Most control properties have a default value. Others are not set by default. You can view a control's property values by clicking on it, and then clicking the **Properties** tab to show the Properties window. Visual Studio displays a list of all of the control's properties and their current values.

To change the value of a property in the Properties window, do the following:

1. Point your mouse cursor at a control and click the main mouse button (the left button if you're right handed).

2. In the pane on the right side of the Visual Studio window, click the **Properties** tab.

3. In the Properties window is a table with the property names in the left column, and their values in the right column. Click the value box to the right of the name of the property you want to change.

4. Enter a value for the property by doing one of the following:

   ◆ Type in a value for the property.

   ◆ If you see a button containing three dots (an ellipsis), click the button to display a dialog box. Use the dialog box to input one or more values.

   ◆ If, instead, you see an arrow pointing down, click it to display a list of possible values for the property. Select one of the values in the list.

The value you set in the Properties window becomes the default value of that property. The program uses that default value every time it runs.

Access on the Run

In addition to setting property values when you design a program, your program can set them as it runs.

Setting default property values is a *design time* activity. Changing them as the program executes is a *run time* activity.

To see how a program can change the property values of controls at run time, try the following activity. This activity is accomplished in three stages. In the first, you put a button control onto a form. Next, you modify the form's code-behind page so that it sets the button's text. Finally, you compile and run the program to see the results.

Stage 1

In this stage, you'll create a Windows Forms program, and place a button on the program's main form.

1. Start Visual Studio and select **File** from the main menu. Click **New**, and then **Project.** Visual Studio displays the New Project dialog box.

2. In the **Project Types** list, choose **Visual C# Projects.**

3. From the Templates list, select the **Windows Application** icon.

4. Type the name of your program into the Name box. At this point, you'll see a blank form in Visual Studio's designer window, as shown in Figure 17.2.

Techno Talk

While you are working in Visual Studio, you are in **design time.** That is, you are designing and building the program.

While the program is running, it is in its **run time.** In programming documentation, you'll often see run time shortened to **runtime.**

Figure 17.2

Visual Studio's designer window displays a program's forms.

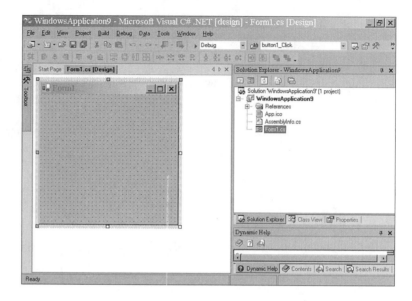

5. Click the **Toolbox** tab on the left side of Visual Studio's main window. The toolbox appears.

6. Drag a Button control from the toolbox onto the form. Try to center the button as well as possible. Your screen should now resemble Figure 17.3.

Figure 17.3

A program's forms contain its other controls. This form contains a button.

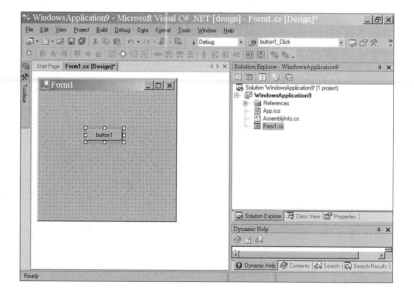

Now that you've got a form with a button on it. You're ready for the next stage of this process.

Stage 2

This stage of the activity demonstrates how to add your program code to a form's code-behind page.

1. Double-click the button on your form. Visual Studio loads the code-behind file and sets your cursor in the button's `Click()` method.

2. Scroll the file upward until you find the **Form** contol's constructor.

3. In the form's constructor, you'll find a comment that says

```
//
// TODO: Add any constructor code after InitializeComponent call
//
```

Highlight the three lines of the comment and press the **Delete** key.

4. Look above the constructor to find the name of the button. If you've been following these steps exactly, the button's name should be `button1`.

5. In the form's constructor, add the following line of code. Be sure you add it *after* the call to `InitializeComponent()`.

```
button1.Text = "A Button That Does Nothing";
```

At this point, your form's constructor should resemble the code shown in Listing 17.1.

> ### From the Knowledge Bank
>
> With the steps you've just completed, you've created a program window (a form) that contains a button. This might not seem like a big deal to you, but it is. When I first started writing Windows programs in C, it literally took hundreds of lines of program code to do what you just did. None of it was particularly easy to write or debug.
>
> My advice: Be grateful for good programming tools. I am.

Listing 17.1   The Form's Constructor

```
1    public Form1()
2    {
3        //
4        // Required for Windows Form Designer support
5        //
6        InitializeComponent();
7        button1.Text = "A Button That Does Nothing";
8    }
```

Data Bit _____

The name that Visual Studio generates for a particular control depends on how many other controls of the same type are on the form. For example, if you add another button to the form in this example, its name will be button2.

Now you're ready for the final stage of this activity.

Stage 3

This stage shows how to compile, link, and run a Windows Forms program.

1. From Visual Studio's **File** menu, select **Save All**.
2. Press **F5.** Visual Studio compiles, links, and runs your program.

When your program runs, it will look like Figure 17.4.

Figure 17.4

The button with its new title.

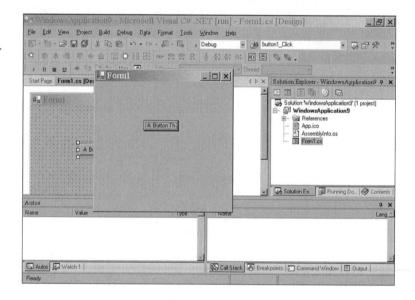

Programming Pitfalls _____

Most controls do not resize themselves when you change their Text property. You must either resize the control in Visual Studio at design time, or your program code must resize it at run time by setting the appropriate properties.

Wait! Something's wrong. The button is not showing the complete title.

The reason for this is that the Button control does not automatically resize itself when you change its title. So whenever you change a button's title, you must resize the button to accommodate the text. You can resize the button at design time (in Visual Studio), or at run time. Just to see how it's done, let's resize it in Visual Studio.

If your program is still running, click on the little X in its upper-right corner. This ends the program and returns you to Visual Studio.

Click the button on the form in Visual Studio's design window. Visual Studio displays a border around the button. In the border are little white boxes. Point your mouse cursor at the middle box on the right side of the button. Drag the box until it's nearly at the edge of the form, as shown in Figure 17.5.

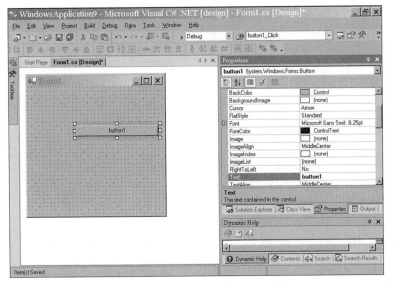

Figure 17.5

Stretching the button to the right.

Now do the same thing to the left edge of the button. Use your mouse cursor to drag the middle white box on the left edge of the button. Stretch the button out until it looks like Figure 17.6.

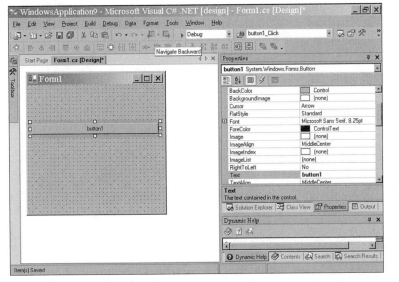

Figure 17.6

The resized button.

Now press F5 to run the program again. This time, the entire title should be visible in the button. You can click the button if you want. But, as its title says, it does nothing.

Data Bit

The little boxes that appear around a control's border when you click the control are its resize handles.

Eventful Programming

In addition to properties, controls have events. An event is a response to an external stimulus. In that respect, controls are rather like living things.

It's Alive! Well, Not Really

Every living thing reacts to changes in its environment. Is there anyone sitting near you now? Go over and tickle him or her. Did she/he react? If you don't know the person you tickled, you might want to run away now.

When you tickled that person, that was an event. The person you tickled handled the event in one way or another. Maybe you just got slapped. Perhaps the police were called. Or maybe you just got yourself a date. Whatever the reaction, the event was handled.

Controls work this same way. When an event occurs that they care about, they react. Their reaction is to call a method. For this reason, the method is called an *event handler*.

To see the events a control supports, drag the control onto a form. Click on the control. If the Properties window is not visible, click its tab. Now look at the top of the Properties window for a button with a yellow lightning bolt on it. Click that button, and the Properties window changes to a list of events. If the event has an event handler, the name of the handler is listed next to the name of the event. If there is nothing next to the event name, the event has no handler.

Techno Talk

An **event handler** is a method that a control calls to react to an event.

Default and Nondefault Events

Every Windows Forms control has a default event. Typically, the default event is the one that gets triggered most often. For instance, a button's default event is called `Click`. When a user selects a button, Windows triggers the button's `Click` event.

To find the default event for a particular type of control, drag the control onto a form. Next, double-click the control. When you do, Visual Studio loads the code-behind page for the form and places its cursor in the default event.

Controls have one, and only one, default event. All of the other events a control supports are nondefault events.

Handling Default Events

If you want your program to handle a control's default event, you need to type some code into its default event handler. Recall that event handlers are methods. For instance, if you create a form with a button on it, the default event handler for the button's `Click` event is a method in the `Form` class.

Data Bit

Visual Studio creates default event handlers for you when you double-click a control.

Use the following steps to see how you can create a default event handler.

1. Create a new Windows Forms application.

2. Drag a button from the Visual Studio Toolbox onto the form.

3. Drag a **Label** control onto the form.

4. Double-click the button to go to the button's `Click` event handler.

5. Type the following line of code into the `button1_Click()` method.

   ```
   label1.Text = "Clicked!";
   ```

6. Go back to the form by clicking the tab for its file name. You'll find it just above the code-behind page's edit window.

7. Click the button, then click the tab for the Properties window. The Properties window displays the button's properties.

8. Change the string in the **Text** property to `Click Me!`.

9. On the form, click the **Label** control.

10. Change the label's **Text** property to `Not Clicked Yet`.

Now run the program. It should look like Figure 17.7.

Now click the button. The result looks like Figure 17.8.

In this activity, you created a form with a button and a label. Windows Forms implements them with **Button** controls and **Label** controls, respectively. When you drag the **Button** and **Label** controls onto the form, the designer generates `private` data members for them in the `form` class. Any method in the `form` class can access these data members. The button's `Click` event handler is a method in the `form` class. As a result, it has access to both the button and the label. This enables the button's `Click` event handler to change the text of the **Label** control.

When you run this program, the default text for the label is `Not Clicked Yet`. Clicking the button triggers its `Click` event, which calls its event handler. The event handler programmatically sets the **Label** control's **Text** property to `"Clicked!"`. Setting a value programmatically means that it's set in the program's source code.

Figure 17.7

What happens when you click the button?

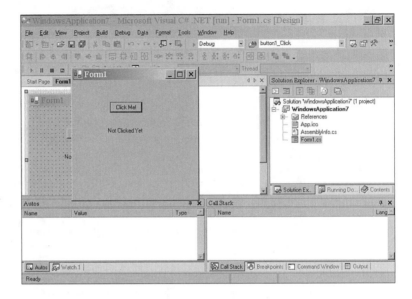

Figure 17.8

Well, now you know.

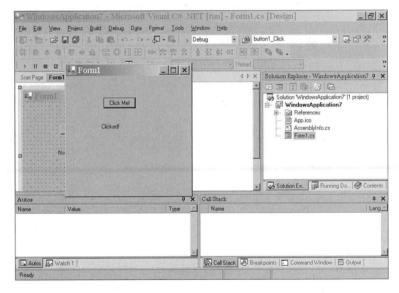

Handling Nondefault Events

Like default events, nondefault events need a method to handle them. However, unlike default event handlers, you've got to create a method from scratch for nondefault events. The easiest way to do that is to copy the default event handler and change its name.

Follow these steps to create a nondefault event handler.

1. Create a new Windows application.

2. Drag a button and a label onto the application's form.

3. Double-click the button.

4. Highlight the button's default event handler.

5. From Visual Studio's **Edit** menu, select **Copy.**

6. In the edit window, move the editing cursor so that it is just below the button's default event handler.

7. From the **Edit** menu, choose **Paste.**

8. Change the name of the method you just pasted to `button1_OnMouseHover()`.

9. Add the following line of code to the `button1_OnMouseHover()` event handler.

   ```
   label1.Text = "Hovering";
   ```

10. Go back to the form by clicking its tab above the Edit window.

11. Click the button.

12. In the Properties window, click the icon that looks like a lightning bolt.

13. Click in the box to the right of the `MouseHover` event. A small arrow appears on the right edge of the box. Click it. Visual Studio displays a list of available methods.

14. Select the name `button1_OnMouseHover`. This sets the `button1_OnMouseHover()` method as the event handler for the `MouseHover` event.

Now compile and run the program. When the program's window pops up, move your mouse cursor so that it points to the button. Don't click your mouse's button. Just let the mouse cursor hover over the button on the form. After a couple of seconds, the **Label** control's text changes to the string `"Hovering"`.

Methods to My Madness

As previously stated, controls are implemented with classes. Classes have methods. In the Windows programs you write, you'll use many methods as event handlers. Others will be called by event handlers.

For example, you might write an event handler for a button's `Click` event. Suppose the button is an OK button on a dialog box. Also imagine that the dialog box has a text box containing the name of the file. Suppose that when the user clicks the button, the event handler must check to see if the filename is valid. Programs usually perform that validation in a method called by the event handler. So, in this example, you would need to write a method to handle the button's `Click` event, and a method to perform the validation.

Data Bit _____

Calling another control's event handler is an easy way to get multiple controls to respond together to a single event.

Whether they are event handlers, or methods called by event handlers, the methods you write can call the methods of any control available. They can even call another control's event handlers. When they do, they essentially simulate an event. This is an easy way to get multiple controls to respond together to one event.

The Least You Need to Know

- Windows Forms controls have properties that keep track of their current state.
- You can set control properties at design time.
- Your program can set control properties at run time.
- Controls also have methods, like classes.
- In addition, Windows Forms controls have events that enable a control to react to changes in their environment.
- When a control responds to an event, it calls an event handler method.
- Controls have one default event. The rest are nondefault events.
- Not all of a control's methods are event handlers. Some methods are called by event handlers.

Chapter 18

Containers: Tupperware for Controls

In This Chapter

◆ Building program windows with the **Form** control

◆ Grouping related controls with the **Panel** control

◆ Visually grouping controls with the **GroupBox** control

In the last chapter, you began building Windows applications with Windows Forms controls. You saw how controls operate, and how easy it is to get them to work for you.

At this point, you're ready to examine specific controls to see how to use them. There are actually too many controls to cover in this book. The individual controls can have literally dozens of properties, methods, and events. A complete reference of all of them would easily be twice as thick as this book!

So we won't try to cover everything related to Windows Forms controls. Instead, the next few chapters introduce you to the most frequently used controls. They present only the properties of each control that programmers use often. Reading these chapters will give you a good foundation for Windows Forms programming. After you have that, you'll know enough of the basics to make learning additional controls (with their properties, methods, and events) easy. Hopefully, you'll learn enough that, when it comes to Windows Forms programming, you'll feel like a complete genius.

Form Controls

You used the **Form** control when you wrote programs in Chapter 17. The **Form** control is a container. Its primary purpose is to hold other controls. However, it does a lot more than that. It has a long list of properties, and a whole host of events it can respond to. Using a form's properties, methods, and events, you can take advantage of powerful techniques for customizing your program.

Windows programs use **Form** controls as their main windows. You can attach menus, toolbars, buttons, and so forth to forms. These, in turn, can pop up other windows, dialog boxes, and message boxes.

Data Bit _____

Other container controls are the **Panel** control and the **GroupBox** control. These are presented later in this chapter. Some Windows Forms programming literature also calls the **PictureBox** control a container. However, the Microsoft documentation doesn't describe it as such.

Data Bit _____

Reminder: If your program sets a property as it runs, software developers often say that it is setting the property *programmatically*. In fact, the Microsoft documentation often refers to setting properties (or doing other tasks) programmatically. It just means that whatever the task is, it's handled in your program's code at run time instead of in the Visual Studio designer.

Form Properties

Form controls have lots of properties. To help give you a feel for how they work, just a few of them are presented here.

The Form.Text Property

The first **Form** control property we'll examine is the **Text** property. The **Form** control uses the string in its **Text** property as its window title. You can set it in Visual Studio's designer, or your program can set it at runtime.

Figure 18.1 shows a form in the Visual Studio's designer. The value of the **Text** property in the Properties window is the string `"New Title"`. As you can see, the new title shows in the form's title bar.

If you want a form to set its title programmatically, put a statement like the following in your program's code.

```
this.Text = "New Title";
```

The C# keyword `this` refers to the current class. So if a **Form** control is setting its own title, `this` refers to the **Form** control. If you want your code to set the title of another form, use a statement similar to the following.

```
form2.Text = "New Title";
```

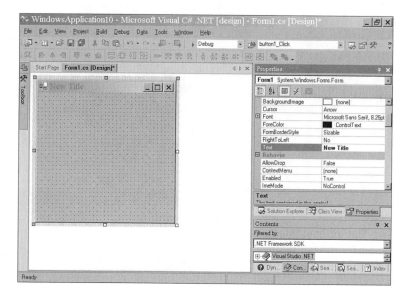

Figure 18.1

Setting a form's title.

The Form.ForeColor and Form.BackColor Properties

The **Form** control's **ForeColor** property sets the color of text on the form. Its **BackColor** property sets the color of the form itself. To see how these work, try the following activity.

1. Create a new Windows application.
2. Click in the application's form.
3. In the Properties window, click the box to the right of the **ForeColor** property. A drop-down arrow appears. Click it.
4. In the list that appears, click the **Custom** tab. Visual Studio shows a collection of colors.
5. Click the white box in the upper left corner of the collection of colors.
6. In the Properties window, click the box to the right of the **BackColor** property.
7. Click the arrow for the drop-down list of colors.
8. Select the **Custom** tab. Click the black box in the collection of colors.
9. Drag a **Label** control from the Toolbox onto the form.

Now run your program. It resembles the one shown in Figure 18.2.

Setting the **ForeColor** property to white and the **BackColor** property to black gives you white text on a black window.

Figure 18.2

Take a look at the program window.

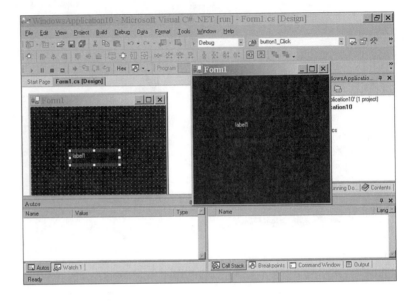

The Form.FormBorderStyle Property

As you might expect, the **FormBorderStyle** property controls a form's border style. Although this might not seem important, you'll see in later chapters that dialog boxes are actually forms. To make them look like dialog boxes, you set their **FormBorderStyle** property to FixedDialog.

With the **FormBorderStyle** property, you can also give your forms a nifty, "sunken" look. Try it and see for yourself by setting the **FormBorderStyle** property to Fixed3D. When you do, you'll find that you cannot resize the form when you run the program.

Data Bit

The default border style forms is Sizable.

Setting **FormBorderStyle** to FixedSingle makes the form look like a normal window. It doesn't have that sunken look. However, like **Fixed3D**, the FixedSingle style prevents the user from resizing the window at runtime.

Form Methods

As you develop your Windows programs, you sometimes need to pop up additional windows. You also need to remove them from the screen. To do this, you use the Form control's Show() and Close() methods.

To see this technique in action, create a new Windows application. Drag a button onto the form, and use the Properties window to set its **Text** property to Open a Form. You need to resize the button so that it displays all of the text. When you've done this, your form resembles Figure 18.3.

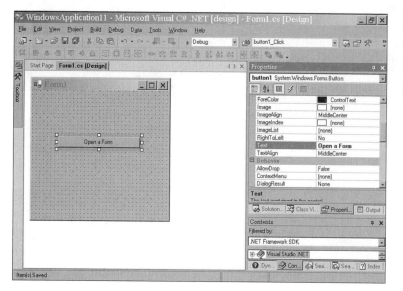

Figure 18.3

The application's form with a button inside it.

Now use the following steps to add another form to your project.

1. From Visual Studio's Project menu, select **Add Windows Form**. Visual Studio displays the Add New Item dialog box.

2. In the Add New Item dialog box, select **Windows Form**, then click the **Open** button. Visual Studio creates a form, called Form2.

3. Now that you have two forms in your program, drag a button onto Form2. Set the button's **Text** property to Close. Double-click the button to bring up its event handler. Add the following line of code to the event handler.

Data Bit

Preview of Coming Attractions: You use the **Form** control's Show() and Close() methods to display additional forms in your program. You don't use this technique for modal dialog boxes. Later chapters present the method Windows Forms programs use for displaying modal dialog boxes.

```
this.Close();
```

This statement tells the form to close itself when the user clicks the button.

4. At this point, you need to return to Form1. You can do that by first clicking the **Solution Explorer** tab. The Solution Explorer displays a list of everything in the current solution, including all of its forms. Double-click the name **Form1** in the Solution Explorer's list. Visual Studio displays Form1.

5. Go to the event handler of Form1's button (double-click the button). Edit the button's event handler so that it matches the following code.

```
private void button1_Click_1(object sender, System.EventArgs e)
{
    Form2 form2 = new Form2();
    form2.Show();
}
```

Data Bit

Reminder: The C# keyword this always refers to the current class.

6. Run the program. Click the **Open a Form** button. When Form2 appears, click the **Close** button. This closes Form2. You can open and close Form2 as many times as you like. When you're ready to end the program, click the X in the upper-right corner of Form1's window.

Form Events

Two of the most important **Form** control events are **Click** and **DoubleClick**. Here's how to use them:

1. Create a new Windows program.

2. Add a **Label** control to its form.

3. Click the form, then press **F7**. This displays the form's code-behind page.

4. Add the two methods shown below to the form's code-behind page right after the Main() method.

```
private void Form1_OnClick(object sender,
                           System.EventArgs e)
{
    label1.Text = "Click";
}

private void Form1_OnDoubleClick(object sender,
                                 System.EventArgs e)
{
    label1.Text = "DoubleClick";
}
```

5. Go back to Visual Studio's designer window by clicking the tab above the edit window.

6. Just to make sure it's selected, click the form again.

7. Go to the Properties window and click the lightning bolt icon at the top.

8. Click the box next to the **Click** event. Use the drop-down list to select the `Form1_OnClick()` method.

9. Click the box next to the **DoubleClick** event. Use the drop-down list to select the `Form1_OnDoubleClick()` method.

Run the program. When its window appears, click the form (not on the **Label** control). The word "Clicked" appears in the **Label** control. When you double-click the form, the word "DoubleClick" appears.

Panel Controls

In addition to **Form** controls, Windows Forms use **Panel** controls as containers. However, panels don't create windows like forms do. You must place panels inside another container, usually a form. You generally use them to group related controls together. They enable you to set the properties of the entire group at once.

For example, sometimes you want a group of controls to be disabled by default. In this case, the user must typically take an action, such as pressing a button, to enable the group of controls. You can disable the entire group by putting them together into a panel and setting the panel's **Enabled** property to `false`. To enable the group, set the panel's **Enabled** property to `true`. By default, a panel's **Enabled** property is `true`.

In addition, panels do not display a border by default. If you want to change that, set the panel's **BorderStyle** property to `FixedSingle` or `Fixed3D`.

> **CAUTION**
>
> **Programming Pitfalls**
>
> If you put a panel into a resizable form, it is possible for users to resize the form so that they can't see the panel. This can cause confusion.
>
> Generally, you should use containers like **Panel** and **GroupBox** controls (**GroupBox** controls are presented in the next section) in dialog boxes that can't be resized.

GroupBox Controls

The **GroupBox** control is very similar to the **Panel** control. Like a panel, it must go inside another container, such as a form. Unlike panels, **GroupBox** controls display a border. In fact, you cannot turn the border off. GroupBox controls have no **BorderStyle** property.

Use the **GroupBox** control to display a group of controls that are visually related. Also use them to make a group of functionally related controls. For example, use a **GroupBox** control to contain a set of **RadioButton** controls (more on these later).

The Least You Need to Know

◆ Containers hold other controls.

◆ Use forms for your program's main window.

◆ Use panels to hold controls whose properties you want to set as a group.

◆ Use the **GroupBox** control to display a group of visually related controls.

19

Buttons: More Than Meets the Eye

In This Chapter

◆ Adding buttons for user input

◆ Using shortcut keys for buttons

◆ Adding images to buttons

◆ Using toolbars as button collections

Buttons are one of the most common user interface elements in Windows programs. The previous chapter used them to demonstrate some of the techniques for working with forms.

In this chapter, you'll get a closer look at buttons, and learn what you can do with them.

Buttons for Basic User Input

As you saw in the previous chapter, buttons generate a **Click** event whenever users select them. You control how the button responds by filling in the code for the **Click** event handler. The event handler can pop up other forms or dialog boxes, load or save files, or do anything else you want it to do.

Of course, users can click buttons with their mice. However, power users often find using the mouse slows them down. They want a method that enables them to use the keyboard to make button selections.

From the Knowledge Bank

Power users are those who are *extremely* familiar with your program. Take my advice, you want to accommodate power users as much as possible. These are people who really put your application through its paces. Some of them can come up with ways to use your program that you would never have imagined.

Power users often have strong opinions about how your program should work. Given a chance, they'll express these opinions. Give them the chance. It is a great benefit to you. It's wise to give them a way to send you feedback on your Web site.

Be aware, however, that power users don't always express their opinions politely. Never mind that fact. Listen to them carefully anyway. Some of the best advice I've ever received about my programs has come in e-mails that began with sentences such as "Dear Stupid" and "You know, you're a complete idiot."

One way users can select buttons from the keyboard is to press the **Tab** key until the button is highlighted. At that point, they can press **Enter**. Although this method works, it is slow. Few users actually do this on a regular basis.

You can make your buttons rapidly selectable through the keyboard with Alt+key combinations. To demonstrate Alt+key combinations, follow these steps.

1. Create a new Windows application.

2. Drag a button onto the form.

3. Set the button's **Text** property to `&Press Me`.

4. Double-click the button.

5. Add the following lines of code to the `button1_Click()` method.
   ```
   Form2 theOtherForm = new Form2();
   theOtherForm.Show();
   ```

6. From Visual Studio's Projects menu, select **Add Windows Form.**

7. Add a button to Form2. Set its **Text** property to `&Close`.

8. Double-click the button.

9. Add the statement …

   ```
   this.Close();
   ```

   … to the button's event handler.

Now run the program. The result looks like Figure 19.1. The underline under the letter P may not be visible when you first start the application. If not, briefly press the **Alt** key to make it appear.

Figure 19.1

A button with an Alt+key combination defined.

When you set the button's Text property to &Press Me instead of just Press Me, you created an Alt+key combination. The user can hold down the Alt key and press the letter **P** to select the button. Give it a try. When you do, another window appears, as shown in Figure 19.2.

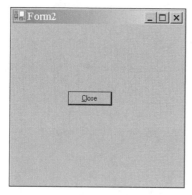

Figure 19.2

To close this window, press Alt+C.

For the button in Figure 19.2, the Alt+key combination is Alt+C. Hold down the Alt key, and briefly press **C**. The dialog box closes, and you're back at the program's main window.

You can define any letter in the string for the button's Text property as an Alt+key combination. Just put the & in front of the letter, and you're done.

Spiffing Up Your Buttons

You can do some pretty fancy things with buttons. For instance, you can emphasize certain buttons on a form by changing their **ForeColor, BackColor,** and **Font** properties. Figure 19.3 shows a form with an emphasized button.

Figure 19.3

Of course, the first thing everyone wants to do is press the button.

To get this effect, I first resized the button in Visual Studio's designer. Next, I clicked the + sign next to the button's **Font** property in the Properties window. This makes a list of font characteristics visible. I set the **Size** property to 36, and the **Bold** property to true. I used red for the **BackColor** property and white for the **ForeColor** property. The result is a button that's just a bit more noticeable than most.

To get even fancier, you can put a bitmapped image on a button. Figures 19.4 and 19.5 show the application you created near the beginning of this chapter.

Figure 19.4

A button with a bitmapped image.

Figure 19.5

Well, at least someone's happy.

To get the program to look like these figures, I set the **Image** properties of both buttons to the names of the files containing the bitmaps. I also resized the buttons to accommodate the images. When put bitmaps on your buttons, you can specify Windows bitmap files (.bmp). Alternatively, you can use other file formats such as GIF (.gif) and JPEG (.jpg).

In addition, I changed the **TextAlign** properties to BottomCenter to center the text along the bottom of the images. This is generally where users expect to find the label of a button that also contains a bitmapped image.

Data Bit _____

When you use bitmapped images for buttons, I recommend that you use either 32x32 or 64x64 pixel bitmaps. These sizes display reasonably well at most screen resolutions.

Alternating Images and Text on Buttons

Adding images to buttons often improves your program's user interface. However, your buttons also take up more room on the screen. You can give your use the option of saving space on the screen by selecting whether or not to display the bitmaps. Here's an activity to demonstrate how.

First, prepare a form with two buttons using the following steps.

1. Create a new Windows application.
2. Drag two buttons onto the form, one above the other.
3. In the Properties window, change the **Text** property of the top button to Bitmaps Only.
4. Change the **Text** property of the lower button to &Press Me.
5. Set the **Image** property of the lower button to a bitmap. I used the sad face from the previous example, but you can use any bitmapped image that fits. Resize the button, if needed.
6. Click **Form1**. Now right-click it (or, if you are using a left-handed mouse, left-click it), and select **View Code** from the context menu.
7. Add the line of code shown below in bold to the Form1 class right at the beginning of the class, like this:

```
public class Form1 : System.Windows.Forms.Form
{
    private int buttonType;
```

The program uses this variable to keep track of what type of button it should display. To see how, let's continue.

8. In the constructor for the Form1 class, type the following line of code immediately *after* the call to InitializeComponent().

```
buttonType = Form2.BITMAPS_AND_TEXT;
```

9. Edit the `button1_Click()` method to read as shown below.

```
private void button1_Click(object sender, System.EventArgs e)
{
    Form2 theOtherForm = new Form2();
     theOtherForm.ButtonType = buttonType;
     theOtherForm.Show();
}
```

10. Right after the `button1_Click()` method, add the following method.

```
private void button2_Click(object sender, System.EventArgs e)
{
    if (button2.Text == "Bitmaps Only")
    {
        buttonType = Form2.BITMAPS_ONLY;
        button2.Text = "Text Only";
    }
    else if (button2.Text == "Text Only")
    {
        buttonType = Form2.TEXT_ONLY;
        button2.Text = "Bitmaps and Text";
    }
    else if (button2.Text == "Bitmaps and Text")
    {
        buttonType = Form2.BITMAPS_AND_TEXT;
        button2.Text = "Bitmaps Only";
    }
}
```

The first form is now ready to roll. Now you need to make another form and configure it with the steps shown here.

1. From the Project menu, select **Add Windows Form**.
2. Drag a button onto the form. Set its **Text** property to &Close.
3. Set the button's **Image** property to a bitmapped image.
4. I used the happy face from the previous example, but you can use any bitmapped image that fits. Resize the button, if needed.
5. Go to the code-behind page for Form2.
6. Add the following code at the beginning of the Form2 class.

```
public const int BITMAPS_AND_TEXT = 0;
public const int TEXT_ONLY = 1;
public const int BITMAPS_ONLY = 2;

private int buttonType;
private int defaultHeight;
```

7. Add these two lines of code to the `Form2` constructor. Put them right after the call to
    `InitializeComponent()`.

    ```
    buttonType = BITMAPS_AND_TEXT;
    defaultHeight = button1.Height;
    ```

8. Go back to the Visual Studio designer. Double-click the button. Use this code for
    the button's **Click** event handler.

    ```
    private void button1_Click(object sender, System.EventArgs e)
    {
        this.Close();
    }
    ```

9. Add the following method to Form2's code-behind page. Put it at the end of the
    class (just before the } symbol).

    ```
    private void button1_Paint(object sender,
                               System.Windows.Forms.PaintEventArgs e)
    {

        if (buttonType == BITMAPS_AND_TEXT)
        {
            button1.Image = Image.FromFile("happy.bmp");
            button1.Text = "&Close";
            button1.Height = defaultHeight;
        }
        else if (buttonType == TEXT_ONLY)
        {
            button1.Image = null;
            button1.Text = "&Close";
            button1.Height = defaultHeight/2;
        }
        else if (buttonType == BITMAPS_ONLY)
        {
            button1.Image = Image.FromFile("happy.bmp");
            button1.Text = "";
            button1.Height = defaultHeight;
        }
    }
    ```

10. Add the following method to Form2's code-behind page at the end of the Form2 class.

    ```
    public int ButtonType
    {
        get
        {
            return (buttonType);
        }
        set
        {
    ```

```
if ((value == BITMAPS_AND_TEXT) ||
    (value == TEXT_ONLY) ||
    (value == BITMAPS_ONLY))
{
    buttonType = value;
}
}
```

11. Go back to the designer view of Form2 by clicking the tab above the edit window
     that reads, "Form2.cs [Design]." (The quoted text is not code. It's just quoted text.)
     Click the button.

12. Go to the Properties window, and click the lightning bolt button to see a list of events.

13. Click in the blank box next to the Paint event and use the drop-down list to set the
     event handler to button1_Paint().

You're ready to run the application. When you start the program, it displays the window
shown in Figure 19.6.

Figure 19.6

*The application's initial
window.*

When the program starts, the constructor initializes a private data member called buttonType
to the value Form2.BITMAPS_AND_TEXT. This tells the program to display both a bitmap and
a text label for the button on Form2.

If you click the lower button, the button1_Click() method creates the second form. It also
initializes the ButtonType property of the Form2 class to the current button type. It then
displays the second form, which is shown in Figure 19.7.

Now close the second form. Click the upper button in the Form1 window. When you do,
the program calls the button2_Click() method. This method checks the text in the upper
button. If the text is currently Bitmaps Only, the method sets the buttonType property of
the Form1 class to Form2.BITMAPS_ONLY. It also sets the **Text** property for button2 to Text
Only.

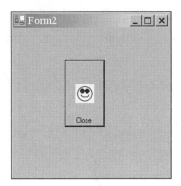

Figure 19.7

The program is currently set to display both a bitmap and text on the button in this form.

What's happening here is that the upper button in the Form1 window always tells you what it will set the buttonType property to next time it's clicked. It doesn't give the current value of the buttonType property. Each time you click the upper button, it sets the buttonType property to whatever is displayed in its Text property. It then changes to display the choice it makes available next time the user clicks the button.

If you click the lower button in the Form1 window, the Form2 window displays its button with only a bitmap. There is no text. An examination of the button1_Paint() method shows why.

When Form1 creates Form2, it sets the button type. Before the program displays Form2 on the screen, it calls the event handler for Form2's **Paint** event, which is called button1_Paint().

The button1_Paint() method checks to determine what type of button to display. If the button contains an image, it sets the image with the statement ...

> **Programming Pitfalls**
>
> Displaying a button that changes its choices like this is kind of a tricky approach to a user interface. If you use it, do it carefully. If you think your users will be confused by this approach, use a radio button control instead. Radio button controls are presented in Chapter 24.

```
button1.Image = Image.FromFile("happy.bmp");
```

This statement assumes that the bitmapped image file is in the same directory as the program.

If the button is supposed to display text, the button1_Paint() method sets the text with the statement

```
button1.Text = "&Close";
```

When the button type is text-only, the button1_Paint() method sets the **Image** property to null. This is a special value defined in the C# language. It literally means nothing. Setting the **Image** property to null means that the property contains no image.

To save space on the screen, the `button1_Paint()` method sets the height of the text-only button to half of its normal value. If the button contains an image, `button1_Paint()` sets the height to its full value.

ToolBar Controls

ToolBar controls are collections of buttons. Writing one used to take literally thousands of lines of source code. With Visual Studio, you can add a toolbar to any form just by dragging and dropping it.

Data Bit

It's wise to provide users with a toolbar in your application. They make it easy to access your program's functionality with a minimum of input. Users generally love them. In fact, it's my opinion that it's better to put too many toolbars into an application than too few.

Your program should give users the option of hiding toolbars. If they prefer not to use it, don't force it on them.

By default, forms display toolbars docked right under the form's title bar or main menu. You can change that with the toolbar's Dock property. Your forms can also dock their toolbars along the bottom, left, or right. If you set the **Dock** property to None, the toolbar floats around the form's window.

To add buttons to a toolbar, go to the Properties window and click in the box to the right of the toolbar's **Buttons** property. A button with an ellipsis (three dots) appears. Click that button, and Visual Studio displays the ToolBarButton Collection Editor dialog box. Click the **Add** button once for each button you want in the toolbar.

Click the individual buttons to display their properties. You can enable the button, disable it, set its text, or even specify a drop-down menu in this dialog box.

The Least You Need to Know

♦ Buttons are one of the most common user interface elements.

♦ There are multiple ways of selecting buttons.

♦ To accommodate power users, add Alt+key combinations to your buttons.

♦ You can emphasize certain buttons by setting their **ForeColor, BackColor,** and **Font** properties.

♦ Buttons can display bitmapped images.

♦ A collection of buttons is called a toolbar. The .NET Framework implements toolbars with the **ToolBar** control.

Chapter 20

Building Character

In This Chapter

- ◆ Using tools for displaying character strings
- ◆ Providing user prompts with the Label control
- ◆ Hyperlinking programs to the World Wide Web
- ◆ Providing the user with a program's current status
- ◆ Text input and editing

The written word is by far the most powerful of all human inventions. It preserves all that we know from generation to generation. Writing gives the human race a memory that extends beyond a single lifetime.

When you think about it, the primary job of a computer is to facilitate communication in one form or another. The user interface of any program is essentially a dialogue between the programmer and the user. A large part of that dialogue involves combining the written word with this new medium of computers. That's what this chapter is about. It introduces the Windows Forms controls that handle character strings.

What's in a Name?

Label controls enable you to provide names for other controls. They also give you an easy way to prompt users for input, or explain output.

You set the string a **Label** control displays by setting its **Text** property. To change the appearance of the text, use the **ForeColor, BackColor,** and **Font** properties.

Data Bit

Use **Label** controls to provide a label in your user interface for controls that don't already have labels. This includes controls such as the **TextBox, PictureBox, DataGrid,** and **ComboBox.**

The previous chapter demonstrated the **ForeColor,** and **BackColor** properties for buttons. It also briefly introduced the **Font** property. Let's take a closer look at the **Font** property using the **Label** control.

Figure 20.1 shows a project in Visual Studio. You can see the Properties window on the right. I've added an arrow to this illustration that points at a small + sign next to the **Font** property.

Figure 20.1

To see what the Font property contains, click the little + sign.

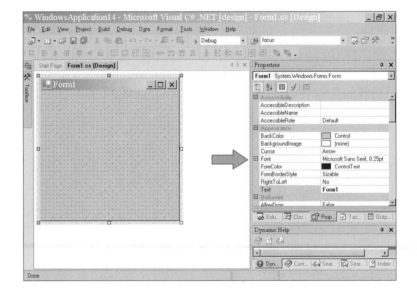

The + sign indicates that the Font property is actually a collection of properties. If you click the + sign, Visual Studio displays the list of properties shown in Figure 20.2.

All controls contain a **Name** property that sets the name of the control in the code-behind page. This is not the same as the **Name** property in the **Font** property's list. You tell the two apart using C# notation. The **Name** property that specifies a control's name is generally just referred to as its **Name** property (if that makes any sense). The **Name** property that sets the name of the **Font** property is referred to as the **Font.Name** property.

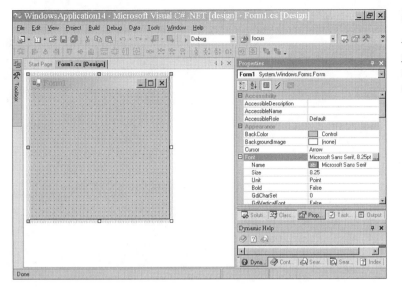

Figure 20.2

*As you can see, the **Font** property is actually a collection of properties that describe a font.*

The font that you specify in the **Font.Name** property can be any font that is installed on the user's computer. Some fonts come with Windows. Others get installed onto a computer when you install software. In particular, installing a word processor, desktop publishing program, or drawing program can install additional fonts on your computer. Be sure you set the **Font.Name** property to one of the fonts that comes with Windows.

You make a **Label** control's text larger by specifying a larger number for the **Font.Size** property. You can also set the **Font.Italic** property to true to get *italic text*. To display ~~strikeout text~~, set the **Font.Strikeout** property to true. If you want the label's text underlined, change **Font.Underline** to true.

In addition to the **Font** property, the **Label** control supports other very useful properties. For example, **Label** controls can display images, as well. Figure 20.3 shows a **Label** control with a bitmapped image.

Data Bit

When you speak of a control's **Name** property, you are talking about the property that sets the control's name in the code-behind page. If you are speaking of the **Font.Name** property, you are talking about the property that sets the font's name.

Programming Pitfalls

Be careful that you do not set the **Font.Name** property to a font the user does not have. The only safe fonts to use are those that come with Windows.

Figure 20.3

Label controls also display bitmapped images.

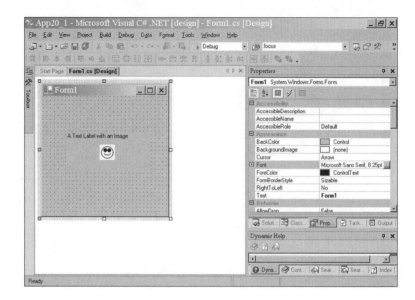

Getting from Here to There

With the advent of hypertext, and especially hyperlinked text on the World Wide Web, hyperlinks have become an important element in the user interface of many programs. To enable your program to use hyperlinks, the .NET Framework provides the **LinkLabel** control.

Your program can use **LinkLabel** controls to link to other forms in your application. They also enable programs to activate the user's default Web browser and jump to any valid universal resource locator (URL). The URL can lead to an item on the computer's hard drive, or it can link to something on the World Wide Web.

If you look for a property in the Properties window that specifies the destination of the **LinkLabel** control, you'll look in vain. The linking is done in the **LinkLabel** control's Click event handler. To see how this works, try the following activity.

> **CAUTION**
>
> **Programming Pitfalls**
>
> If a **LinkLabel** control links to something on the World Wide Web, you must warn the user to make sure they are connected to the Internet before they click the link.
>
> Also, you must make sure that the link jumps to a valid destination. It is wise to link only to Web sites controlled by you or the company you work for.

1. Create a new Windows application.

2. Drag a **LinkLabel** control onto the form.

3. Set the **LinkLabel** controls Text property to Next Form.

4. Double-click the **LinkLabel** control.

5. Use the code below for the **Click** event handler.

```
private void linkLabel1_LinkClicked(
    object sender,
    System.Windows.Forms.LinkLabelLinkClickedEventArgs e)
{
    Form2 secondForm = new Form2();
        secondForm.Show();
    linkLabel1.LinkVisited = true;
}
```

6. Add a second form to the project (reminder, select **Project**, then **Add Windows Form**).

7. Drag a button onto the second form.

8. Set the button's **Text** property to Close.

9. Double-click the button.

10. Add the statement …

```
this.Close();
```

… to the button's event handler for the Click event.

When you compile and run the program, it displays its main form with a **LinkLabel** control. If you click the link, the second form appears. Click the button to close the second form.

To link to a destination in the World Wide Web, you follow a similar procedure. First, you create your project, then you drag a **LinkLabel** control onto it. Because you're linking to a URL on the Web, you don't need a second form. The **LinkLabel** control's **Click** event handler would use code similar to the Listing 20.1.

Listing 20.1   A LinkLabel Control's Click Event Handler That Links to the World Wide Web

```
1    private void linkLabel1_LinkClicked(
2        object sender,
3        System.Windows.Forms.LinkLabelLinkClickedEventArgs e)
4    {
5        linkLabel1.LinkVisited = true;
6        System.Diagnostics.Process.Start("http://www.idiotsguides.com/");
7    }
```

The event handler in Listing 20.1 uses the Start() method to start the user's default Web browser. It also passes the browser the destination URL. In this case, the URL leads to the Web site for *The Complete Idiot's Guide* series.

Data Bit

To use the `System.Diagnostics.Process.Start()` method, you must add the statement shown below in bold to your program. Put it at the beginning of the code-behind page for the form on which the **LinkLabel** control appears.

```
using System;
using System.Drawing;
using System.Collections;
using System.ComponentModel;
using System.Windows.Forms;
using System.Data;
using System.Diagnostics;     // Add this statement.
```

If you want to set the colors the **LinkLabel** uses to display the link, you can. The properties you set are **VisitedLinkColor, LinkColor, DisabledLinkColor,** and **ActiveLinkColor.** However, I recommend that you don't alter these colors. Use the default colors provided by Windows. The user chooses these colors. If your program uses different link colors, it often irritates users.

Programming Pitfalls

Don't let your program appear to be doing nothing unless it is really doing nothing. Give feedback to your users. If your program looks like it's locked up, it's likely that users will end the program with the Windows Task Manager, or reboot their computers.

Data Bit

Users are accustomed to seeing status bars at the bottom of a program window. It's been the convention for many years. If you put the status bar anywhere else, it can confuse users. Your program should follow the convention of putting it on the bottom of the window unless you have a *really* good reason not to.

How's Everything?

One of the most important things your program can do while it is working on something is to give feedback to the user. I don't known how many times I've terminated a program (or rebooted a computer) because I thought it was locked up when it wasn't.

One way to give feedback to your users it through the status bar. Most programs today have a status bar, and users generally expect to see them in your program. The .NET Framework provides status bars through the use of the **StatusBar** control.

Figure 20.4 shows a program with a status bar across the bottom of its window. It contains a simple text message that tells the user the program is doing something.

Almost all programs display their status bars at the bottom of their windows. You can change that by changing the value of the status bar's **Dock** property. It enables you to dock the status bar on the left, right, top, or bottom. You can even have a floating status bar.

Figure 20.4

The status bar indicates that the program is doing something.

Users will only wait for about 20 to 30 seconds when you show them a message like the one in Figure 20.4. It's better to keep them constantly updated. For example, when your program has a long task to complete, it can display its progress in the status bar. Figure 20.5 shows such a program.

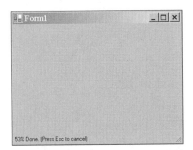

Figure 20.5

Displaying your programs progress lets the user know it's not locked up.

To make more complex status bars, you can divide the **StatusBar** control into what Microsoft calls "panels." In my opinion, this is an unfortunate choice of terms. It confuses developers. The panels in a status bar have no connection at all to **Panel** controls.

The panels in a **StatusBar** control enable you to divide the status bar into multiple message areas. Each of these message areas can be dedicated to the status of particular aspects of the program. You can even use them to tell users about the state of their hardware. The status bar in Figure 20.6 shows the status of the program, and indicates that the user's **CapsLock** key is on.

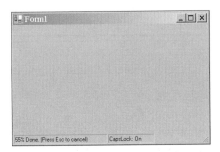

Figure 20.6

The two panels in this status bar help keep the user informed.

To make the **StatusBar** control display panels, set its **ShowPanels** property to true. You can then add the individual panels with the **Panels** property. Click the box to the right of the **Panels** property in the Properties window. Visual Studio displays a button with an ellipsis in it. Click the button to display the StatusBarPanel Collection Editor dialog box. Clicking the **Add** button adds panels.

> **Programming Pitfalls**
>
> Don't confuse the panels in a **StatusBar** control with the panels displayed by the **Panel** control. They are not the same thing at all.

The list on the right side of the dialog box displays the panel's properties. You can output messages to the user by setting or updating a panel's **Text** property. For long messages, increase the width of the panel with its **Width** property.

Let's Talk

If you need to get a string from your user, then add a **TextBox** control to your form. The **TextBox** control enables users to type in a single string, or multiple lines of text.

Here's an activity that demonstrates the **TextBox** control.

1. Create a new Windows program.

2. Add a **Label** control onto the form. Set its **Text** property to `Please enter a string:`.

3. Set the **Label** control's **TextAlign** property to `TopCenter`.

4. Add a **TextBox** control under the **Label** control. Set its **Text** property to `Type a string here`.

5. Add a button to the form just below the **TextBox** control. Set its **Text** property to `&Done`.

6. Arrange these three controls as shown in Figure 20.7.

7. In Visual Studio's designer, click the **TextBox** control.

8. Click Visual Studio's **Properties** tab to show the Properties window.

9. Click the **lightning bolt** button to see the list of events the **TextBox** control supports.

10. Scroll to the **KeyDown** property and double-click it. Be sure you double-click the word `KeyDown` in the list. Visual Studio starts an event handler for the **KeyDown** event and takes you to the code-behind page.

11. Edit the event handler for the **KeyDown** event to read as follows:

```
private void textBox1_KeyDown(
    object sender,
    System.Windows.Forms.KeyEventArgs e)
{
```

```
        if (e.KeyCode == Keys.Enter)
        {
            this.button1_Click(sender,(System.EventArgs)e);
        }
    }
```

12. Go back to the designer and double-click the **Button** control on Form1. Visual Studio returns you to the code-behind page, starts the Click event handler for you, and connects the event handler to the event.

13. Add the code shown in bold below to the Click event handler.

```
private void button1_Click(object sender, System.EventArgs e)
{
    string tempString = textBox1.Text;
    if ((tempString.Length > 0) &&
        (tempString != "Type a string here."))
    {
        this.Close();
    }
    else
    {
        label1.Text = "Error: No string entered.";
        textBox1.Text = "Type a string here.";
    }
}
```

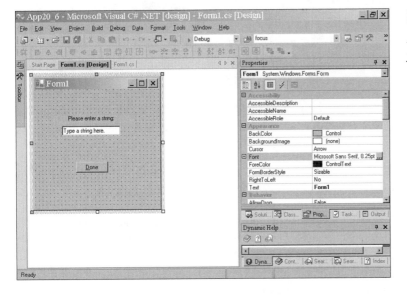

Figure 20.7

Arrange your controls so that your form looks like this.

Run the program. It does a lot with very little code. If you click the **Done** button, the program calls the `button1_Click()` method. This method uses an `if-else` statement to test the string in the text box. The `if-else` statement provides a simple form of data input validation.

Before we go on, there's a term I need to define. The term is *input focus*. If a control has input focus, it receives characters from the keyboard.

So, with that term defined, we're ready to see how the `if-else` statement performs its data validation.

Techno Talk _____

A control that has **input focus** receives characters from the keyboard.

If the string is empty, or if it is still set to the default string, the method executes the `else` clause of the `if-else` statement. This sets the text of the **Label** control to `Error: No string entered.`, and sets the **Text** property of the **TextBox** control back to its default value. The statement ...

```
textBox1.Focus();
```

... sets the input focus back to the text box. This enables the user to just start typing a string. It saves them from having to click the **TextBox** control before they type text.

On the other hand, if you type a string into the **TextBox** control and click the **Done** button, the program executes the `if` clause in the `if-else` statement. The `if` clause contains a call to the `Close()` method that ends the program.

Now prepare yourself for something a bit tricky. While the program runs, it generates a **KeyDown** event every time you type a letter into the **TextBox** control. The **KeyDown** event handler checks the character you enter. The event handler has a parameter called `e`.

Data Bit _____

When a user makes a mistake involving a **TextBox** control, it's good practice to set the input focus back to the **TextBox** control. This enables the user to just start typing. They do not have to click the **TextBox** control to give it the input focus.

The `e` parameter is of type `System.Windows.Forms.KeyEventArgs`. One of the properties of the `e` parameter is called `KeyCode`. It contains the character you entered. All of the characters are specified in the `Keys` type, which is part of the .NET Framework.

Ready for the tricky bit? Here it comes. If the key you pressed is `Key.Enter`, which represents the Enter key (imagine that!), the **KeyDown** event handler calls the `button1_Click()` method. Calling the `button1_Click()` method essentially simulates the user pressing the **Done** button. This speeds data entry on your form. The user simply types a string and presses Enter.

Recall that the e parameter is of type `System.Windows.Forms.KeyEventArgs`. The Microsoft documentation shows that the second parameter to the `button1_Click()` method is of type `System.EventArgs`. How can the **KeyDown** event handler pass e as a parameter to the `button1_Click()` method when they are not the same type?

The C# compiler doesn't complain because of the type cast. The `System.Windows.Forms.KeyEventArgs` class inherits from `System.EventArgs`. You can always type cast a derived class to its base type. The C# compiler doesn't mind a bit.

Data Bit _____

Calling the `Close()` method on the main form window of a program causes the program to end.

Striking It Rich

The **RichTextBox** control is like a **TextBox** control on steroids. It does everything a **TextBox** control does, and more. It provides much greater text formatting capabilities. It can even load and save files.

Data Bit _____

For those of you who've been around as long as I have, dust off your memories of the days before HyperText Markup Language (HTML) came along. Remember Rich Text Format (RTF)? That's what the **RichTextBox** control uses.

For those too young to remember RTF, it is a well-established markup language (but we didn't call it a markup language in the Old Days) for producing platform-independent documents. It was in wide use before HTML.

With RTF, you can produce documents that contain formatting information. When you load it into a program, that program renders the document in a way that best suits the particular operating system and computer.

In addition to enabling users to enter or edit text, the **RichTextBox** control also displays fonts, colors, and links in text. By default, the **RichTextBox** control lets users do multi-line editing. If the user enters more text than will fit on one line, it wraps words onto the next line. It also provides both vertical and horizontal scroll bars. With its `LoadFile()` and `SaveFile()` methods, your program can use the **RichTextBox** control very much like a word processor.

If you do want to make the **RichTextBox** control function more like a word processor, set its **AcceptsTab** property to true. This means you won't be able to tab from control to control on the form. However, most word processing programs don't allow that anyway.

One feature that I really like is the **ZoomFactor** property. By default, its value is 1, which displays the text at a size of 100 percent. If you want to display the text at 50 percent of its normal size, set **ZoomFactor** to 0.5. To get a zoom of 200 percent, set it to 2.

The Least You Need to Know

- The .NET Framework provides a variety of controls for working with character strings.
- The primary use of the **Label** control is to provide names for other controls, and for user prompts.
- The **LinkLabel** control performs the same functions as the **Label** control. In addition, it enables your program to hyperlink to other forms, and to URLs on the Internet.
- The status bar displays messages to the user. You can use it as a single bar, or section it into panels.
- To get plain text strings from users, use the **TextBox** control.
- Use a **RichTextBox** when you want to enable users to input or edit formatted text.

21

What's on the Menu Today?

In This Chapter

◆ Adding menus to forms

◆ Responding to menu item selection

◆ Assigning accelerator keys to menu items

◆ Implementing a simple calculator

Before graphical user interfaces, computer programs primarily took input from
the command line. Some power users still prefer to work this way. However,
today's average user wants programs with clear and concise menus. Therefore,
you need to put menus in your programs. This chapter shows you how.

MainMenu Controls

The .NET Framekwork's **MainMenu** control makes for easy menu system
creation. Past versions of Visual Studio required that you use a special menu
editor. This is no longer the case. You can now just drag a **MainMenu** control
onto a form. As Figure 21.1 shows, menus in the designer contain boxes displaying the text "Type Here." You can add entries to menus by clicking any of
these boxes and typing the item's text.

Figure 21.1

Enter menu items in the rectangle containing the words "Type Here."

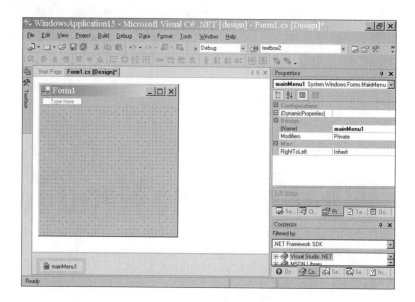

The structure of your menus can go as deep as you need. In other words, your main menu can have submenus, which can have submenus, and so on.

Each menu item has a **Click** event, and a corresponding event handler. To make a menu item respond when the user selects it, you write C# source code in its **Click** event handler. Menu item event handlers can bring up additional forms, dialog boxes, or do whatever else you need them to.

Accelerator Keys

There are two ways of defining keystrokes that speed up access to your programs. The first, Alt+key combinations, is one you've already seen. You can define an Alt+key combination for any item in a menu. This enables power users to select menu items from the keyboard very rapidly. In fact, people who are extremely familiar with your application can often select menu items faster than the program can respond (power users love to move faster than programs, it impresses onlookers).

In addition, you can define special shortcut keys for actions the user performs often. For instance, people who have been around computers for a while know that you save your data as often as possible. When I'm writing, I save my file at the end of every paragraph.

For tasks that users do repeatedly, such as saving important data, you should define shortcut keys.

The **MainMenu** control makes this very easy. Just click an item in the menu for which you want to define a shortcut key. Go to Visual Studio's Properties window and click in the box next to the **Shortcut** property. Use the drop-down list to select a shortcut key.

A wide variety of shortcut keys is available. You can use the function keys F1 through F12. You can also use Ctrl plus a function key, Ctrl plus Shift plus a function key, or Alt plus a function key. In addition, you can use Ctrl plus a letter or Ctrl plus a number. You can even use such keystrokes as the Insert or Delete keys.

Be aware that some shortcut keys are used by Windows. For example, if you press Alt+Spacebar, Windows displays your program window's System menu. If you press Ctrl+Esc, Windows pops up its start menu.

Other shortcut keys are used by most applications for a certain task. For instance, most programs that display multiple windows use Ctrl+F6 to switch from window to window. Check the Windows developer documentation for more information.

Data Bit

Good shortcut keys for saving data are Ctrl+S or Alt+S.

Programming Pitfalls

Be careful that you do not try to use shortcut keys normally used by Windows. For a complete list of these keys, please see the Windows developer documentation.

Practice Makes Perfect

Now that you know what some of the Windows Forms controls do, let's use them to write a program. In this activity, you create a simple calculator. You'll probably be surprised how easy this is.

The calculator program, called LittleCalc, will add and subtract integers. The techniques for building multiplication and division into the program are the same as putting in addition and subtraction. To gain some additional experience with Windows Forms programming in C#, try enhancing this program so that it does multiplication and division.

To write the calculator program, you create a form, add controls to it, and set their properties. When that's finished, you write the code for the code-behind page.

Creating the User Interface

Like nearly all applications, the LittleCalc program needs a main menu. The main menu will have two items, **File** and **Edit**. The **File** and **Edit** menus will have one item each, **Exit** and **Clear**, respectively. When users select **File** and then **Exit**, the program ends. If users choose Edit and then Clear, the program clears the contents of its output display.

LittleCalc will display its output in a **TextBox** control. The text box appears just under the main menu. All of the calculator's buttons will be grouped together in a **Panel** control. The program needs buttons for the numbers 0–9. It will also show buttons for addition and subtraction. In addition, it will display a button for clearing the contents of the **TextBox** control.

To create the user interface for the LittleCalc program, use the following steps.

1. Create a new Windows application.

2. Set the form's **Name** property to MainForm, and its **Text** property to LittleCalc.

3. Drag a **MainMenu** control to the form.

4. In the main menu, add the an item named &File. This creates a File menu and sets the Alt+key combination to the letter F.

5. Add an item named E&xit to the File menu.

6. In the main menu, add an item named &Edit.

7. Add an item named C&lear to the Edit menu.

8. Drag a **TextBox** control to the form. Place it immediately below the main menu.

9. Set the **TextBox** control's **Font.Size** property to 12. Set its **RightToLeft** and **ReadOnly** properties to true.

10. Drag a **Panel** control to the form. Position it just below the **TextBox** control, and set its **BorderStyle** property to Fixed3D.

11. Drag 14 buttons onto the Panel control. Position them as shown in Figure 21.2.

Figure 21.2

Make your calculator look like this.

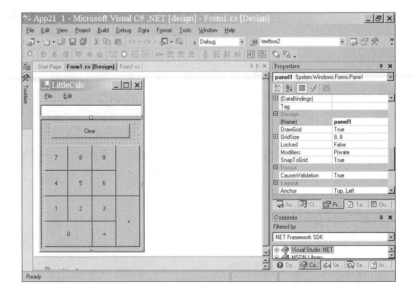

12. Label each button as shown in Figure 21.2 by setting their **Text** properties.

13. Rename each of the buttons on the panel as shown in Table 21.1.

Table 21.1

Button Label	Name Property
Clear	clearButton
0	zeroButton
1	oneButton
2	twoButton
3	threeButton
4	fourButton
5	fiveButton
6	sixButton
7	sevenButton
8	eightButton
9	nineButton
+	plusButton
-	minusButton
=	equalButton

After completing these steps, you should have a calculator that resembles Figure 21.2. You're ready to start writing code to make it work.

Writing the Code

At this point, LittleCalc is nothing more than a pretty face. To actually do anything, it needs a **Click** event handler for each of its buttons and menu items. Also, LittleCalc requires a handler for its **Paint** event.

Use the following steps to write LittleCalc's event handlers.

1. Double-click the **0** button. Use the following code for its **Click** event handler:

```
private void zeroButton_Click(object sender, System.EventArgs e)
{
    string tempString = textBox1.Text;

    if ((tempString.Length < MAX_STRING_LENGTH) &&
        (tempString.Length > 0))
    {
        tempString+='0';
        textBox1.Text = tempString;
    }
    panel1.Focus();
}
```

2. Go back to the designer, and double-click the **1** button. Use the following code for its **Click** event handler:

```
private void oneButton_Click(object sender, System.EventArgs e)
{
    string tempString = textBox1.Text;

    if (tempString.Length < MAX_STRING_LENGTH)
    {
        tempString+='1';
        textBox1.Text = tempString;
    }
    panel1.Focus();
}
```

3. Go back to the designer and double-click the **2** button. Use the following code for its **Click** event handler:

```
private void twoButton_Click(object sender, System.EventArgs e)
{
    string tempString = textBox1.Text;

    if (tempString.Length < MAX_STRING_LENGTH)
    {
        tempString+='2';
        textBox1.Text = tempString;
    }
    panel1.Focus();
}
```

4. Go back to the designer, and double-click the **3** button. Use the following code for its **Click** event handler:

```
private void threeButton_Click(object sender, System.EventArgs e)
{
    string tempString = textBox1.Text;

    if (tempString.Length < MAX_STRING_LENGTH)
    {
        tempString+='3';
        textBox1.Text = tempString;
    }
    panel1.Focus();
}
```

5. Go back to the designer, and double-click the **4** button. Use the following code for its **Click** event handler:

```
private void fourButton_Click(object sender, System.EventArgs e)
{
```

```
        string tempString = textBox1.Text;

        if (tempString.Length < MAX_STRING_LENGTH)
        {
            tempString+='4';
            textBox1.Text = tempString;
        }
        panel1.Focus();
    }
```

6. Go back to the designer and double-click the **5** button. Use the following code for its **Click** event handler:

```
private void fiveButton_Click(object sender, System.EventArgs e)
{
    string tempString = textBox1.Text;

    if (tempString.Length < MAX_STRING_LENGTH)
    {
        tempString+='5';
        textBox1.Text = tempString;
    }
    panel1.Focus();
}
```

7. Go back to the designer and double-click the **6** button. Use the following code for its **Click** event handler:

```
private void sixButton_Click(object sender, System.EventArgs e)
{
    string tempString = textBox1.Text;

    if (tempString.Length < MAX_STRING_LENGTH)
    {
        tempString+='6';
        textBox1.Text = tempString;
    }
    panel1.Focus();
}
```

8. Go back to the designer and double-click the **7** button. Use the following code for its **Click** event handler:

```
private void sevenButton_Click(object sender, System.EventArgs e)
{
    string tempString = textBox1.Text;

    if (tempString.Length < MAX_STRING_LENGTH)
    {
        tempString+='7';
```

```
        textBox1.Text = tempString;
    }
    panel1.Focus();
}
```

9. Go back to the designer and double-click the **8** button. Use the following code for its **Click** event handler:

```
private void fourButton_Click(object sender, System.EventArgs e)
{
    string tempString = textBox1.Text;

    if (tempString.Length < MAX_STRING_LENGTH)
    {
        tempString+='8';
        textBox1.Text = tempString;
    }
    panel1.Focus();
}
```

10. Go back to the designer and double-click the **9** button. Use the following code for its **Click** event handler:

```
private void fourButton_Click(object sender, System.EventArgs e)
{
    string tempString = textBox1.Text;

    if (tempString.Length < MAX_STRING_LENGTH)
    {
        tempString+='9';
        textBox1.Text = tempString;
    }
    panel1.Focus();
}
```

11. Go back to the designer and double-click the **+** (plus) button. Use the following code for its **Click** event handler:

```
private void plusButton_Click(object sender, System.EventArgs e)
{
    operand1 = textBox1.Text;
    operation = '+';
    textBox1.Text = "";
    panel1.Focus();
}
```

12. Go back to the designer and double-click the **–** (minus) button. Use the following code for its **Click** event handler:

```
private void minusButton_Click(object sender, System.EventArgs e)
{
```

```
        operand1 = textBox1.Text;
        operation = '-';
        textBox1.Text = "";
        panel1.Focus();
    }
```

13. Go back to the designer and double-click the **=** (equal) button. Use the following code for its **Click** event handler:

```
    private void equalButton_Click(object sender, System.EventArgs e)
    {
        operand2 = textBox1.Text;

        long num1, num2, answer=0;
        num1 = Convert.ToInt64(operand1);
        num2 = Convert.ToInt64(operand2);

        if (operation == '+')
        {
        answer = num1 + num2;
        }
        else if (operation == '-')
        {
        answer = num1 - num2;
        }

        textBox1.Text = Convert.ToString(answer);
        operand1 = "";
        operand2 = "";
        operation = '\0';
        panel1.Focus();        .
    }
```

14. Go back to the designer and double-click the **Clear** button. Use the following code for its **Click** event handler:

```
    private void clearButton_Click(object sender, System.EventArgs e)
    {
        textBox1.Text = "";
        operand1 = "";
        operand2 = "";
        operation = '\0';
        panel1.Focus();
    }
```

15. Go back to the designer and double-click the **Exit** item in the **File** menu. Use the following code for its **Click** event handler:

```
    private void fileExit_Click(object sender, System.EventArgs e)
    {
```

```
        this.Close();
    }
```

16. Return to the designer yet again. Double-click the **Clear** item in the **Edit** menu. Use the following code for its **Click** event handler:

```
private void editClear_Click(object sender, System.EventArgs e)
{
    clearButton_Click(sender,e);
}
```

17. One final time, return to the designer. Double-click the panel. Use the following code for its **Paint** event handler:

```
private void panel1_Paint(
    object sender,
    System.Windows.Forms.PaintEventArgs e)
{
    panel1.Focus();
}
```

Data Bit

Spend a moment to take stock of what you've just done. By dragging and dropping controls, you created the entire user interface for this program. By adding short methods, you made a simple, yet functional, calculator.

You've come a long way since you started this book.

Data Bit

When writing programs that deal with numbers, you usually want to throw away leading 0s.

Compile, link, and run the program. You've got a calculator that adds and subtracts integers.

This nifty little calculator actually operates very simply. Clicking buttons 0 through 9 calls their associated **Click** event handlers.

An examination of the event handler for the 0 button shows how simple it is. It copies the current contents of the text box into a temporary string variable. This isn't strictly necessary. However, it doesn't add much extra overhead to the program, and it makes the code clearer.

Next, the zeroButton_Click() method tests the string to see if it is less than the maximum number of digits allowed. I arbitrarily set this limit to 10. If the string is less than 10 digits long, the method checks to see if its length is greater than 0. This prevents a user from entering 0s when there are no other digits in the string. In our number system, we don't display leading 0s.

If the string's length is less than then maximum and greater than zero, the zeroButton_Click() method adds the character '0' onto the end of the string.

The event handler then stores the new string back into the text box. Before it ends, it calls the Focus() method for the variable panel1. If this call were absent, the program's input focus would stay on the 0 button. Windows programs highlight buttons that have input focus. For calculators, that looks funny. Shifting input focus back to the panel keeps any of the buttons from being highlighted.

Data Bit

Reminder: The character '0' is not the same as the number 0. The number 0 has an actual value of 0. The character '0' has a Unicode value of 48.

The **Click** event handlers for the buttons 1–9 are even simpler than the one for the 0 button. All they do is test to ensure that the text box's string is less than the maximum length. If it is, they add their respective characters ('1' through '9') to the end of the string. They then put the string back into the text box, and shift input focus to panel1.

The calculator program lets the user type in a number, and displays the number in the text box. You don't want users to be able to type directly into the text box; that's why you set its **ReadOnly** property to true.

Data Bit

Setting a text box's **ReadOnly** property to true prevents users from typing numbers into it. However, if they click it, the text box still receives input focus. To see for yourself, run the calculator program and click its text box. It displays a cursor, but it doesn't let you enter any data.

In the case of this calculator program, you can solve that by adding an event handler for the text box's **Enter** event. It's triggered when the text box receives input focus. Inserting the statement

```
panel1.Focus();
```

into the event handler for the **Enter** event prevents the text box from receiving input focus.

When the user presses the plus button, its **Click** event handler copies the string of digits in the text box into a private data member called operand1. It sets the private data member operation to the character '+'. It also clears out the contents of the text box, and shifts the input focus back to the panel.

There is only one difference between the **Click** event handler for the plus button and the **Click** event handler for the minus button. The minus button event handler stores the '-' character in operation rather than the '+' character.

After users input a number, click the **+** or **–** button, and input another number, they click the equal button. The **Click** event handler for the equal button does most of the calculator's work. It begins by copying the string in the text box into the data member operand2. It declares three variables of type long. Next, the equalButton_Click() method makes two calls to the ToInt64() method, which is a member of the Convert class.

The .NET Framework's Convert class converts data from one type to another, somewhat like a type cast. In this case, the equalButton_Click() method needs to convert the strings operand1 and operand2 to long integers. So it uses the Convert.ToInt64() method.

After the equalButton_Click() method has two numbers to work with, it checks operation to see whether it should add or subtract them. Whichever it does, it stores the result in a variable called answer. To display the result, it calls Convert.ToString() to change the number in answer to a string. It stores the string containing the result in the text box.

Data Bit

When you need to convert data from one type to another, you'll find helpful methods in the Convert class.

After users perform a calculation, they must clear the result to continue using the calculator. They can do that in two ways. The first is to click the **Clear** button. The button's **Click** event handler sets the text box's **Text** property to an empty string. It does the same for operand1 and operand2. It also stores a null character in operation. The method ends by shifting input focus to the panel.

The other way for users to clear the result of a previous calculation is to select **Clear** from the **Edit** menu. The handler for the **Clear** item just calls the clearButton_Click() method, which is the **Click** event handler for the **Clear** button.

The Least You Need to Know

The least you need to know about menus is:

- The **MainMenu** control implements menus for your forms.
- You type menu items directly into the **MainMenu** control in Visual Studio's designer.
- When selected, menu items generate **Click** events.
- Your program responds to menu item selections in their **Click** event handlers.
- You can assign Alt+key combinations to all menu items.
- You can also assign shortcut keys to menu items.

Chapter 22

And Now, This Message ...

In This Chapter

- ◆ Displaying simple messages with message boxes
- ◆ Using message boxes to give users simple choices
- ◆ Using dialog boxes for input
- ◆ Displaying dialog boxes
- ◆ Retrieving input from dialog boxes
- ◆ Modal and modeless dialog boxes

After forms, message boxes and dialog boxes are two of the most important tools programs use for communicating with users. Message boxes display short messages to users (surprise!). You can also use them to give the user a choice before they commit to an action ("Do you really want to reformat your hard drive? Yes/No").

Dialog boxes get more complex information from users. They can contain almost any type of control. They can also pop up other message and dialog boxes.

This chapter introduces the basics of both message boxes and dialog boxes.

Message Boxes the Easy Way

Basic message boxes are simple to use. And with very little extra effort, you can fancy them up quite a bit. In fact, the .NET Framework provides a wide range of options for message boxes.

Data Bit

Use message boxes to display error messages or warnings. You can also use them to ask simple questions.

Displaying Message Boxes

You do not need to create a form to make a message box. You don't have to declare a variable. You don't need to use the C# new keyword. All you really have to do is call the MessageBox.Show() method.

To make your first message box, give the following steps a try:

1. Create a new Windows application.

2. Drag a button onto the form.

3. Set the button's text to Message in a Button. Resize the button so that all of the text shows.

4. Double-click the button and add the following line of code to the button's **Click** event handler.

```
MessageBox.Show("Hi!");
```

Go ahead and run the program. Click the button on the main form. Your program displays the message box shown in Figure 22.1.

Figure 22.1

A message box with an OK button.

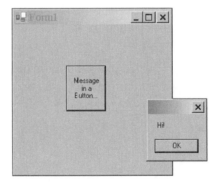

The message box displays the string it gets from the Show() method's parameter list. In this case, it displays the string "Hi". The message box automatically puts an OK button into its window. When you click the button, the box closes (also automatically). What could be simpler than that?

More Complex Message Boxes

Perhaps you want your application to do a bit more with its message boxes. Well, you can. Very easily, I might add. Here's how.

1. Create a new Windows application.

2. Drag a button onto the form.

3. Set the button's **Text** property to Message in a Button. Resize the button so that all of the text shows.

4. Double-click the button and use the code in Listing 22.1 for the button's **Click** event handler.

Listing 22.1   New and Improved Message Boxes

```
1     private void button1_Click(object sender, System.EventArgs e)
2     {
3         DialogResult result;
4
5         result = MessageBox.Show(
6             "Teleport you instantly to Tahiti for the day?",
7             "You Deserve a Break",
8             MessageBoxButtons.YesNo,
9             MessageBoxIcon.Question,
10            MessageBoxDefaultButton.Button1);
11
12        if (result == DialogResult.Yes)
13        {
14            MessageBox.Show(
15                "Transport failed. You're stuck here with me.",
16                "Error!",
17                MessageBoxButtons.OK,
18                MessageBoxIcon.Error);
19        }
20        else if (result == DialogResult.No)
21        {
22            MessageBox.Show(
23                "Good. You can stay here with me.",
24                "Hooray!",
25                MessageBoxButtons.OK,
26                MessageBoxIcon.Exclamation);
27        }
28    }
```

Running the program displays the program's main form. When you click the button, the program displays a message box with **Yes** and **No** buttons, as shown in Figure 22.2. The message box also has a title bar (complete with title) and an icon with a question mark.

Figure 22.2

A message box with a title, icon, and buttons.

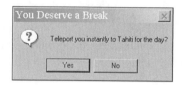

The `button1_Click()` method contains three calls to the `Show()` method. The first call produces the message box in Figure 22.2. It begins on line 5 of Listing 22.1. The first parameter to `Show()` appears on line 6. It specifies the message that `Show()` displays. The second parameter is a string containing the message box's title.

Line 8 contains a parameter that selects the buttons the `Show()` method adds to the message box. The `MessageBoxButtons` type defines which buttons `Show()` can display. On line 8, the constant `MessageBoxButtons.YesNo` tells the `Show()` method to display Yes and No buttons.

Data Bit

For complete lists of the buttons and icons that the `Show()` function displays, see Visual Studio's online documentation for the `MessageBoxButtons` and `MessageBoxIcon` types.

The parameter on line 9 specifies the icon for `Show()` to display. It is defined in a type called `MessageBoxIcon`.

The fifth parameter selects the message box's default button. The default button is the button that is highlighted when the message box appears. Valid values for this parameter are `MessageBoxDefaultButton.Button1`, `MessageBoxDefaultButton.Button2`, and `MessageBoxDefaultButton.Button3`. Button 1 is the first button you added, button 2 and button 3 are the second and third buttons you added, respectively.

When you click one of the message box's buttons, the box closes. The `Show()` method returns a value indicating which button you selected. The `DialogResult` type defines the values that the `Show()` method returns.

Your programs can test the `Show()` method's return value and react based on which button the user selected. This is exactly what the `button1_Click()` method does. If the user clicks the **Yes** button, the `if-else` statement beginning on line 12 of Listing 22.1 displays another message box with an error message.

This call to the `Show()` method, which begins on line 14, displays a message box with just one button (an **OK** button). It does not need to specify a default button. Therefore, I omitted the fifth parameter to the `Show()` method.

This message box appears in Figure 22.3. Instead of a question mark icon, this message box displays a red circle with a white X in it. Windows uses this as its error symbol.

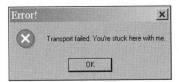

Figure 22.3

An error message box.

Data Bit

If your computer has speakers, you can hear sounds when a message box appears. These sounds are defined by Windows. The sound that the `Show()` method plays depends on which icon you select for the message box.

Users can set the Windows system sounds, so there's no way for you to know what sound the user hears. For example, the default sound for an error message box is a ding. On my computer, it's the digitized voice of the animated Bit character from the movie *Tron* saying "No."

If the user selects the **No** button in the first message box, the `button1_Click()` method executes the `else` clause of the `if-else` statement. It displays a message box with the call to the `Show()` method that begins on line 22. This message box, which appears in Figure 22.4, displays an **OK** button. It also shows an icon containing a yellow triangle with a black exclamation point inside.

Figure 22.4

An exclamation message box.

Dialog Boxes

When you need to get more input from your users than just a simple yes or no, try dialog boxes. You can use dialog boxes to collect nearly any type of input that computers allow. Common uses of dialog boxes are such tasks as entering text, selecting text characteristics (fonts, text color, and so on), controlling printers, selecting colors, and much, much more.

Programming Pitfalls

Using menus in your dialog boxes should be the exception rather than the rule. It can lead to overly complex dialog boxes and confused users. If you are absolutely sure you have a very good reason to add menus to your dialog boxes, add them. Otherwise, don't.

Most dialog boxes do not have menus. However, I have seen some programs that use dialog box menus. Visual Studio allows you to add them to your dialog boxes. Although it is unconventional, menus in dialog boxes can be a useful technique.

Typically, dialog boxes are not resizable. They usually do not have control boxes in their title bars. The control box is the set of symbols on the right end of the title bar that minimizes, maximizes, and closes the window.

Making Your Own

A dialog box is nothing more than a specialized **Form** control. I'll bet that doesn't surprise you. To make a form into a dialog box, you just need to:

◆ Set the form's **FormBorderStyle** property to FixedDialog.

◆ Set its **ControlBox** property to false.

◆ Add at least one button to close the dialog box.

◆ Add any other controls you need.

◆ Add C# source code to the form's code-behind page.

To get some practice applying these steps, try the following activity, which is accomplished in two stages. In the first, you create the form that calls up the dialog box. In the second stage, you create the dialog box.

Stage 1

Begin this stage of the activity by creating the application. Next, add a button, set it's **Text** property, and use its **Click** event handler to call up the dialog box.

1. Create a new Windows application.

2. Drag a button onto the form.

3. Set the button's **Text** property to Let's have a dialog. Resize the button so that all of the text shows.

4. Double-click the button and use the following code for the button's **Click** event handler.

```
private void button1_Click(object sender, System.EventArgs e)
{
    Form2 aDialogBox = new Form2();
    aDialogBox.ShowDialog();

    if (aDialogBox.DialogResult == DialogResult.OK)
    {
        MessageBox.Show(
```

```
            aDialogBox.TextBoxText,
            "Dialog Box Results",
            MessageBoxButtons.OK,
            MessageBoxIcon.Information);
    }
    else if (aDialogBox.DialogResult == DialogResult.Cancel)
    {
        MessageBox.Show(
            "Canceled",
            "Dialog Box Results",
            MessageBoxButtons.OK,
            MessageBoxIcon.Information);
    }
}
```

The main form is now complete. It displays the dialog box when a user clicks the button. Now you're ready to make the dialog box.

Stage 2

For this stage of the activity, create another form and style it as a dialog box.

1. Add a new form to the project. (Reminder: Choose **Add Windows Form** from Visual Studio's **Project** menu.)

2. Set the form's **FormBorderStyle** property to FixedDialog.

3. Set its **ControlBox** property to false.

4. Set its **Text** property to Dialog Box.

5. Drag a **Label** control onto the form. Set its property to &Enter Text Here:. Place it as shown in Figure 22.5.

6. Add a **TextBox** control to the form. Delete the text from its **Text** property. Place the text box as shown in Figure 22.5.

7. Add two buttons to the form. Place them as shown in Figure 22.5.

8. Set the **Text** property of the left button to "&OK". Set the button's **Name** property to OKButton. Change its **DialogResult** property to OK.

9. Set the **Text** property of the left button to &Cancel. Set the button's **Name** property to CancelButton. Change its **DialogResult** property to Cancel.

10. Click the dialog box's form. Set its **AcceptButton** property to OKButton.

11. Click the dialog box's form. Set its **CancelButton** property to CancelButton.

12. Double-click the **OK** button. Use the following code for its Click event handler.

```
private void OKButton_Click(object sender, System.EventArgs e)
{
    textBoxText = textBox1.Text;
    this.Close();
}
```

Figure 22.5

A dialog box for text entry.

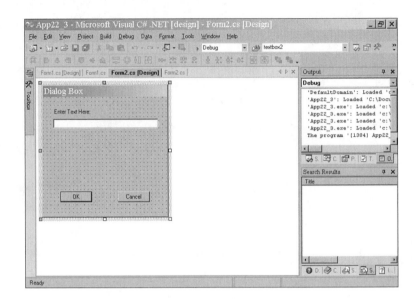

13. Double-click the **Cancel** button. Add the statement …

```
this.Close()
```

… to its Click event handler.

14. At the beginning of the Form2 class, add the following statement:

```
private string textBoxText;
```

15. Add the property method below at the end of the Form2 class.

```
public string TextBoxText
{
    get
    {
        return (textBoxText);
    }
}
```

Go ahead and run this program. When its main window appears, click the button. The program calls the button's **Click** event handler. The code for the event handler is shown in step 4 of Stage 1 of this activity.

The first thing the **Click** event handler does is create a dialog box. It displays the dialog box with a call to the ShowDialog() method rather than the Show() method. The reason for this is explained in the "Modal and Modeless Dialog Boxes" section later in this chapter.

Calling `ShowDialog()` displays the dialog box on the screen. By default, the text box has input focus. You'll see a cursor inside it. Press the Tab key twice. Input focus shifts to the **Cancel** button. Hold down the Alt key. Notice that the Label control displays an underline under the letter E in its text. Press Alt+E. Input focus shifts back to the textbox control.

What happened?

This is one of the nice features of the **Label** control. It's most often used in dialog boxes, so it's presented here rather than in Chapter 20. If you put an ampersand (&) in the text of a Label control, it defines an Alt+key combination for the control next to it. This is how you define Alt+key combinations for controls that don't have their own labels, like the **TextBox** control.

Let's get back to the sample program. Type some text into the dialog box's **TextBox** control. Now click the **OK** button. This calls the button's **Click** event handler. The event handler is called `OKButton_Click()`. It saves the text from the **TextBox** control into a data member called `textBoxText`. Next, it closes the dialog box.

Data Bit _____

The **Label** control can define an Alt+key combination for the next control in the dialog box.

Closing the dialog box returns program execution to the `button1_Click()` method. This method is the **Click** event handler for the button on the program's main form.

When a dialog box ends, it stores its result in a property called **DialogResult.** You can see what happened with the dialog box by checking this property. That's exactly what the `button1_Click()` method does. Its `if-else` statement determines whether the user clicked the **OK** button or the **Cancel** button.

If the user clicks the **OK** button, the `button1_Click()` method displays a message box. It calls the `TextBoxText` property, which is defined in step 15 of Stage 2 of this activity. This property enables the `button1_Click()` method to retrieve the contents of the text box. Recall that the text was stored in the private data member `textBoxText` when you clicked the **OK** button.

Data Bit _____

Your dialog boxes collect information. But the information is private to the dialog box's class (in this example, `Form2`). To make the information available outside the dialog box's class, store it in private data members and define properties. Methods from other classes call the dialog box class's properties. They use the properties to get the information the dialog box stores in the class's private data members.

The message box created in the if clause of the `button1_Click()` method displays the text you typed in the dialog box. But that only happens if users click the OK button. What happens if they click the **Cancel** button?

Nothing. That's what's supposed to happen.

Okay, so something does happen, but not much. In Form2's `CancelButton_Click()` method, you can see that it just closes the dialog box. When it does, program execution returns to Form1's `button1_Click()` method. This method executes its `else` clause. The `else` clause displays a message box stating that the dialog box was canceled.

Out of Sight, but Not Out of Mind

It's important to understand that dialog boxes do not go away when you close them. They just get removed from the screen. This is because the **Form** control's `ShowDialog()` method works differently than its `Show()` method.

When the `ShowDialog()` method ends, it hides the dialog box. However, it keeps the dialog box in memory. That's why you can get access to the dialog box's **DialogResult** property. This also gives you access to the properties that you define for the dialog box's class. In the example program, the **TextBoxText** property could still get text because the dialog box was still in memory.

Data Bit

When the `ShowDialog()` method ends, it does not release the memory allocated to the dialog box. This is different than the `Show()` method. `Show()` releases the memory allocated to a form when the form is closed.

Another advantage of this is that, when the program calls the dialog box again, its memory is already allocated. The program can pop it up faster.

The Windows and the .NET Framework automatically release the memory for the dialog box when the program ends. If you want to manually release the memory, you can. Just call the dialog box's `Dispose()` method. If your program uses the dialog box again after you call `Dispose()`, it has to allocate memory again with the C# `new` keyword, like this:

```
aDialogBox = new Form2();
```

Modal and Modeless Dialog Boxes

Windows defines two types of dialog boxes: modal and modeless. A modal dialog box is what most of us think as a "normal" dialog box. It keeps input focus to itself. It won't let you switch to any other window in the program. To get access to the program's other windows, you have to close the dialog box.

A modeless dialog box does not hold on to the input focus. You can switch to other windows in the program with no problem.

If you want your dialog box to be modal (you usually do), display it on the screen with the ShowDialog() method. If you want it to be modeless, call Show().

The Least You Need to Know

- ◆ Message boxes contain short text messages to the user.
- ◆ Message boxes can give users simple choices.
- ◆ You can display message boxes by calling MessageBox.Show().
- ◆ For more complex input, use dialog boxes.
- ◆ Dialog boxes can be modal or modeless. Modal dialog boxes keep input focus until they are closed. Modal dialog boxes don't hold on to input focus.
- ◆ Display modal dialog boxes by calling the **Form** control's ShowDialog() method.
- ◆ Display modeless dialog boxes by calling the **Form** control's Show() method.

Chapter 23

You're at the Top of My List

In This Chapter

◆ Displaying lists

◆ Retrieving list selections

◆ Selecting multiple items with CheckedListBox controls

◆ The often-renamed ComboBox control

Suppose you're writing a program that does cool visual effects on bitmapped images. From the program's main menu, users can make selections from an **Effects** menu such as **2-D Effects, 3-D Effects,** and **Color Transformations.** Each of these selections specifies a category of special effects. Selecting any one of them opens a dialog box. The individual dialog boxes enable the user to select an effect, apply it to the image, and view a preview of the results.

The question is, when the users are looking at the individual dialog boxes, how do they select the specific effect they want?

Do you show them a group of buttons? That takes a lot of space on the screen.

Do you put a menu on your dialog box? You can, you know. But that can confuse users. They're not used to dialog boxes with menus.

Data Bit _____

One of the great advantages of list controls is that they can display long lists without taking up much screen space.

How about a list of effects? It would be especially good if the dialog box could have a scrollable list of effects. That way, you could make the list really long, but it would only take up a little room in the dialog box.

This chapter introduces some of the Windows Forms list controls provided by the .NET Framework.

Just Lists

The simplest list control is the **List** control. For such a simple control, it does a lot. To see what I mean, try the following activity. In these two stages, you create a form that calls up a dialog box, and make a dialog box containing a list of TV shows.

Stage 1

In this stage of the activity, you create your Windows Forms application. The application's main form will contain a button that launches a dialog box. It will then use a message box to report the user input it retrieved from the dialog box.

1. Create a new Windows program.

2. Drag a button onto the form.

3. Set the button's **Text** property to Show Me the Dialog Box!. Resize the button so that all of the text is visible.

4. Double-click the button and use the following code for its **Click** event handler.

```
private void button1_Click(object sender, System.EventArgs e)
{
    Form2 showList = new Form2();
    showList.ShowDialog();

    MessageBox.Show(
        showList.SelectedShow,
        "This is the show you selected",
        MessageBoxButtons.OK,
        MessageBoxIcon.Information);
}
```

Your main form should resemble the one shown in Figure 23.1.

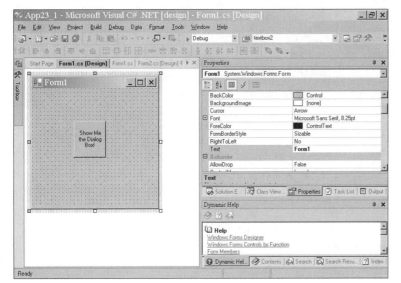

Figure 23.1

Your main form should look like this.

Stage 2

1. Add another form to the project.
2. Set the form's **Text** property to Show List.
3. Set the form's **FormBorderStyle** property to FixedDialog.
4. Set the form's **ControlBox** property to false.
5. Drag a **Label** control onto the form and position it as shown in Figure 23.2.

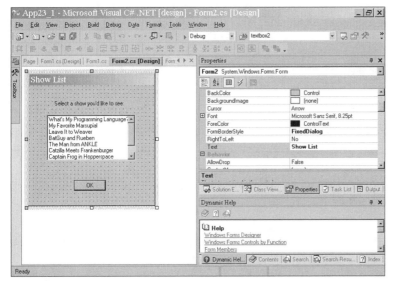

Figure 23.2

The Show List dialog box.

6. Set the **Label** control's **Text** property to `Select a show you'd like to see:`.

7. Drag a **List** control onto the form and position it as shown in Figure 23.2. Set its **HorizontalScrollbar** property to `true`.

8. In the **Properties** window, click in the box next to the **List** control's **Items** property. Click the button that appears.

9. Enter the following strings into the String Collection Editor dialog box. Click the **OK** button when you're finished.

```
What's My Programming Language?
My Favorite Marsupial
Leave It to Weaver
BatGuy and Rueben
The Man from ANKLE
Catzilla Meets Frankenburger
Captain Frog in Hopperspace
Plant 9 from Otter Space
Day of the Limpet
```

10. Drag a button onto the form. Position it as shown in Figure 23.2.

11. Set the button's **Text** property to `&OK`.

12. Double-click the **OK** button and add the statement …

```
this.Close();
```

… to the **Click** event handler.

13. Go back to the designer and double-click the **List** control. Add the code below to its **SelectedIndexChanged** event handler.

```
showSelected = (string)listBox1.SelectedItem;
```

14. Add the statement

```
private string showSelected;
```

to the beginning of the `Form2` class.

15. Add the following code to the end of the `Form2` class:

```
public string SelectedShow
{
    get
    {
        return (showSelected);
    }
}
```

16. Go back to the designer and click the form. Set its **AcceptButton** property to `button1`.

You're ready to compile, link, and run the program. When it starts up, the program displays its main window. Click the button to make the dialog box appear. Now select an item in the list. Each time you do, it triggers the list's **SelectedIndexChanged** event. The **List** control responds by calling the event handler for that event.

The listBox1_SelectedIndexChanged() method does only one thing. It copies the contents of the **List** control's **SelectedItem** property into a private data member called showSelected. Because it does this, the **SelectedItem** property always contains the item in the **Items** property that is currently selected.

The **Items** property holds a group of items of type object. Every class in C# is automatically derived from the object type. You don't have to specify that in your classes. In fact, even the built-in types like int and double are ultimately derived from the object type. This means that object is a generic type. Because the **List** control's **Items** property holds items of type object, it can hold data of any type.

Data Bit

In C#, the object type is a generic type from which all others are derived. Any type can be type cast to object. The reverse is also true.

In this program, the list's **Items** property contains a group of strings. But the **List** control stores them as a group of items of type object. As a result, you must type cast the item you get from the **SelectedItem** property. The listBox1_SelectedIndexChanged() event handler type casts it to string.

The statement in the listBox1_SelectedIndexChanged() method ensures that showSelected always contains the list's currently selected item. When the user clicks the **OK** button, showSelected still has the last item that was selected. The dialog box ends and program execution returns to the button1_Click() method.

Remember button1_Click()? It's the **Click** event handler for the button on the main form. It was the function that called the ShowDialog() method.

After the dialog box ends, the button1_Click() method calls the SelectedShow property from the Form2 class. The SelectedShow property returns the string for the item that was selected when the user pressed the **OK** button in the dialog box. The button1_Click() method passes that string to the MessageBox.Show() method. The MessageBox.Show() method displays a message box with the name of the TV show the user selected.

Check, Please

In addition to plain old **List** controls (which aren't actually plain or old), the .NET Framework offers a **CheckedListBox** control. These two controls are very similar. However, there are some important differences.

As the name implies, the items in the **CheckedListBox** control can be checked or un-checked. The user must double-click an individual item to get the check mark to appear. By default, the **CheckedListBox** control enables users to select more than one item in the list. You can get the **List** control to do this too, but it isn't the default behavior.

Here's a short activity that demonstrates a checked list.

1. Create a new Windows program.

2. Drag a **Label** control onto the form. Set its **Text** property to Select one or more shows:. Resize it so the entire string shows.

3. Drag a **CheckedListBox** control onto the form. Position it underneath the **Label** control. Set its ThreeDCheckBoxes property to true.

4. In the Properties window, click the box next to the **CheckedListBox** control's **Items** property. A button appears; click it.

5. In the String Collection Editor dialog box, type the following list of strings. When you're done, click the dialog box's **OK** button.

   ```
   What's My Programming Language?
   My Favorite Marsupial
   Leave It to Weaver
   BatGuy and Rueben
   The Man from ANKLE
   Catzilla Meets Frankenburger
   Captain Frog in Hopperspace
   Plant 9 from Otter Space
   Day of the Limpet
   ```

6. Add a button to the form. Position it underneath the **CheckedListBox** control.

7. Set the button's **Text** property to &Done.

8. Double-click the button. Use the following code for its **Click** event handler.

   ```
   private void button1_Click(object sender, System.EventArgs e)
   {
       if(checkedListBox1.CheckedItems.Count != 0)
       {
           string tempString = "";

           for(int i = 0;
               i < checkedListBox1.CheckedItems.Count;
               i++)
           {
               tempString +=
                   checkedListBox1.CheckedItems[i].ToString() +
                   "\n";
   ```

```
        }
        MessageBox.Show(
            tempString,
            "Checked Items",
            MessageBoxButtons.OK,
            MessageBoxIcon.Information);
    }
}
```

Compile, link, and run the program. The result looks similar to Figure 23.3. Select items in the list and press the **Done** button. This calls the button's **Click** event handler.

Figure 23.3

A form with a CheckedListBox control.

The **Done** button's **Click** event handler, button1_Click() uses an if statement to test whether the user selected any items. The **CheckedListBox** control keeps number of items that are currently selected in a property called **CheckedItems.Count**. If one or more items were selected, the method enters a for loop.

Inside the loop, it builds a string. The string contains the names of each selected item. The button1_Click() method gets the individual items by using the **CheckedListBox** control's **CheckedItems** property. This property is written to behave like an array so you can use array notation to get each item.

The return value of **CheckedItems[i]** is of type object. It needs to be converted to a string. You can do that with a type cast. Or you can call the object class's ToString() method. Either way works.

After the button1_Click() method converts the item to a string, it concatenates that string onto the end of the variable tempString. The button1_Click() method then appends a new-line.

Data Bit

Because all types in C# are ultimately derived from the object class, most data can be converted to a string by calling the object class's ToString() method.

When the `for` loop ends, `tempString` contains the names of all the items that the user checked. The `button1_Click()` method uses `tempString` to display a message box containing all of the checked items.

Longer, Yet Shorter, Lists

If you want to compact a list into an even smaller screen area and still display a large number of items, you need the **ComboBox** control. In spite of the name, it actually displays a list. The list is compact because it only displays one item at a time. Yet the **ComboBox** control easily displays long lists.

From the Knowledge Bank

The name combo box is a relic from the Old Days of Windows programming. When I started writing documentation for Microsoft about five years ago, the Official Name of combo boxes had recently become "pull-down lists." About a year ago, the "new and improved" Official Name became "drop-down lists." I found this out when all of the editors suddenly started bouncing the documentation I wrote back at me with red marks everywhere the words "pull-down list" appeared. I took the hint.

To make a short story shorter, you'll see combo boxes referred to as combo boxes, drop-down lists, and pull-down lists in Windows programming literature. They're all talking about the list that the **ComboBox** control displays.

Figure 23.4 shows a form with a combo box (pull-down list, drop-down list, or whatever you want to call it). It has an edit box that displays the item that is currently selected. Next to the edit box, is a downward-pointing arrow. If you click the arrow, the **ComboBox** control displays a scrollable list of items.

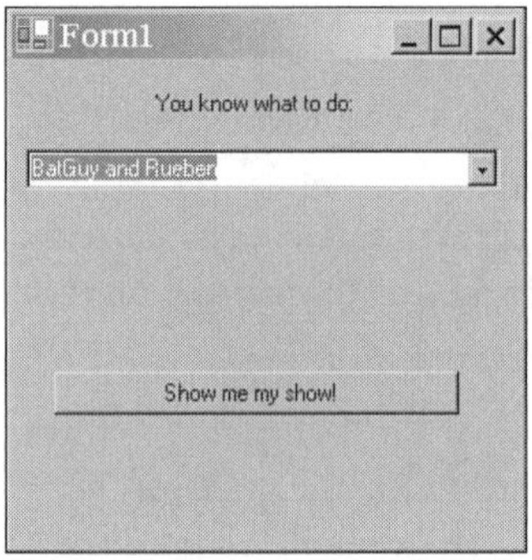

Figure 23.4

A form with a ComboBox control.

Enough rambling about names already. Let's take a look at how to use this thing.

1. Create a new Windows application.

2. Drag a **Label** control onto the application's form. Set its **Text** property to `"You know what to do:"`, and resize it so that all of the text shows.

3. Drag a **ComboBox** control onto the application's form. Position it underneath the label. Resize it so that it's nearly the width of the form.

4. Set the **ComboBox** control's **Text** property to (`Select a Show`). Be sure to type in the parentheses. They are a standard part of the user interface associated with the **ComboBox** control.

5. In the Properties window, click the box next to the **Items** property. A button appears. Click it.

6. In the String Collection Editor dialog box, type the following list of strings. When you're done, click the dialog box's **OK** button.

```
What's My Programming Language?
My Favorite Marsupial
Leave It to Weaver
BatGuy and Rueben
The Man from ANKLE
Catzilla Meets Frankenburger
Captain Frog in Hopperspace
Plant 9 from Otter Space
Day of the Limpet
```

7. Add a button to the form. Position it underneath the **ComboBox** control, as shown in Figure 23.5.

8. Set its **Text** property to `Show me my show!`. Resize the button so that it displays all of the text.

9. Double-click the button. Add the statement ...

```
MessageBox.Show(
    (string)comboBox1.SelectedItem,
    "You Selected This Show",
    MessageBoxButtons.OK,
    MessageBoxIcon.Information);
```

Figure 23.5

Your form should resemble this one.

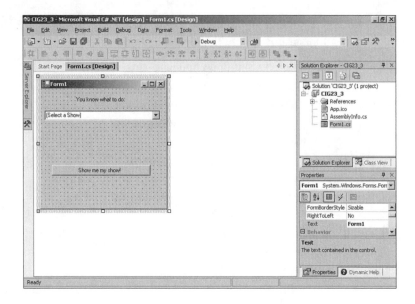

Run the program. If you click the button before selecting an item in the list, the program displays a message box with no string in it. That's because the text in the **ComboBox** control's **Text** property is not one of the choices in the list. It's considered a prompt that tells the user what to do.

Data Bit

The string in a **ComboBox** control's **Text** property is not a list item. Users cannot select it. It's a prompt to get them to choose a list item.

Drop down the list and select an item. Next, click the button. The program displays a message box showing your selection. The button's Click event handler uses the ComboBox control's SelectItem property to get the string that you selected. As in the previous example, it must be type cast to the string type or you'll get a compile error.

The Least You Need to Know

- ◆ Lists provide a way to present users with a group of choices without taking up lots of room on the screen.
- ◆ Your program can use the **List** control to let the user select a single item from a list.
- ◆ The **List** control can also let the user select multiple items, but that's not the default.
- ◆ By default, the **CheckedListBox** control enables users to select multiple items.
- ◆ The **ComboBox** control displays lists that drop down. When the downward-pointing arrow is clicked, it reveals a scrollable list. The item that is currently selected is always in the list's edit box.

24

Valuable Information

In This Chapter

- ◆ Controls for retrieving values from users
- ◆ Getting simple true/false values with the **CheckBox** and **RadioButton** controls
- ◆ Getting exact values with the **NumericUpDown** control
- ◆ Getting relative values with the **TrackBar** control

The .Net Framework contains a group of controls that the Microsoft documentation calls "value setting controls." This is something of a catch-all category of controls that take on some type of value. The value can be as simple as yes/no or true/false; it can be an actual number, or it can be relative values like more/less or louder/softer.

This chapter introduces the value setting controls and provides demonstrations of how to use them.

Just Checking In

Windows programs use the **CheckBox** control for such tasks as turning on and off program options. It answers simple yes/no or true/false questions. Your program uses the **CheckBox** control's **Checked** property to determine whether the box is checked or not. The **Checked** property can be either true or false.

Try the following activity to become more familiar with the **CheckBox** control.

1. Create a new Windows application.

2. Set the form's **Text** property to `Warp Field Regulator`. Resize the form so that the entire title shows.

3. Drag a **CheckBox** control onto the form and position it near the top.

4. Set the **CheckBox** control's **Text** property to `&Dump warp core 10 seconds before breach`. Resize it so that all of the text shows.

5. Set the **CheckBox** control's **CheckState** property to true. A check appears in the check box.

6. Drag two buttons onto the form. Position them as shown in Figure 24.1.

Figure 24.1

Your warp field regulator should resemble this illustration.

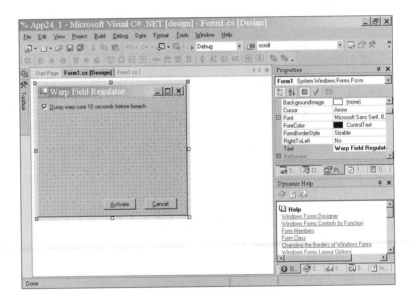

7. Set the **Text** property of the left button to `&Activate`. Set the **Text** property of the right button to `&Cancel`.

8. Double-click the **CheckBox** control. Add the statement ...

```
changesMade = true;
```

... to its **CheckedChanged** event handler.

9. Go back to the designer. Double-click the **Activate** button. Use the code below for its **Click** event handler.

```
private void button1_Click(object sender, System.EventArgs e)
{
    if (changesMade == true)
```

```
        {
            string tempString = "";

            if (checkBox1.Checked == true)
            {
                tempString =
                  "Warp core will be dumped 10 seconds before breach.";
            }
            else
            {
                tempString =
                  "You must manually dump the warp core.";
            }

            MessageBox.Show(
                tempString,
                "Settings Changed",
                MessageBoxButtons.OK,
                MessageBoxIcon.Information);

            changesMade = false;
        }
        else
        {
            MessageBox.Show(
                "No Changes Made",
                "Settings Changed",
                MessageBoxButtons.OK,
                MessageBoxIcon.Information);
        }
    }
```

10. Go back to the designer. Double-click the **Cancel** button. Use the code below for its Click event handler.

```
private void button2_Click(object sender, System.EventArgs e)
{
    MessageBox.Show(
        "No Changes Made",
        "Settings Changed",
        MessageBoxButtons.OK,
        MessageBoxIcon.Information);

    this.Close();
}
```

11. Go to the code-behind page for Form1. Add the statement ...

```
private bool changesMade;
```

... at the beginning of the `Form1` class.

12. Add the statement ...

```
changesMade = false;
```

... to the `Form1` constructor. Put it right after the call to the `InitializeComponent()` method.

Running the program displays its main form. When the program creates the form, it calls the `Form1` class's constructor. Inside the constructor, the statement you added in step 11 sets a private data member called `changesMade` to `false`.

If you click the **Activate** button, its event handler, `button1_Click()`, gets called. The `button1_Click()` method tests `changesMade`. Because you made no changes to the check box, `changesMade` still contains `false`. As a result, the method executes the statement in the `else` clause of its outer `if-else` statement. It displays a message box stating that no changes were made.

Clicking the main form's check box calls `checkBox1_CheckedChanged()`. This method is the check box's **CheckedChanged** event handler. The statement in the `checkBox1_CheckedChanged()` method sets `changesMade` to `true`. The next time you click the **Activate** button, the `button1_Click()` method executes the `if` clause of its outer `if-else` statement. Because the check box is now unchecked, the method displays the message, "You must manually dump the warp core." Before it finishes, the `checkBox1_CheckedChanged()` method sets `changesMade` to `false`.

Data Bit _____

The **CheckBox** control generates a **CheckedChanged** event each time the user toggles the check mark on or off.

If you click the check box again, its `checkBox1_CheckedChanged()` method executes once more. The method again sets `changesMade` to `true`. Clicking the **Activate** button causes the `button1_Click()` method to display the message "Warp core will be dumped 10 seconds before breach."

Tuning in with Radio Buttons

The **RadioButton** control is, in many respects, very much like the **CheckBox** control. The most important difference between the two is that you can select more than one check box in a group of **CheckBox** controls. On the other hand, you can only select one radio button in a group of **RadioButton** controls.

Like the **CheckBox** control, the **RadioButton** control has a **Checked** property and a **CheckChanged** event. You use these events in essentially the same manner as a **CheckBox** control.

1. Create a new Windows program.

2. From the **File** menu, select **Save All**.

3. From the **File** menu, choose **Close Solution**.

4. Use Windows Explorer to copy the file Form1.cs from the directory containing the program you wrote for the check box activity. Copy Form1.cs to the directory Visual Studio created for the program for this example. When Windows Explorer asks you if you want to replace the file, choose **Yes**.

> ## From the Knowledge Bank
>
> The name "radio button" comes from the buttons on a car's radio. Naturally, car radio buttons only let you select and listen to one station at a time. A group of **RadioButton** controls acts the same way. Only one of them can be selected at a time. They are said to be mutually exclusive.

5. Open the solution for this program. When you do, Visual Studio displays the form from the previous program. It contains all of the controls and code it had in the check box program.

6. Add a **GroupBox** control to the form. Resize the form and the group box as shown in Figure 24.2.

7. Place four **RadioButton** controls in the group box. Arrange them as shown in Figure 24.2.

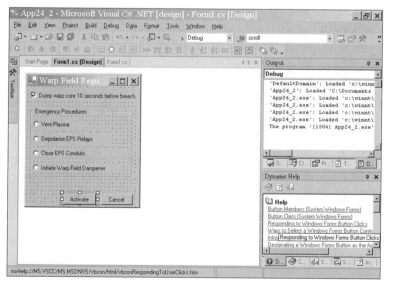

Figure 24.2

The Warp Field Regulator with a set of radio buttons.

8. Change the **Text** properties of the four radio buttons to the following strings.

```
"&Vent Plasma"
"&Depolarize EPS Relays"
"C&lose EPS Conduits"
"&Initiate Warp Field Dampener"
```

9. Click the first radio button. In Visual Studio's Properties window, click the **lightning bolt** icon (at the top of the Properties window).

10. Click in the box next to the **CheckChanged** event. Use the drop-down list to select the checkBox1_CheckedChanged() method.

11. Repeat steps 9 and 10 for the rest of the radio buttons.

12. Go to the code-behind page for Form1. Use the code below for the button1_Click() method. The portion of this method that is different than the previous version is shown in bold.

```
private void button1_Click(object sender, System.EventArgs e)
{
    if (changesMade == true)
    {
        string tempString = "";

        if (checkBox1.Checked == true)
        {
            tempString =
                "Warp core will be dumped 10 seconds before breach.";
        }
        else
        {
            tempString =
                "You must manually dump the warp core.";
        }

        if (radioButton1.Checked == true)
        {
            tempString +=
                "\nVenting plasma.";
        }
        else if (radioButton2.Checked == true)
        {
            tempString +=
                "\nDepolarizing EPS Relays.";
        }
        else if (radioButton3.Checked == true)
        {
            tempString +=
```

```
            "\nClosing EPS Conduits.";
        }
        else if (radioButton4.Checked == true)
        {
            tempString +=
            "\nInitiating Warp Field Dampener.";
        }

        MessageBox.Show(
            tempString,
             "Settings Changed",
            MessageBoxButtons.OK,
            MessageBoxIcon.Information);

        changesMade = false;
    }
    else
    {
        MessageBox.Show(
        "No Changes Made",
        "Settings Changed",
        MessageBoxButtons.OK,
        MessageBoxIcon.Information);
    }
}
```

This program extends the program from the previous activity. It adds a group of radio buttons to the form. The group is contained in a **GroupBox** control.

Run this program and click one of the radio buttons. Now click the **Activate** button. When you do, the chain of if-else statements in the button1_Click() method tests to see which radio button is checked. It appends a string for that radio button that the button1_Click() method prints in the message box.

Data Bit _____

For a group of radio buttons to be considered a group, they must be together in a **GroupBox** or **Panel** control. A form can display multiple groups of radio buttons. Each group must be in a different group box or panel.

Pick a Number, Any Number

Another value control that programmers use a lot is the **NumericUpDown** control. It presents the user with an edit box that they can type a value into. On one side of the edit box (usually the right side), the **NumericUpDown** control displays a set of up and down arrows. Users can click the arrows to increase or decrease the value in the edit control.

In dealing with the **NumericUpDown** control, the most important things you need to worry about are the **Value** property and the **ValueChanged** event. You use the **Value** property to set or get the current value of a **NumericUpDown** control. Every time its values changes, the **NumericUpDown** control triggers a **ValueChanged** event. The following steps demonstrate how to use these two items:

1. Create a new Windows program.

2. From the **File** menu, select **Save All.**

3. From the **File** menu, choose **Close Solution.**

4. Use Windows Explorer to copy the file Form1.cs from the directory containing the program you wrote for the previous activity. Copy Form1.cs to the directory Visual Studio created for this program. When Windows Explorer asks you if you want to replace the file, choose **Yes.**

> **Data Bit**
>
> Use the numeric value control to get an exact number from the user.

5. Open the solution for this program. When you do, Visual Studio displays the form from the previous program. It contains all of the controls and code it had in the previous program.

6. Resize the form and add a **NumericUpDown** control, as shown in Figure 24.3.

Figure 24.3

The Warp Field Regulator with a NumericUpDown control.

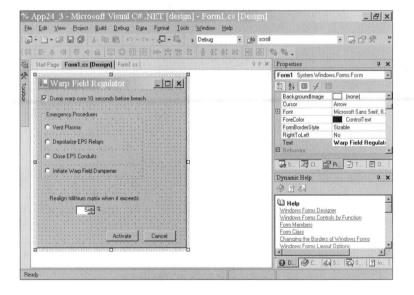

7. Click the **NumericUpDown** control. In the Properties window, set its **TextAlign** property to Right.

8. Set the **NumericUpDown** control's **Value** property to 5. Set its **Minimum** property to 3.

9. Click the **lightning bolt** icon at the top of the Properties window. Set the **NumericUpDown** control's **ValueChanged** event handler to `checkBox1_CheckedChanged`.

10. Drag a **Label** control onto the form just above the **NumericUpDown** control. Position it as shown in Figure 24.3. Set its **Text** property to `"&Realign trilithium matrix when it exceeds:"`.

11. Drag another **Label** control onto the form next to the **NumericUpDown** control. Position it as shown in Figure 24.3. Set its **Text** property to `"%."`.

12. Go to the code-behind page for Form1. Use the following code for the `button1_Click()` method. The portion of this method that is different than the previous version is shown in bold.

```
private void button1_Click(object sender, System.EventArgs e)
{
    if (changesMade == true)
    {
        string tempString = "";

        if (checkBox1.Checked == true)
        {
            tempString =
              "Warp core will be dumped 10 seconds before breach.";
        }
        else
        {
            tempString =
                "You must manually dump the warp core.";
        }

        if (radioButton1.Checked == true)
        {
            tempString +=
                "\nVenting plasma.";
        }
        else if (radioButton2.Checked == true)
        {
            tempString +=
                "\nDepolarizing EPS Relays.";
        }
        else if (radioButton3.Checked == true)
        {
            tempString +=
                "\nClosing EPS Conduits.";
```

```
        }
        else if (radioButton4.Checked == true)
        {
            tempString +=
                "\nInitiating Warp Field Dampener.";
        }

        tempString +=
            "\n" +
            "Trilithium matrix will be realigned " +
            "when it exceeds " +
            numericUpDown1.Value.ToString() +
            "%.";

        MessageBox.Show(
            tempString,
            "Settings Changed",
            MessageBoxButtons.OK,
            MessageBoxIcon.Information);

        changesMade = false;
    }
    else
    {
        MessageBox.Show(
            "No Changes Made",
            "Settings Changed",
            MessageBoxButtons.OK,
            MessageBoxIcon.Information);
    }
}
```

Compile, link, and run this program. Changing the value in the **NumericUpDown** control triggers its **ValueChanged** event. This calls the checkBox1_CheckedChanged() method. As in previous versions, the checkBox1_CheckedChanged() method sets the changesMade private data member to true.

Data Bit _____

Reminder: Because all of the types in C# are derived from the **object** class, you can use the **object** class's ToString() method to convert many types to a string.

Clicking the **Activate** button triggers its **Click** event, which calls the button1_Click() method. The majority of this method is the same as the version in the previous activity. The difference in this version is that it uses the **NumericUpDown** control's **Value** property to get the control's current value. It calls the ToString() method to convert the value from a string to a number. It then prints the string in a message box.

Sliding Scales

The last of the value controls to be demonstrated in this chapter is the **TrackBar** control. This control presents users with a horizontal or vertical slider. The individual positions on the slider's scale each have a unique value. By moving the slider, users can select any value on the scale. You can set the minimum and maximum values for the slider's scale. To do so, set the **TrackBar** control's **Minimum** and **Maximum** properties.

Data Bit

You should use track bars when you do not need an exact numeric value from the user. For instance, track bars make good volume controls for music or sound effects programs. With volume controls, the user communicates the commands, "Make it louder" or "Make it softer." Exact numeric values are not needed.

If your program needs exact numeric values, do not use a track bar. Instead, use a **NumericUpDown** control.

Your program can get or set the slider's current value with the **TrackBar** control's **Value** property. Any time a user moves the **TrackBar** control's slider, it triggers a **Scroll** event. Of course, you can assign a handler to this event to enable your program to react to the change in the slider's value.

To demonstrate the **TrackBar** control, let's add one to the program we've been using throughout this chapter.

1. Create a new Windows program.
2. From the **File** menu, select **Save All**.
3. From the **File** menu, choose **Close Solution**.
4. Use Windows Explorer to copy the file Form1.cs from the directory containing the program you wrote for the previous activity. Copy Form1.cs to the directory Visual Studio created for this program. When Windows Explorer asks you if you want to replace the file, choose **Yes**.
5. Open the solution for this program. When you do, Visual Studio displays the form from the previous program. It contains all of the controls and code it had in the previous version of the program.
6. Resize the form and add a **TrackBar** control as shown in Figure 24.4.
7. In the Properties window, set the **TrackBar** control's **Orientation** property to `Vertical`.
8. Set its **Maximum** property to 25.

Figure 24.4

The Warp Field Regulator with a TrackBar control.

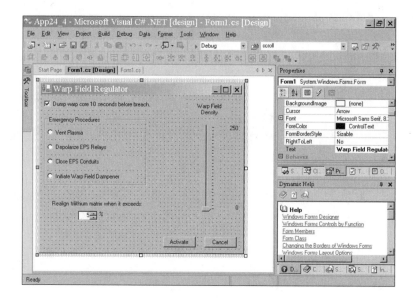

9. Click the lightning bolt icon at the top of the Properties window. Set the **TrackBar** control's **Scroll** event handler to `checkBox1_CheckedChanged`.

10. Drag a **Label** control onto the form and position it above the **TrackBar** control, as shown in Figure 24.4. Set its **Text** property to `&Warp Field Density`.

11. Put another **Label** control on the form. Position it to the top right of the **TrackBar** control. Set its Text property to 250, and its **TextAlign** property to `TopRight`.

12. Put one more Label control on the form. Position it to the bottom right of the **TrackBar** control. Set its **TextAlign** property to **TopRight**.

13. Double-click the **Activate** button on the form. Add the code shown in bold in Listing 24.1 to the `button1_Click()` method.

Listing 24.1 The Updated Click Event Handler for the Activate Button

```
1    private void button1_Click(object sender, System.EventArgs e)
2    {
3        if (changesMade == true)
4        {
5            string tempString = "";
6
7            if (checkBox1.Checked == true)
8            {
9                tempString =
10                   "Warp core will be dumped 10 seconds before breach.";
11           }
12           else
```

```
13          {
14              tempString =
15                  "You must manually dump the warp core.";
16          }
17
18          if (radioButton1.Checked == true)
19          {
20              tempString +=
21                  "\nVenting plasma.";
22          }
23          else if (radioButton2.Checked == true)
24          {
25              tempString +=
26                  "\nDepolarizing EPS Relays.";
27          }
28          else if (radioButton3.Checked == true)
29          {
30              tempString +=
31                  "\nClosing EPS Conduits.";
32          }
33          else if (radioButton4.Checked == true)
34          {
35              tempString +=
36                  "\nInitiating Warp Field Dampener.";
37          }
38
39          tempString +=
40              "\n" +
41              "Dilithium matrix will be realigned " +
42              "when it exceeds " +
43              numericUpDown1.Value.ToString() +
44              "%.";
45
46          int fieldDensity = trackBar1.Value * 10;
47
48          tempString +=
49              "\n" +
50              "Warp Field Density is " +
51              fieldDensity.ToString();
52
53          MessageBox.Show(
54              tempString,
55              "Settings Changed",
56              MessageBoxButtons.OK,
57              MessageBoxIcon.Information);
58
59          changesMade = false;
```

continues

Listing 24.1   The Updated Click Event Handler for the Activate Button   (continued)

```
60        }
61        else
62        {
63            MessageBox.Show(
64                "No Changes Made",
65                "Settings Changed",
66                MessageBoxButtons.OK,
67                MessageBoxIcon.Information);
68        }
69    }
```

With very little additional code, this example program demonstrates the properties and use of a **TrackBar** control. In particular, it shows the **Text, Maximum, Orientation,** and **Value** properties. It also demonstrates the use of the **Scroll** event. As you can see, using the **TrackBar** control in a program is very similar to using the other value setting controls.

The Least You Need to Know

- ◆ Use the **CheckBox** control to answer simple yes/no or true/false questions.
- ◆ Use the **RadioButton** control to select one of a group of options. To group **RadioButton** controls together, use a **GroupBox** or Panel control.
- ◆ The **NumericUpDown** control gets exact values from the user.
- ◆ The **TrackBar** control gets relative values from the user.

Chapter 25

Almost Containers (But Not Quite)

In This Chapter

- ◆ Adding more controls to a form by making it a tabbed page
- ◆ Using the Tab control, the container-like noncontainer
- ◆ Illustrating your application with the **PictureBox** control

One of the things you might have noticed in the last chapter was how quickly controls can fill up a page. Each time you add additional controls, you have to increase the size of the form. Adding still more controls could make a form too big to be usable.

There is a simple way to solve this problem. The .NET Framework provides a **Tab** control. The purpose of a **Tab** control is to display a tabbed page. Your form can have as many tabbed pages as you need. Each page has its own controls. Because the **Tab** control displays one page at a time, the entire group of pages only takes up the space of one page.

The **Tab** control is not considered a container. I don't know why. In my opinion, it should be. This chapter presents the use of the **Tab** control. It also demonstrates another control that is very similar to a container—the **PictureBox** control.

Tabbed Pages

Programs use the **Tab** control to present lots of other controls in a small space. To use a **Tab** control, you must be able to group the other controls you want to display into specific categories. You'll put each category of controls together onto one tabbed page.

The **Tab** control can display its tabs with a button-style appearance. To see what that looks like, set a **Tab** control's property to Buttons or FlatButtons. In addition, you can make the **Tab** control display its tabs along its top, bottom, left, or right. Simply set the **Alignment** property to Top, Bottom, Left, or Right.

Data Bit

When using the **Tab** control, each tabbed page should contain a group of related controls.

Here's an application to demonstrate the **Tab** control. Actually, it's a new version of the Warp Field Regulator program from Chapter 24. You create the application in two stages.

Stage 1

In this stage, you create a Windows Forms application, and build the program's user interface.

1. Create a new Windows application.
2. Set the form's **Text** property to Warp Field Regulator. Resize the form so that the entire title shows.
3. Drag a **Tab** control onto the form. Click it once.
4. In the Properties window, click the box next to the name of the **TabPages** property. A button appears, click it.
5. In the TabPage Collection Editor dialog box, click the **Add** button three times to add three tabbed pages.
6. Set the names of the tabbed pages to emergencyPage, trilithiumPage, and fieldPage respectively.
7. Set the text properties of the three pages to Emergency Procedures, Trilithium Matrix, and Field Control, respectively.
8. Click the tab for the **Emergency Procedures** page. Add controls as shown in Figure 25.1.
9. Click the tab for the **Trilithium Matrix** page. Add controls as shown in Figure 25.2.
10. Click the tab for the **Field Control** page. Add controls as shown in Figure 25.3.

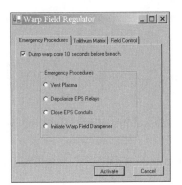

Figure 25.1

The Emergency Procedures page.

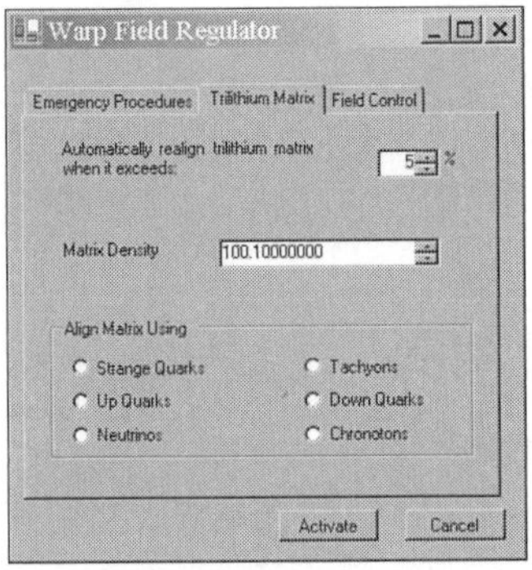

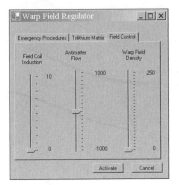

Figure 25.2

The Trilithium Matrix page.

Figure 25.3

The Field Control page.

Stage 2

Now that you've got the user interface for the Warp Field Regulator program, you need to add some code to make it all work. The steps in this stage show how to accomplish that.

1. Double-click the check box on the **Emergency Procedures** page. Add the statement

   ```
   changesMade = true;
   ```

   to the event handler.

2. At the beginning of the Form1 class, add the statement ...

```
private bool changesMade;
```

3. Insert the statement ...

```
changesMade = false;
```

... into the constructor for the Form1 class immediately after the call to the InitializeComponent() method.

4. Set the default event handlers for all of the controls on the tabbed pages to checkBox1_CheckedChanged.

5. Double-click the **Activate** button. Use the following code for its **Click** event handler.

```
private void button1_Click(object sender, System.EventArgs e)
{
    if (changesMade == true)
    {
        string tempString = "";

        tempString = Page1Report();

        tempString += Page2Report();

        tempString += Page3Report();

        MessageBox.Show(
            tempString,
            "Settings Changed",
            MessageBoxButtons.OK,
            MessageBoxIcon.Information);

        changesMade = false;
    }
    else
    {
        MessageBox.Show(
            "No Changes Made",
            "Settings Changed",
            MessageBoxButtons.OK,
            MessageBoxIcon.Information);
    }
}
```

6. Go back to the designer and double-click the **Cancel** button. Use the following code for its **Click** event handler.

```
private void button2_Click(object sender, System.EventArgs e)
{
    MessageBox.Show(
        "No Changes Made",
        "Settings Changed",
        MessageBoxButtons.OK,
        MessageBoxIcon.Information);

    this.Close();
}
```

7. Insert the code in Listing 25.1 just before the closing brace of the form1 class.

Listing 25.1 Report Generation Functions for the Warp Field Regulator

```
1    private string Page1Report()
2    {
3        string tempString = "";
4
5        if (checkBox1.Checked == true)
6        {
7            tempString =
8                "Warp core will be dumped 10 seconds before breach.";
9        }
10       else
11       {
12           tempString =
13               "You must manually dump the warp core.";
14       }
15
16       if (radioButton1.Checked == true)
17       {
18           tempString +=
19               "\nVenting plasma.";
20       }
21       else if (radioButton2.Checked == true)
22       {
23           tempString +=
24               "\nDepolarizing EPS Relays.";
25       }
26       else if (radioButton3.Checked == true)
```

continues

Listing 25.1 Report Generation Functions for the Warp Field Regulator (continued)

```
27          {
28              tempString +=
29                  "\nClosing EPS Conduits.";
30          }
31          else if (radioButton4.Checked == true)
32          {
33              tempString +=
34                  "\nInitiating Warp Field Dampener.";
35          }
36
37          return (tempString);
38      }
39
40      private string Page2Report()
41      {
42          string tempString = "";
43
44          tempString =
45              "\n" +
46              "Trilithium matrix will be realigned " +
47              "when it exceeds " +
48              numericUpDown1.Value.ToString() +
49              "%.";
50
51          tempString +=
52              "\n" +
53              "Matrix Density is: " +
54              numericUpDown2.Value.ToString();
55
56          if (radioButton5.Checked == true)
57          {
58              tempString +=
59                  "\nUsing strange quarks to realign " +
60                  "trilithium matrix.";
61          }
62          else if (radioButton6.Checked == true)
63          {
64              tempString +=
65                  "\nUsing up quarks to realign " +
66                  "trilithium matrix.";
67          }
68          else if (radioButton7.Checked == true)
```

```
69          {
70              tempString +=
71                  "\nUsing neutrinos to realign " +
72                  "trilithium matrix.";
73          }
74          else if (radioButton8.Checked == true)
75          {
76              tempString +=
77                  "\nUsing tachyons to realign " +
78                  "trilithium matrix.";
79          }
80          else if (radioButton9.Checked == true)
81          {
82              tempString +=
83                  "\nUsing down quarks to realign " +
84                  "trilithium matrix.";
85          }
86          else if (radioButton10.Checked == true)
87          {
88              tempString +=
89                  "\nUsing chronotons to realign " +
90                  "trilithium matrix.";
91          }
92
93          return (tempString);
94      }
95
96      private string Page3Report()
97      {
98          string tempString = "";
99          int fieldDensity = trackBar1.Value * 10;
100         double antimatterFlow = trackBar2.Value * 100;
101         int fieldCoilInduction = trackBar3.Value;
102
103         tempString =
104             "\n" +
105             "Warp Field Density is " +
106             fieldDensity.ToString();
107
108         tempString +=
109             "\n" +
110             "Antimatter Flow is " +
111             antimatterFlow.ToString();
112
113         tempString +=
114             "\n" +
115             "Field Coil Induction is " +
```

continues

Listing 25.1   Report Generation Functions for the Warp Field Regulator   (continued)

```
116              fieldCoilInduction.ToString();
117
118        return (tempString);
119    }
```

This version of the Warp Field Regulator uses most of the Windows Forms controls we've discussed so far. Using a **Tab** control enables the program to contain a quite a few controls. However, it doesn't take up any more screen real estate than it did before. The program clearly demonstrates the value of the **Tab** control.

Because this program uses so many controls, the code for generating the report is too long to fit in **Click** event handler for the **Activate** button. Extremely long methods tend to be hard for other programmers to read and maintain. Therefore, I divided most of the code into three other methods, Page1Report(), Page2Report(), and Page3Report(). These method are called by the **Click** event handler for the **Activate** button.

The Page1Report(), Page2Report(), and Page3Report() methods build a report for their respective pages. Each stores the report information in their own local variable called tempString. The report information is based on the current state of the controls on their respective pages. When the report is compiled, these functions return each return the contents of their tempString variable to the **Click** event handler for the **Activate** button.

When you run this program, try resizing the form's window. Notice that the **Tab** control does not get resized. For this reason, it's generally best to use **Tab** controls in dialog boxes rather than resizable forms.

Data Bit

It's better to use **Tab** controls in dialog boxes than on resizable forms. It's possible that a user can make the form smaller, and then become confused because the **Tab** control is no longer visible.

Although this is off the topic a bit, I'm going to point out something else to note about this program. The **Trilithium Matrix** page uses a **NumbericUpDown** control that contains floating point numbers. If you want a **NumbericUpDown** control to use numbers with decimal points, set its **DecimalPlaces** property to a number other than 0. If you do, you should generally also set its **Increment** property to a number be-tween 0.0 and 1.0.

Picture Boxes

PictureBox controls are not true containers. Nevertheless, they do hold graphic images. The images can be in a variety of formats. The most common are Windows Bitmap (BMP), JPEG (JPG), and GIF.

By default, the **PictureBox** control loads an image as is. If the image is too big for the picture box, only part of it will show. To make the entire image show in the box, set the **PictureBox** control's **SizeMode** property to StretchImage. This makes the image larger or smaller, according to the size of the control. Figure 25.4 shows a JPG image that is stretched down to the size of the **PictureBox** control.

Figure 25.4

*A **PictureBox** control with the **SizeMode** property set to StretchImage and the **BorderStyle** property set to Fixed3D.*

If you prefer that the **PictureBox** control scale itself to the size of the image, set the **SizeMode** property to AutoSize.

The Least You Need to Know

- The **Tab** control and the **PictureBox** control are not considered true containers.
- Like containers, the **Tab** control holds other controls. It displays them on one or more tabbed pages.
- Using the **Tab** control enables your program to display many controls in a small amount of screen space.
- The **PictureBox** control holds graphic images.
- **PictureBox** controls can scale the image to the size of the control, or the control to the size of the image.

26

Common Dialog Boxes

In This Chapter

- ◆ What the Common Dialog Boxes are
- ◆ Why they save you time and effort
- ◆ Leveraging the power of the Common Dialog Boxes in your programs

Remember back in previous chapters when I talked about being successfully lazy? Hardworking programmers jump right into writing code. They seldom look around for shortcuts. Successfully lazy programmers try to get as much mileage out of their efforts as possible.

In this chapter, we're going to look at the Common Dialog Boxes. While doing so, we'll be taking laziness to a high art.

Complex Tasks Made Incredibly Easy

There are certain tasks that the vast majority of programs perform. Nearly every program loads and saves data files. Because we are extremely dependent on the written word, most programs process text to one degree or another. As a result, a majority of programs enable you to set text properties.

The Common Dialog Boxes handle all of these tasks and more. They are a set of dialog boxes that Windows provides for you. It saves you from having to write your own dialog boxes to accomplish these tasks.

Windows doesn't provide the Common Dialog Boxes for only your use. It uses them itself. So using the Common Dialog Boxes not only saves you effort, it gives your program a familiar "look and feel" to users from the very first time they fire it up.

Windows Forms provides the Common Dialog Boxes shown in Table 26.1.

Table 26.1   The Common Dialog Boxes

Name	Description
FileOpenDialog	Opens a file.
FileSaveDialog	Saves a file.
FontDialog	Select font properties such as **Font.Name, Font.Size,** and so forth.
ColorDialog	Pick a color from a color palette.
PrintDialog	Select print-related settings in Windows.
PrintPreviewDialog	See what a document will look like when you print it.
PageSetupDialog	Sets page characteristics for printing.

The .NET Framework SDK documentation calls the Common Dialog Boxes components rather than controls. Be that as it may, you'll find them in the System.Windows.Forms namespace. They're so handy that I just can't help demonstrating how to write a text editor with them. The name of your program will be MOE, which stands for My Own Editor. You'll be amazed at how easy this is to do.

How to Write a Text Editor Without Really Trying

All text editors open and save files, so that's where we'll start the discussion of the Common Dialog Boxes. The following activity uses the **RichTextBox** control to provide the basic functionality of the editor. To enable you to easily load and save files, it uses the **FileOpenDialog** and **FileSaveDialog** components.

You do this activity in two stages. In the first, you create the form, then add a main menu and a **RichTextBox** control. Next, you configure the **RichTextBox** control.

In the second stage, you add menu items and their event handlers. This is where you use the **FileOpenDialog** and **FileSaveDialog** components.

Stage 1

In this stage you being the activity by creating a Windows Forms program. You then add a menu and a **RichTextBox** control to the form. In addition, you define the private data member isDirty in the Form1 class.

1. Create a new Windows application.

2. Drag a **MainMenu** control onto the form.

3. Drag a **RichTextBox** control onto the form. Resize it so that it takes up the entire form below the main menu.

4. Delete the string in the **RichTextBox** control's **Text** property.

5. Click the **lightning bolt** icon at the top of the Properties window to view the **RichTextBox** control's events.

6. Double-click the **TextChanged** event.

7. Add the statement

   ```
   isDirty = true;
   ```

   to the **TextChanged** event's handler method.

8. Scroll to the beginning of the Form1 class. Insert the statement

   ```
   bool isDirty;
   ```

   on the line after the class's opening brace.

9. In the constructor for the Form1 class, add the statement

   ```
   isDirty = false;
   ```

   just after the call to InitializeComponent().

10. Go back to Visual Studio's designer. Click the form, and change its **Text** property to MOE.

After you've completed the steps in this stage, your text editor will resemble Figure 26.1.

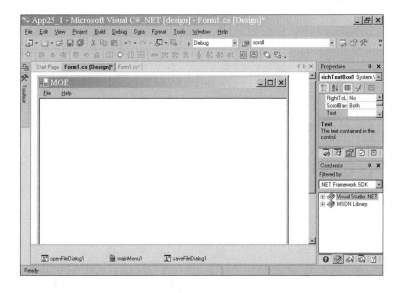

Figure 26.1

The beginning of MOE.

Stage 2

1. In the designer, add an item to the main menu. Set its text to `&File`.

2. Add an item named `&Open` to the **File** menu. Set its **Name** property to `FileOpenItem`.

3. Add an item named `&Save` to the **File** menu. Set its **Name** property to `FileSaveItem`.

4. Add an item named `E&xit` to the **File** menu. Set its **Name** property to `FileExitItem`.

5. In the main menu, add an item named `&Help`.

6. Add an item named `&About` to the **Help** menu. Set its **Name** property to `HelpAboutItem`.

7. Double-click the **Open** item in the **File** menu. Use the following code for its **Click** event handler:

```
private void FileOpenItem_Click(object sender, System.EventArgs e)
{
    openFileDialog1.DefaultExt = "*.rtf";
    openFileDialog1.Filter =
        "RTF Files|*.rtf|txt files (*.txt)|*.txt";

    if((openFileDialog1.ShowDialog() == DialogResult.OK) &&
       (openFileDialog1.FileName.Length > 0))
    {
        richTextBox1.LoadFile(
            openFileDialog1.FileName,
            RichTextBoxStreamType.PlainText);
        isDirty = false;
    }
}
```

8. Double-click the **Save** item in the **File** menu. Use the following code for its **Click** event handler:

```
private void FileSaveItem_Click(object sender, System.EventArgs e)
{
    saveFileDialog1.DefaultExt = "*.rtf";
    saveFileDialog1.Filter =
        "RTF Files|*.rtf|txt files (*.txt)|*.txt";

    if((saveFileDialog1.ShowDialog() == DialogResult.OK) &&
       (saveFileDialog1.FileName.Length > 0))
    {
        richTextBox1.SaveFile(
            saveFileDialog1.FileName,
            RichTextBoxStreamType.PlainText);
        isDirty = false;
        }
}
```

9. Double-click the **Exit** item in the **File** menu. Use the following code for its **Click** event handler:

```
private void FileExitItem_Click(object sender, System.EventArgs e)
{
    if (isDirty)
    {
        string saveMessage =
            "Do you want to save changes to this " +
            "file before you exit?";

        DialogResult answer;

        answer = MessageBox.Show(
                    saveMessage,
                    "File Not Saved",
                    MessageBoxButtons.YesNo,
                    MessageBoxIcon.Question);

        if (answer == DialogResult.Yes)
        {
            FileSaveItem_Click(sender,e);
        }
    }
    this.Close();
}
```

10. Double-click the **Exit** item in the **File** menu. Use the following code for its Click event handler:

```
private void HelpAbout_Click(object sender, System.EventArgs e)
{
    MessageBox.Show(
        "My Own Editor",
        "About MOE");
}
```

11. Drag a **FileOpenDialog** onto the form.

12. Drag a **FileSaveDialog** onto the form.

Compile, link, and run your program. You've done it! You've got a working text editor.

To see how it works, try typing some text into the MOE program. Each time you enter a character, it triggers the **RichTextBox** control's **TextChanged** event. This, in turn, calls the `richTextBox1_TextChanged()` method. This method contains a statement that sets the `Form1` class's private data member `isDirty` to `true`. The default value for `isDirty` is `false`, which is the value it gets in the constructor for the `Form1` class.

Data Bit _____

The `Form1` class's `isDirty` member lets MOE know when the user changes the text in the editor. If `isDirty` is `false`, it means the document is "clean," which is another way of saying that no changes have occurred since it was last saved.

When `isDirty` is `true`, it means the user changed some text in the editor. The document in the editor is newer than the file on the disk. The program needs to save the document before it exits.

After you type some text into the editor, choose **Save** from MOE's **File** menu. This calls the `FileSaveItem_Click()` method. This method uses the **FileSaveDialog** component.

First, though, the `FileSaveItem_Click()` method sets the **DefaultExt** property of the **FileSaveDialog** component to the string `*.rtf`. The **DefaultExt** property contains the default file extension that the File Save dialog box uses to save files. The `FileSaveItem_Click()` method also sets the **FileSaveDialog** component's **Filter** property to `RTF Files|*.rtf|txt files (*.txt)|*.txt`. This tells the File Save dialog box what types of files to look for in the current directory.

The `if` statement in the `FileSaveItem_Click()` method tests to ensure the user typed in a valid filename. It also checks the length of the name to make sure it's greater than zero. If both of these conditions are met, the `FileSaveItem_Click()` method calls the **RichTextBox** control's `SaveFile()` method to save the text you typed. After the text is saved, it sets `isDirty` to `false` to indicate that no changes were made since the file was last saved.

Now try opening the file you just saved. From the **File** menu, choose **Open**. When you do, the main menu calls the `FileOpenItem_Click()` method. This method works almost identically to the `FileSaveItem_Click()` method. The only difference is that it calls the **RichTextBox** control's `LoadFile()` method rather than `SaveFile()`.

Data Bit _____

Notice that the `FileOpenItem_Click()` method sets the `isDirty` member to `false`. When your program calls the **RichTextBox** control's `LoadFile()` method, it triggers a **TextChanged** event. Recall that the event handler for the **TextChanged** event sets the `isDirty` member to `true`. Your program must fix this. The `isDirty` member should be `false` until the user changes something in the document. Remember, the purpose of `isDirty` is to indicate when the document in memory is newer than the file on the disk.

Type some more text into the document, then choose **Exit** from the **File** menu. Before it exits, MOE tests to see if the document is dirty (needs to be saved). If so, it displays a message box and asks the user if the document should be saved. If the user says yes, MOE saves the document by calling `FileSaveItem_Click()`. If the user says no, it just goes on to the end of the method. At the end of the event handler method, it closes the application's main form. This causes the program to end.

Getting Richer

The version of MOE in the previous section loads and saves text files, not rich text format files. It's time to change that, and to add some simple formatting to MOE's documents.

We'll use the **FontDialog** component to enable users to set a document's font. To keep things simple, the entire document will be in the same font.

After we add the **Font** dialog box, we'll make some modifications to MOE to enable it to load and save RTF documents.

1. Create a new Windows program.

2. From the **File** menu, select **Save All.**

3. From the **File** menu, choose **Close Solution.**

4. Use Windows Explorer to copy the file Form1.cs from the directory containing the program you wrote for the previous activity. Copy Form1.cs to the directory Visual Studio created for this program. When Windows Explorer asks you if you want to replace the file, choose **Yes.**

5. Open the solution for this program. When you do, Visual Studio displays the form from the previous program. It contains all of the controls and code it had in the previous version of the program.

6. Add an item named F&ormat to the main menu. Drag it so that it appears between the File and Help menus, as shown in Figure 26.2.

7. In the **Format** menu, add an item named `"Fon&t"`. Use the Properties window to rename this item to `FormatFontItem`.

8. Double-click the **Font** item in the designer. Use the following code for its **Click** event handler.

```
private void FormatFontItem_Click(object sender,
                                  System.EventArgs e)
{
    if(fontDialog1.ShowDialog() != DialogResult.Cancel )
    {
        richTextBox1.Font = fontDialog1.Font ;
    }
}
```

Figure 26.2

Add a Format menu to MOE.

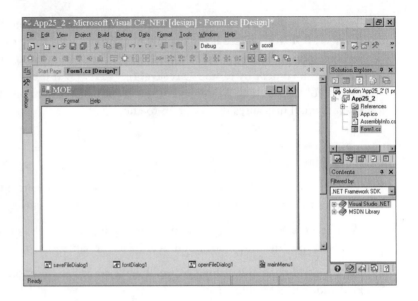

9. Modify the `FileSaveItem_Click()` method as shown in the following code. The changes you need to make are shown in bold.

```
private void FileSaveItem_Click(object sender, System.EventArgs e)
{
    saveFileDialog1.DefaultExt = "*.rtf";
    saveFileDialog1.Filter = "RTF Files|*.rtf";

    if((saveFileDialog1.ShowDialog() == DialogResult.OK) &&
        (saveFileDialog1.FileName.Length > 0))
    {
        richTextBox1.SaveFile(
            saveFileDialog1.FileName,
            RichTextBoxStreamType.RichText);
        isDirty = false;
    }
}
```

10. Edit the `FileOpenItem_Click()` method as shown in the following code. The changes you need to make are shown in bold.

```
private void FileOpenItem_Click(object sender, System.EventArgs e)
{
    openFileDialog1.DefaultExt = "*.rtf";
    openFileDialog1.Filter = "RTF Files|*.rtf";

    if((openFileDialog1.ShowDialog() == DialogResult.OK) &&
        (openFileDialog1.FileName.Length > 0))
    {
```

```
richTextBox1.LoadFile(
    openFileDialog1.FileName,
    RichTextBoxStreamType.RichText);
    isDirty = false;
    }
}
```

11. Drag a **FontDialog** component onto the form.

Recompile, link, and run the program. Type some text into the **RichTextBox** control. Now choose **Font** from the **Format** menu. Voilà, you've got a **Font** dialog box. You can set the font characteristics used by the entire document. After you do, try saving and then loading the file. When the file is opened, you can see that MOE saved your file with the font characteristics you selected.

Good ol' MOE.

How Lazy Can You Be?

You've created a program with an incredible amount of functionality while writing a very small amount of program code. It might help you get a good perspective on just how amazing this is if you have a bit of background.

The first Windows program I ever wrote was a text editor almost exactly like the one in this chapter. I did this as an exercise to teach myself Windows programming. I wrote it in C, and it was in excess of 10,000 lines of code! Yes, 10,000. It took me weeks to complete.

With C#, the .NET Framework, and the Common Dialog Boxes, you've written a text editor with just a few hundred lines of code. You could easily complete this project in an afternoon. It doesn't get much better than that.

The Least You Need to Know

- ◆ The Common Dialog Boxes are provided by the .NET Framework.
- ◆ They perform tasks that are common to most programs.
- ◆ Programs use the **FileOpenDialog** and **FileSaveDialog** to enable users to input the names of files to load or save.

Speak Like a Geek Glossary

.NET Framework A set of classes, types, and other tools that you can use and reuse in your programs.

.NET Platform A development environment composed of CLS-compliant languages (Visual C# and Visual Basic), the .NET Framework, and the CLR.

access modifier A C# keyword that specifies the scope of a program element such as classes, member data, and member functions.

accessor method See *property*.

allocate memory To devote memory to a variable.

application See *program*.

application program See *program*.

application prototyping Creating a program that presents your application's user interface. The user program does nothing but display menus, dialog boxes, and other user interface elements.

application software See *program*.

array element A single item in an array.

Assembler Another name for assembly language.

assembly Not the same as Assembler or Assembly language. An assembly is a library containing C# components.

assembly language Not the same as an assembly. Assembly language is a more English-like version of binary instructions processed by a microprocessor.

base class A class from which other classes are derived through inheritance.

bit A binary digit. Binary digits can be a 0 or a 1.

black box function A function that hides its internal workings. All functions should be black box functions.

branching statement A C# statement that causes a block of code to be conditionally executed, depending on the evaluation of a condition.

breakpoint   A debugger command that enables you to suspend program execution. It does not end the program. You can resume execution when you are ready.

buffer   An area of memory dedicated to holding input or output data for a while.

bus   A path that connects a microprocessor to memory. Data and program instructions flow across the bus.

byte   A group of eight bits.

child class   See *derived class*.

class   A C# object.

code-behind page   A file containing the methods and event handlers associated with a WinForm control.

Common Language Runtime (CLR)   An execution platform that uses a JIT compiler to compile programs from IL into executable binary programs.

Common Language Specification (CLS)   A document that defines IL.

compiler   A program that translates source code, written in languages such as C, C++, or C#, into binary. Compilers translate entire programs at one time. The translated binary program can be executed over and over.

compound assignment operator   An operator composed of an assignment operator prefixed with another operator.

constant   Opposite of a variable. Its value does not change while the program runs.

data type   A specifier that defines the kind of data a variable can hold. String variables hold string data, numeric variables hold numbers, and so on.

debugger   A program that helps you find and remove errors from other programs.

debugging program   See *debugger*.

decrement   To decrease the contents of a variable by 1.

derived class   A class that uses inheritance to obtain part or all of its functionality.

design time   The interval of time in which you are designing and developing a program.

encapsulation   Hiding program data or implementation, typically in an object.

escape sequence   A sequence of special characters that the C# language sees as a single character.

event handler   A method that a Windows Forms controls calls to react to an event.

field   See *member data*.

file handling   The technique of reading data from and writing data to files on external devices such as disks.

function   A reusable block of program code with a name, parameter list, and return type.

gigabyte   A group of 1,000 megabytes.

I/O   Input and output.

implementation hiding   The technique of writing black box functions.

increment   To increase the contents of a variable by 1.

input focus   When a window or control has input focus, it can receive characters from the keyboard.

instance   A variable for which memory is allocated in a program.

Intermediate Languge (IL)   A binary programming language similar to object code. To be executable, IL programs must be compiled by the CLR's JIT compiler.

interpreter   A program that translates source code into binary. Unlike a compiler, an interpreter translates a statement, executes the binary, then moves onto the next statement. It repeats this process until the program ends.

iterate   To do something more than once.

Just in Time (JIT) Compiler   A compiler in the CLR that translates IL programs into executable binary programs.

kilobyte   A group of 1,024 bytes.

line feed   The act of moving the cursor to the beginning of the next line.

linker   A program that converts object code into executable code.

logical error   An incorrect instruction in a program.

looping statement   A C# statement that causes a block of code to be executed repeatedly, depending on the evaluation of a condition.

magic number   A number in a computer program that does not explain itself. Almost no numbers explain themselves.

megabyte   A group of 1,000 kilobytes.

member data   One or more data items contained in a class.

member function   A function that is a member of a class.

method   See *member function*.

microprocessor   A microchip that can execute instructions.

multidimensional array   An array of arrays.

object   A programmer-defined data type that contains member functions, called methods, and member data. The data describes the state of the object. The method forms the set of valid operations that programs can perform on the object.

overloading   See *polymorphism*.

overriding   Overloading a method inherited from a base class.

parent class   See *base class*.

polymorphism   A one-to-many mapping. In C#, this refers to having more than one method or operator with the same name.

port   To move a program, possibly by rewriting it, to a different type of computer or operating system.

portable   A program that can be ported easily.

postdecrement   Causes the value in a variable to be used for other operations first, then decremented.

postincrement   Causes the value in a variable to be used for other operations first, then incremented.

post-test loop   A loop whose condition is tested after at least one iteration.

precedence   The order of operator evaluation in a program.

predecrement   Causes the value in a variable to be decremented first, then used for other operations.

preincrement   Causes the value in a variable to be incremented first, then used for other operations.

pretest loop   A loop whose condition is tested before the loop's code block is executed.

primary storage   A computer's memory (RAM). This is where it stores its programs and data while it's running.

program   A collection of instructions for the computer's microprocessor. The instructions tell the computer how to accomplish a particular task.

project   A file used by Visual Studio .NET that contains the names of one or more source files. When you build a project, you compile and link the source files into a program.

property   A specialized type of function used to set or get the value of member data items.

RAM   Random access memory. While they are running, computers store programs and data in RAM.

rapid application development (RAD)   A tool or development environment that enables you to quickly develop your application by providing code for most of the common tasks your program performs.

runtime, run time   The time interval in which the program executes.

scope   The visibility of program elements—such as classes, member data, and member functions—within a program.

secondary storage   A computer's disk (hard or floppy). This is where programs and data are stored while the computer is turned off.

simple data type   A data type that is build into the C# language.

software   See *program*.

software object   See *object*.

solution   A collection of projects in Microsoft Visual Studio .NET.

source code   C# instructions in a source file. Source code can also be written in other languages, such as Basic, Pascal, Cobol, C, or C++.

source file   A text file containing statements in a programming language such as C#.

syntax error   An error made by typing invalid C# statements into a source file.

type cast   A C# statement that changes the type of a variable or function for one statement only.

variable   A named memory location used to store program data.

virtual machine (VM)   A generic computer that is simulated by software such as the CLR.

whitespace   Indentation, spaces, and newlines.

WinForm control   An abbreviation for a Windows Form control.

What Are Binary and Hexadecimal?

All program instructions and data are stored in computers as binary numbers. However, programmers often represent binary numbers with hexadecimal numbers. Because of this, programmers must have at least a minimal familiarity with the binary and hexadecimal number systems.

Beginning with Base 10

The number system that you and I count with is called base 10, because it has 10 digits. Those digits are 0, 1, 2, 3, 4, 5, 6, 7, 8, and 9. Believe it or not, those are the only digits we have in the base 10 counting system. We represent all other numbers using those 10 digits.

For instance, we represent the number ten with the 10, which means 1 ten and 0 ones. Eleven is 1 ten and 1 one, or 11.

When we get to 99, we need an additional decimal place. Each decimal place is a power of ten. The ones' place is 10^0. The tens' place is 10^1. The next decimal place is 10^2, or 100. One more decimal place is 10^3, which is 1,000.

You're probably saying, "Why are you telling me this? I learned it in grade school." The reason is simple. All number systems work this same way. So the easiest way to understand other number systems is to review the one we're already familiar with.

Counting in Binary

Binary numbers are numbers in base 2. Base 2 contains only two digits. Those digits are 0 and 1. To represent any other numbers in base 2, we use combinations of these two digits.

For instance, the number two in base two is 10, which is 1 two and 0 ones. Three is 11, or 1 two and 1 one. Quick. What would four be? Remember, you can only use the digits 0 and 1 to make numbers in base 2.

Time's up. The answers is 100. We can only represent four numbers with two binary digits, zero, one, two, and three. Remember that, in base 10, we add additional decimal places to represent bigger numbers.

We do the same thing in base 2. However, we increase each place by a power of two rather than a power of 10. The ones place is 2^0. The twos place is 2^1. The next position is 2^2, which is 4. The next is 2^3, which is 8. We continue to increase them in powers of 2.

Longtime programmers usually learn to recognize binary numbers almost as well as they recognize numbers in base 10. However, to make things easier, Table B.1 shows how to count to 16 in binary.

Table B.1 Counting to 16 in Binary

Base 2	Base 10
0	0
1	1
10	2
11	3
100	4
101	5
110	6
111	7
1000	8
1001	9
1010	10
1011	11
1100	12
1101	13
1110	14
1111	15
10000	16

Representing Binary Numbers in Hexadecimal

Base 16 works just like base 2 and base 10. In base 16, we need 16 digits. They are 0, 1, 2, 3, 4, 5, 6, 7, 8, 9, A, B, C, D, E, and F.

Say! What's with the letters A–F?

In base 16, the number 10 is sixteen, not ten. We need to use something to represent the numbers ten through fifteen. Instead, we use A through F as digits in the base 16 numbering system. So in base 16, A1 is not just a steak sauce, it's also a valid hexadecimal number. It's A (10) sixteens and 1 one. Sixteen times 10 is 160 (base 10), plus 1 is 161.

Recall that, in base 10, we use additional decimal places to represent higher numbers. Each one is a power of ten. Base 16 works the same way, only they additional places are powers of 16.

We use hexadecimal (hex, for short) because most programmers find it easier to read than binary. And it's easy to convert numbers between binary and hexadecimal. If you have a binary number, just start from the right and gather its digits into groups of four. Each group of four binary digits converts directly to one hexadecimal digit.

For example, to convert the binary number 1010101 to hex, start from the right and gather the digits into groups of four. Put a space between each group. That gives 101 0101.

Notice that the leftmost group only has three digits. That's okay. We can fill in the fourth digit by adding a leading zero onto the number. Doing so does not change its value. When we add the leading zero, we get 0101 0101.

Now we can use Table B.2 to convert the individual digits to hex. The table shows us that 0101 in binary is 5 in hex. So the number 1010101 in binary is 55 in hex.

Table B.2   Counting to 16 in Binary, Hexadecimal, and Decimal

Base 2	Base 16	Base 10
0000	0	0
0001	1	1
0010	2	2
0011	3	3
0100	4	4
0101	5	5
0110	6	6
0111	7	7
1000	8	8

continues

Table B.2 Counting to 16 in Binary, Hexadecimal, and Decimal (continued)

Base 2	Base 16	Base 10
1001	9	9
1010	A	10
1011	B	11
1100	C	12
1101	D	13
1110	E	14
1111	F	15
10000	10	16

ASCII Chart

C# programs use Unicode characters. The complete set of Unicode characters includes thousands of individual characters. Most programmers who speak English only need to be familiar with the first 127 of them. However, if you write software for those who do not speak English, it is wise to obtain a complete copy of the Unicode character set.

The Unicode character set includes the ASCII characters set for its first 127 characters. ASCII stands for the American Standard Code for Information Interchange. The ASCII character set contains all of the uppercase and lowercase characters in the English alphabet. It also includes numbers, punctuation, and some other useful characters.

In addition, the ASCII character set contains some characters that were specifically intended for accessing the features of the old character terminals that were common in the 1960s.

The first column of the ASCII table shows the ASCII characters. The second column displays their numeric values. The third column contains a brief description of what the ASCII character represents.

Character	Decimal Value	Represents
NUL	0	Null character
SOH	1	^A
STX	2	^B
ETX	3	^C
EOT	4	^D
ENQ	5	^E
ACK	6	^F

Character	Decimal Value	Represents
BEL	7	^G, Rings bell or beeps speaker
BS	8	^H, Backspace
HT	9	^I, Tab
LF	10	^J, Linefeed
VT	11	^K, Vertical tab
FF	12	^L. Form feed
CR	13	^M, Carriage return
SO	14	^N
SI	15	^O
DLE	16	^P
DC1	17	^Q
DC2	18	^R
DC3	19	^S
DC4	20	^T
NAK	21	^U
SYN	22	^V
ETB	23	^W
CAN	24	^X
EM	25	^Y
SUB	26	^Z
ESC	27	Escape
FS	28	^/
GS	29	^]
RS	30	^=
US	31	^-
SP	32	Spacebar
!	33	!
"	34	"
#	35	#
$	36	$
%	37	%
&	38	&
'	39	'
(	40	(
)	41	)
*	42	*
+	43	+
,	44	,
-	45	-
.	46	.

Character	Decimal Value	Represents
/	47	/
0	48	0
1	49	1
2	50	2
3	51	3
4	52	4
5	53	5
6	54	6
7	55	7
8	56	8
9	57	9
:	58	:
;	59	;
<	60	<
=	61	=
>	62	>
?	63	?
@	64	@
A	65	A
B	66	B
C	67	C
D	68	D
E	69	E
F	70	F
G	71	G
H	72	H
I	73	I
J	74	J
K	75	K
L	76	L
M	77	M
N	78	N
O	79	O
P	80	P
Q	81	Q
R	82	R
S	83	S
T	84	T
U	85	U
V	86	V

Character	Decimal Value	Represents
W	87	W
X	88	X
Y	89	Y
Z	90	Z
[	91	[
\	92	\
]	93	]
^	94	^
_	95	_
`	96	`
a	97	a
b	98	b
c	99	c
d	100	d
e	101	e
f	102	f
g	103	g
h	104	h
i	105	i
j	106	j
k	107	k
l	108	l
m	109	m
n	110	n
o	111	o
p	112	p
q	113	q
r	114	r
s	115	s
t	116	t
u	117	u
v	118	v
w	119	w
x	120	x
y	121	y
z	122	z
{	123	}
|	124	|
}	125	}
~	126	~
DEL	127	Delete

Index